C000255016

LONDON BOOKBINDERS

1780–1840

LONDON
BOOKBINDERS

1780-1840

By

CHARLES
RAMSDEN

LONDON
B. T. BATSFORD LTD

© Charles Ramsden 1956
First published 1956
Reprinted 1987

ISBN 0 7134 5078 9

All rights reserved. No part of this publication
may be reproduced, in any form or by any means,
without permission from the Publisher

PRINTED AND BOUND IN GREAT BRITAIN BY
ANCHOR BRENDON LTD, TIPTREE, ESSEX
FOR THE PUBLISHERS
B. T. BATSFORD LTD
4 FITZHARDINGE STREET, LONDON, W1H 0AH

CONTENTS

v

ACKNOWLEDGMENTS

IN the Introduction I have already expressed my profound gratitude to Mr. Ellic Howe and Mr. H. M. Nixon for their unstinting kindness and readiness to assist me with their experience and counsel.

I am also deeply indebted to the librarians and officials of the British Museum, the Guildhall, the House of Lords, Westminster Abbey, the Stationers' Company, Manchester University, the Bishopsgate and St. Bride's Foundation Institutes, Eton College, and a number of other similar foundations, as well as the Yale University Library, the Folger-Shakespeare Library, the Henry E. Huntington Library, etc., in the U.S.A.

To refer to individuals who have helped me must be necessarily invidious, but I should like at least to mention the following:

Mr. C. C. Blagden, Mr. M. Craig, Mr. M. Cohen, Mr. H. W. Davies, Mr. A. Ehrman, Mr. H. Fletcher, Mr. A. Hobson, Dr. W. S. Mitchell, Mr. P. Muir, Mr. A. Munby, Mr. J. Oates, Mr. J. B. Oldham, and Mr. Graham Pollard.

Finally, may I thank Mr. John Hayward who kindly undertook a large measure of stylistic, and even grammatical revision of the original draft of the Introduction.

C. RAMSDEN

Spring, 1956

LIST OF ILLUSTRATIONS

Note.—Actual overall dimensions of the bindings in inches are given in brackets.

x

xi

INTRODUCTION

IN compiling my two previous books on (1) *French Bookbinders, 1789–1848* (1950); and (2) *United Kingdom Bookbinders (outside London) 1780–1840* (1954), I was fortunate to be in each case dealing with what was largely virgin territory. In preparing the second work, especially while working through the directories from about 1815, I found myself making notes of London binders of the last twenty-five years of a period which has been of special interest to me. I had also accumulated a number of examples of London bookbinders' work between the approximate dates of 1780–1840, and the temptation to compile a book on the London bookbinders of that period was therefore very strong.

I did, however, find myself faced with a situation which gave me ground for considerable hesitation. Mr. Ellic Howe, in his Bibliographical Society Publication: *A List of London Bookbinders of 1648–1815* (1950), had recorded the vast majority of London bookbinders active up to 1815 and had in many cases pursued their careers for ten or fifteen years later. Was I justified in dealing with the binders who came into prominence after 1815 and at the same time giving such additional information on the binders already noted by Mr. Howe, as had come my way?

Mr. Howe most generously encouraged me to pursue my further studies in a field at least three-quarters of which he had made particularly his own. I, as indeed all who are interested in London bookbinding, am deeply in his debt for his work, much of which is of a pioneering nature and without which the present volume would not have been written, at least by me. Mr. Howe has put me further in his debt by most helpful advice and by giving me a number of most valuable introductions to sources of information. (Readers will notice that, where information is available in Howe's List, or indeed in his later publication—with Mr. Child—on *The Society of London Bookbinders, 1780–1951* (1952), I have not repeated the same, but merely given the appropriate reference.)

I would also wish to acknowledge my indebtedness to Mr. H. M. Nixon, of the British Museum. He not only encouraged me to undertake the present work but also buoyed me up during the periods of depression and even hopelessness, which were all too frequent—especially as regards the study of binding styles from 1765–1840, the undertaking of which was an addition to my original ideas. He not only encouraged me *ab initio* but he was always ready with wise counsel and equally ready to help materially by placing relevant bindings at my disposal.

HOW FAR CAN THE NAMES IN THE ALPHABETICAL LIST BE REGARDED AS THOSE OF PERSONS OR FIRMS POSSESSING THEIR OWN BINDERIES?

This is a question similar to that with which I have already dealt at some length in *Bookbinders of the United Kingdom (outside London), 1780–1840*. In the case of London, however, greater information, of a more regular nature, is not unnaturally available as a result of the greater number and higher degree of organisation of the London bookbinders, as compared with those of other cities, large or small, elsewhere in the country.

There is available on the one hand the large mass of documents in the possession of the London Bookbinders' Branch of the National Union of Printing, Bookbinding and Paper Workers, including many records of the Society of London Bookbinders and the invaluable Jaffray MSS, which Mr. Howe, with the assistance of Mr. John Child, has analysed in his *Society of London Bookbinders, 1780–1951*.

Further, there are two important printed sources of contemporary information, which are dealt with in detail under separate headings, viz.: (1) the Directories, which become increasingly comprehensive after about 1817; and (2) Cowie's *Bookbinders' Manual*, first published in 1828. The *Manual* was primarily intended for sale to bookbinders, and I venture to think would hardly have been popular with them if it had listed any perceptible proportion of "spurious" binders.

Lastly, it is worth recording that the original Masters' Association founded in 1794 did not disappear till about 1824. Though it was not refounded till 1837 (an association of smaller binders was founded in 1839), the Lodges, and later (from about 1811) the Trade Committee, existed over the whole period from 1780–1840. It would therefore seem curious that "spurious" entries in either the Directories or Cowie, if such existed, were not (within my knowledge) the subject of adverse criticism.

PLATE I   BAUMGARTEN   (5″ × 7½″)

PLATE II   CAUMONT, de $(5\frac{1}{4}'' \times 8\frac{3}{4}'')$

Previous to 1817 the London Directories are not drawn up on a "trades" basis and it requires laborious search, item by item, to trace such few bookbinders as are recorded among the alphabetical lists of London tradesmen. Having made a fairly extensive sampling of the earlier London directories from 1780 I can only report that the results are most disappointing, and I am forced to assume that bookbinding was regarded by the compilers of the directories, if not as a disreputable, at least as an unimportant trade activity.

Apart from the eight bookbinders listed in Boyle's *General London Guide* of 1794, the first London directory to include a "trades" section on bookbinders, etc., was Johnstone's *London Commerical Guide and Street Directory* of 1817. It included bookbinders under the headings "Bookbinders", "Bookbinders & Stationers", and "Vellum binders"; also one entry under "Book Toolmakers".

Slightly later, Robson's *Classification of Trades, London Commercial Directory*, 1821. Vol. II, contained headings for "Bookbinders" and "Vellum Binders".

A year or two later Pigot's *London and Provincial New Commercial Directory* for 1822–23 contained headings for "Bookbinders", "Vellum Binders", "Book Edgegilders" and "Book Claspmakers". A few booksellers were also noted as "Binders".

Not till 1840 did the *P.O. Directory* contain a "trades" section which listed bookbinders, indicating with an asterisk those who were also booksellers, or stationers. It also listed ploughknife and pressmakers, as well as toolcutters and engravers.

COWIE'S BOOKBINDER'S MANUAL

The first edition of this work was published in 1828 and contained a list of 295 bookbinders and 56 members of ancillary trades. Second, third, and fourth editions followed rapidly in 1829, 1831, and 1832. No doubt fifth and sixth editions were published (though I have not been able to trace copies) before the "7th and New" edition, which is unfortunately not dated. This seventh edition contains a reference to J. Zaehnsdorf at his Drury Lane address, which would seem to place it between 1842–45 (though some authorities date it as late as 1852). In any case it dates outside the limits of the present work. I have therefore decided not to quote entries in COWIE/7 except in cases where the binder in question is known from other sources to have been working not later than 1840. Where a change of address is indicated, I have marked it as "(ca. 40)", but give no guarantee as to the exact date of the change. Other entries in COWIE/7 I have ignored.

Howe in his BS/HOWE/LBB. expresses some doubt as to whether *all* the "bookbinders" listed in Cowie's *Manual* were really bookbinders. I feel that doubtful entries in a work primarily addressed to bookbinders might well have brought about Cowie's ears a storm of angry hornets, and there is no evidence of this having happened. The various editions seem to have been conscientiously kept up to date and they record considerable alterations, deletions or additions both in the names and the addresses given. Most of the entries in COWIE are supported by the Directories or by other sources. Elsewhere in this Introduction I have explained in some detail how far I consider the names, etc., which I have listed as being those of "substantial" binders.

MASTER BOOKBINDERS' ASSOCIATIONS

The question of the authenticity of firms claiming to be "bookbinders" between the dates of 1825–40 is not made clearer by the fact that the original Master Bookbinders' Association founded in 1794 seems to have disappeared about 1824 (see BS/HOWE/LBB. p. XXI). In 1837 it was refounded with 40 members (for partial list of same, see SLB. pp. 109–110), rising a year later to 57. On 13th February, 1839, the smaller binders formed the Friendly Society of Master Bookbinders with an initial membership of only 28, though a few days later they appear to have got together 85 subscribers to their views, and possibly to their funds. I have unfortunately not been able to obtain access to the relevant lists.

A SPECIMEN ANALYSIS OF THE SOURCES OF INFORMATION
REGARDING 200 LONDON BOOKBINDERS
OF THE 1780–1840 PERIOD

As one method of checking the extent to which the entries in the alphabetical list which forms the latter part of this volume are "truly" or "substantially" bookbinders, I have analysed the first 200 entries, but have treated as a single entry the various members of a family who can be reasonably considered to have been bookbinders by training, etc.

(1) Out of these first 200 entries, 58 (29%) are mentioned in BS/HOWE/LBB. I have not automatically accepted these 58 entries as being necessarily "true" bookbinders, but have re-examined them from other aspects and find that supplementary evidence is available regarding about half of them. Bearing in mind that many of them date back to a period when "Directory" evidence was not available, I feel justified in accepting Howe's verdict in those cases with which he has dealt.

(2) Of the remaining 142 specimen entries, 63 (or $31\frac{1}{2}$%) are mentioned in Cowie's *Manual* (for editions consulted see p. 26), *and* in one or more of the Trade Directories.

(3) A further 69 (or $34\frac{1}{2}$%) figure mainly in the Trade Directories. An estimate of the value both of Cowie's *Manual* and of the Trade Directories from the point of view of this analysis is given earlier in this Introduction, so I will only say here that I regard the evidence of both favourably.

(4) The remaining 10 (5%) have been culled with due care from a variety of sources. Such evidence as tickets, showcards, catalogues, etc., is the *main* source, though, of course, for a number of the specimens in Classes 1 to 3 useful supporting evidence has also been forthcoming from such sources.

A SKETCH OF STYLISTIC DEVELOPMENTS IN LONDON BOOK-BINDING BETWEEN 1765 AND 1840

To the best of my knowledge, no one has yet made a serious attempt to describe the stylistic pattern to which the varying taste and skill of the more important bookbinders of 1765–1840 did not necessarily conform, but by which at any rate they were largely influenced. I have been tempted to essay the task, but have found myself more than once appalled by the difficulty of planning the sketch in a way which would be both reasonably logical and sufficiently comprehensive.

Eventually I decided to operate on lines which I can perhaps best explain by an analogy. It seemed to me that I might work as if I were studying a large bed of flowers of a single genus over a season. I would try to set out their common features and their varieties, how far they followed common lines of development and how far they were affected by idiosyncracies, or by outside circumstances.

I have divided my sketch into four parts: (I) (1765–80); (II) (1780–1810); (III) (1810–30); and (IV) (1830–40), without pretending that the dates as applied to the binders of 1765 to 1840 can be regarded as any more definite than the floral stages. In studying the styles of the periods as they merge one into another, I will endeavour to show how far the more important binders fit into the general picture and how far they are indirectly responsible for the changes which can be noted.

PERIOD I: THE REVIVAL OF ENGLISH BOOKBINDING
FROM ABOUT 1765 TO 1780

It would have been tempting to begin the present book from a date fifteen years or so before 1780. Although, for reasons of symmetry, etc., I decided against antedating the alphabetical index of binders, I have felt that it would be well to indicate the extent of the work done by the London bookbinders between 1765 and 1780, to which Mr. G. D. Hobson had drawn some attention in the Introduction to his 1940 book on the *English Bindings in the J. R. Abbey Collection*.

My reason for going back to the rather odd year of 1765 is the categorical statement in the "Address to the Booksellers of London & Westminster" of 1st November, 1781 (BS/HOWE/LBB. p. XXVI) to the effect that "It cannot be disputed that Bookbinding has arrived at a degree of Perfection in the course of the last 16 years unknown to any period, both in the useful, as well as the ornamental Part." It is easier to deduct 16 from 1781 and to arrive at 1765, than to arrive at the precise reasons for which the author of the "Address" apparently chose 1765 so definitely as the opening year of the new period.

It does, however, seem that at least in England (though not in Scotland and Ireland) a very dull period of binding dates from about 1741 (when Edward Harley, 2nd Earl of Oxford, died) to about 1760 or 1765. (It may seem that this rather sweeping statement excludes the work, illustrated in R. R. Holmes, *Specimens of Bookbinding*, Windsor Castle, 1893, of Andreas Linde, for George II; and of another unknown binder on Faerno's *Fabulae*, 1743, for Frederick, Prince of Wales, but, even if executed in this country, they appear to me to show no London influence.) Perhaps the revival can to some extent be ascribed to the emergence of a fresh set of collectors and bibliophiles, rich but hardly extravagantly so, who had the taste to select their binders with care and often with considerable variation. Among them may be noted Hollis, Hanway, Cracherode, and Wodhull (whose binding attributions in notes in his own handwriting in many of his volumes are of the utmost value). The 3rd Duke of Roxburghe

6

and William Beckford seem also to have chosen their binders with imagination.

Between 1765 and 1780 a number of first-class London binders were already working, and coming into prominence, about some of whom we know a little, and about others little more than their names. Robiquet, Johnson, Payne, and Baumgarten are cited in the 1781 "Address" as the brightest stars in the 1765–81 "Hemisphere of Bookbinding". Other London binders of eminence during the period were R. Wier, J. Lovejoy, and R. Black.

Of at least equal interest is the outstanding work of anonymous binders, nearly all on presentation copies and therefore probably contemporaneous with publication. They include the "coffin" bindings on Robert Adam's *Ruins of the Temple of Diocletian at Spalato* (1764); the "Minerva" bindings on James Stuart-Nicolas Revett's *Antiquities of Athens* (1762–87); the binding on the George III copy of the Strawberry Hill-printed *Life of Lord Herbert of Cherbury* (1762); and on a copy of Vol. I of Stuart's *Antiquities* in the Soane Museum combining different features of the two previously quoted bindings; the "Fasces" bindings on Rutherford's *Cicero* (1781); Admiral Keppel's *Freedom Box* (1779), with its elaborate shell and anchor pattern; the Chinoiserie bindings (ca. 1775) connected with the initials "J.B.".

As all the bindings mentioned in this paragraph are uncommon, it may be of interest to readers to know where illustrations of them can be found: (*a*) R. Adam's "coffin" bindings (variants with or without the "coffin" or the Royal Arms exist), see *Talks on Bookcollecting*, Cassell, 1952, facing p. 70; (*b*) "Minerva" bindings, for reproduction, see No. 684 in Sotheby Sale Catalogue of 27th April, 1948; (*c*) binding on George III's copy of *Life of Lord Herbert of Cherbury*, see *Book Collector*, Spring, 1953, facing p. 66. The Soane variant shows the same surround as on (*b*), and combines the two tools, shown concentrically on the illustration of (*c*), into a longitudinal pattern on the spine; (*d*) "Fasces" binding, see Plate XXXII; (*e*) Keppel's *Freedom Box*, one binding version is reproduced in HOB/ABB: No. 92; (*f*) Chinoiserie bindings, two different forms are reproduced in HOB/ABB: Nos. 93 and 94.

BINDERS OF 1765–80

At this point it seems desirable to pass to the principal individual binders of the 1765–80 period known to us. They can be first divided into two classes: (*a*) those regarding whom our present knowledge is very limited, or whose influence on the subsequent period is believed to be slight; and (*b*) those who appear to have exercised an important formative influence on their successors after 1780.

(*a*) Under this class the most obscure is Robiquet, mentioned in the Holkham Hall accounts for 1738 as binding in red morocco, and elsewhere in the accounts styled Jean Roubiquet (presumably a Frenchman). Richard Dymott is only known by one handsome binding (HOB/ABB/77). Of Richard Montague only the bindings sent by Thomas Hollis, now in the Biblioteca Nazionale at Florence, and one other (see BS/HOWE/LBB. p. XXI) have been traced to date. To Johnson, also a leading craftsman of the 1765–80 period, only two very dilapidated and rather uninteresting bindings in the Yale University Library can at present be attributed with any degree of certainty (see Plate XIV).

(*b*) The 1765–80 binders exercising an important formative influence on their successors may be classed as: (i) native; and (ii) German binders, though, as time passes, their respective influences naturally tend to intermingle.

(i) Of the native binders the outstanding figures are Roger Payne and, to a far lesser degree, Richard Wier, or Weir. The former, and probably the latter, were handicapped as leaders of a movement by the fact that (except in so far as Mrs. Wier and, possibly, their son may have learned their binding skill from Richard) they appear to have trained or in fact had no apprentices to carry on their tradition. Any influence they exercised (and Payne's was obviously enormous) was therefore due to their innate genius. An attempt to summarise the principal features of Payne's style is in the first place rendered very difficult by the very plainness of Payne's early work, its similarity to that of Wier and Mrs. Wier, and that of many of his contemporaries or near successors. It is also closely paralleled by much of the plainer work of members of the Derome Family. As regards Payne's more decorated work, complications arise from doubts as to its earliest date and the fact that Charles Hering, the closest imitator in this latest style, was already working some years before Payne's death, and that Walther at least, and possibly others, were probably capable of closely imitating Payne's pointillé effects. Certainly the impact of Payne's leadership is very apparent for at least twenty years after his death.

Richard Wier (or Weir) had a far less important and lasting influence on English binding. His earlier work, of which some specimens are known, authenticated by his signature on the spine or the endpapers, is almost identical with that of Payne, with whom he worked for a time either before or after his return from Toulouse. The bindings which he executed for Count MacCarthy are now easily recognisable, and are markedly individual. The tools which he employed are limited in number but combined with great skill and variety. What happened to these tools on his return to England is unknown, and indeed only one specimen of Wier's post-Toulouse style has been identified to date (see article in Winter 1953 number, *Book Collector*).

(ii) Of the foreign binders working in this country during the 1765–80 period, Baumgarten was an early arrival and was internationally famous by 1770. Of the known specimens of his work one is in smooth red morocco, another in marbled calf, and the third and fourth (neither certainly ascribed) in morocco and calf respectively. Knowledge of a wider range of his work will, however, be necessary before an accurate view can be formed of his style, which was much appreciated by his contemporaries. One finds occasionally bindings which appear with little doubt to date between the years 1760–70 and where certain very high standards are reached in the leather used and in the forwarding and the fineness of the tooling. Where we are unable with our present knowledge of the binders of those years to attribute them to definite binders, it is, I admit, tempting, rightly or wrongly, to ascribe them to Baumgarten, however slender the evidence we possess as to his own style. Whether such guesses, due as they must often be to a sense of "*faute de mieux*", are correct or not, there can be no doubt that Baumgarten's lasting influence on English binding was very great and was not confined to that exercised through Kalthoeber, who succeeded to his business, and through Walther who worked under him for a time.

PERIOD II: 1780–1810

There seems no doubt that during these years binders of German origin were predominant, among them Baumgarten, Walther, Kalthoeber, Staggemeier, Welcher, Benedict, the two Bohns, Kappelmann, Meyer, Bielefeld, and Deschlein. Charles Lewis was the son of a German from Hanover, while Charles Hering and Fargher and Lindner were also probably German at least by descent.

It is perhaps useful to examine at least some of the different styles used by Walther, since he is believed to have worked for fifty years from about 1790 or even earlier, and signed specimens of his work are numerous. His styles include: (1) plain morocco with a minimum of gilt straight lines on spine and sides, resembling the work of the Frenchman Antoine Chaumont, but with the double spine bands for which Walther seems to have had a special liking; (2) somewhat similar bindings, but with more, but still restrained straight and curved lines with ornamentation, which occasionally takes a convolute form; (3) bindings mainly in straight-grained morocco, often dark blue (a colour which Walther seems to have affected), decorated with a series of architectural tools, embodying a variety of steeples and spires (see Plate XXV). This tooling is usually executed in blind, but there are a number of bindings known (e.g., in the Storer Bequest at Eton College Library) which are tooled in gilt and from a close examination must be by Walther; to whom can also be creditably attributed (4), a series of bindings (see Plate XXXVIII), also exemplified in the Storer Collection, covered with a close pattern of diagonal crossed lines with a small dot or ornament in the centre of each diamond so formed. (This style was also used by the elder Bozérian (see Descamps = Scrive Cat., Part 1, No. 193) and Bradel Aîné (see Rylands: Sp. 15467).). (5) A number of "mosaic" bindings "à répétition" closely allied to the earlier French productions attributed to Padeloup and Monnier. Perhaps the best known example, that in the collection of the late J. W. Hely-Hutchinson, is dated 1791, which is probably early in Walther's career as an independent London binder. He may, however, well have then been about forty years of age, which would explain the consummate craftmanship of this specimen.

ENGLISH BINDERS 1780–1810

It is a curious phenomenon that outside a very narrow range of binders, which I will deal with later, London binders of English origin between the above dates are either not known by sufficient authenticated specimens of their work, or have little or no definite style to distinguish them. When one looks at the very large body of binding of excellent quality in great libraries obviously executed between these dates, one asks oneself whether, apart from the close copying by bookbinders of the tools and general styles of their competitors, our lack of information is not due to a dislike by patrons to see their books "disfigured" by binders' tickets, etc. I believe that it is quite possible that a patron, having extensive binding and rebinding undertaken for him, definitely objected to having bookbinders' labels stuck in them. I have therefore thought it worthwhile to illustrate a considerable number of anonymous bindings.

There were, however, a number of well-authenticated "English" binders of this period, including Payne and Wier, who have been dealt with under the preceding period: Mrs. Wier, who does not seem to have signed her bindings, and Robert Black, whose best known binding dates before 1780. There seems no doubt that several were working up to, and in some cases beyond, 1800. Of the leading "English" binders of the 1780–1810 period (among which I include Charles Hering, see next cross-heading below), Dillon (of Chelsea) is known by numerous examples, but, apart from his attractive two-colour calf bindings, seems to have no distinctive style; Lovejoy is well known for his masonic bindings, mostly unsigned; Mackinlay was a first-class binder, but only a handful of authenticated specimens of his work are known; the two Faulkners were evidently excellent craftsmen. There were others, who will be found in the Alphabetical Index.

THE TRANSITION FROM THE 1780–1810 PERIOD TO THE 1810-30 PERIOD, AND THE ACTIVITY OF CHARLES HERING

It is obviously a matter of considerable difficulty to draw a definite line between two periods of artistic development, and in taking 1810 as a dividing point I go no further than to claim that there is a very recognisable difference in style between the bindings, say, of 1805 and those of 1815 and after. Further-more, it is, I think, possible to find one binder, Charles Hering, Sr., who seems to furnish the connecting link between the two periods.

Charles Hering was certainly established on his own in 1799 and probably as early as 1795 (see BS/HOWE/LBB. p. 46) and can therefore be taken as over-lapping with Payne, who died in 1797 in St. Martin's Lane, in or near which Hering seems to have set up on his own (Howe gives addresses for Hering in St. Martin's Street or Lane).

If 1809 is accepted as the date of the removal of the Hering business to Newman Street and Timperley is correct in stating that Charles Hering died in that year, he can have made little use himself of what Wheeler (in WH/CAT/1932) calls ticket "C" reading "Bound by Hering, 9 Newman St.". Even if Dibdin is more correct in placing his death about 1812 (a recently acquired binding in my own collection on an 1811 publication with the "B" ticket lends some support to the Dibdin dating), it seems likely that the "C" ticket was mostly used by his brother John and possibly by other members of the family. We should there-fore be on safer ground in attributing with certainty to Charles Hering, Sr., only the bindings having the "A" and "B" labels, and leaving an element of doubt regarding those bearing the "C" label.

11

Two of what are probably among Hering's earliest bindings show influence by Walther and (possibly) by Edwards respectively. The first has the "A" label (see notes in Alphabetical Index under Charles Hering). It is a dark blue straight-grained morocco in my own collection on the 1794 *Aristotelis de Poetica,* with Walther's characteristic double spinebands. The second, on R. Baxter's *Apparitions,* 1691, also in my own collection and with the "A" label (see Plate XI), has a modern spine, but mottled calf sides, with "shadow" winged devils produced by an acid process akin to Edwards' Etruscan bindings. It also carries gilt skulls, owls, and other necromantic tools.

Also with the earliest "A" label is the *Callimachus* (Utrecht, 1797: BM. G. 8650), bound in green straight-grained morocco. The spine carries elaborate but somewhat commonplace tooling, while the sides are plain but for Payne-like corner ornaments.

Another series of bindings shows an even closer affiliation to Payne. One of the earliest, with the "A" label, is illustrated in sch/s. de r/iv, No. 28; and a much plainer russia binding, with the "B" label ("Bound by C. Hering"), is to be found in my own collection on Knight's *Life of Erasmus,* 1726.

Another red straight-grained morocco binding, also in my possession, with the "B" label, is to be found on Gale's *History . . . Cathedral Church of Winchester,* with endpapers watermarked 1801. It shows the fine pointillé work on the spine which was becoming common both here and in France about that date, which is hard to ascribe to any one binder, though the style probably originates with Payne.

Here is perhaps the place to refer to a highly original binding on *A True Report . . . Captain Frobisher* (1577. BM. G. 6479). It is in olive straight-grained morocco and carries the "B" label. The sides are boldly decorated with a minimum of diagonal lines, which is quite original for its date, and which may have inspired C. Lewis's earliest known binding dated 1812. Strangely enough, the elaborate gilt inner dentelles also anticipate Lewis's style.

Two bindings with the Newman St labels showing italianate influence, are probably early productions from that address, but may for reasons explained elsewhere be either by Charles Hering, or his brother and successor, John. Both are in olive straight-grained morocco. The first covers Boccaccio, *Laberinto d'Amore* (1516: BM. C. 72. a. 16). It has elaborate and mostly blind-stamped, stylised sides and the ornate inside dentelles found on the last described binding. The other is on the *Ars Moriendi* (Nuremberg(?), 1480: BM. C. 23. a. 25) and has a completely blind-stamped centre with double and treble gilt architectural surrounds and gothic corners.

Finally two almost unclassifiable productions in the British Museum. The first is in red straight-grained morocco carrying the "B" label on *Homer* (Oxford, 1801: BM. G. 8833). The sides are elaborate, but the doublures are as magnificent as they are lacking in taste. They consist of red morocco with blue inlays, highly gilt with tools inspired by, or imitated from Walther, Staggemeier, and others. The fly-leaves facing them are of gilt paper. The second, also in red straight-grained morocco, on the Bensley *Bible* (1795: BM. 675. h. 5), has a Paynesque spine, plainish geometrically ruled sides, blue silk endpapers with Staggemeier corner tools and a red morocco inside surround with lily tools "à la de Caumont".

Both the above bindings are sumptuous and of very fine workmanship, but in their lack of refinement can be considered as forerunners of the highly decorated productions by Charles Lewis at his Duke St. shop for his many patrons with more money than taste.

The preceding paragraphs make no attempt (such would, in fact, be quite impossible) to list more than a few of the principal classes of binding produced by Charles Hering, with some indication of their relevant dates. I have purposely refrained from ascribing to Charles Hering many of the styles emanating from 9 Newman St., because of the comparatively short time that Charles can have worked there. The vast majority of the bindings bearing one or other indication that they were bound by "Hering, 9, Newman St." are almost certainly the work of John, Charles's brother, or other members of the family who continued to work at the same address till well after 1840.

PERIODS (III) 1810–30 AND (IV) 1830–40

I do not wish to emphasise the date 1830 as marking a definite break in continuity, and for practical purposes I propose, whenever necessary, to treat the two periods as one. But I think that the year 1830 does to some extent mark a dividing line. Such faults, especially of taste, as mar bindings of the 1810–30 period are mainly due to exuberance, while those of the 1830–40 period are rather to be ascribed to dullness and lack of enterprise. I know myself that I approach bindings dating after 1830 with a considerable measure of reserve.

By about 1810 any dividing line between the English and German binders of the previous period had virtually disappeared. On the one hand the binders of German origin (as, for example, both C. Hering and C. Lewis doubtless were) had become naturalised both actually and artistically. On the other hand the principal binders of the post-1810 period had no hesitation in taking ideas from abroad, notably from France and Italy.

Another outstanding feature already existing well before 1810, but intensified thereafter, is the almost feverish haste and complacency with which most book-binders in London rushed to have the successful tools of their trade rivals (whether at home or abroad) copied and to apply them to their own productions. No doubt this copying is almost as old as are tooled bindings themselves, but in the early nineteenth century the copying of tools reached a new level of accuracy. This is what makes it so hard to say, especially before 1810, whether the bindings with pointillé backs or sides such as Renouard possessed in large numbers (see Plate XXVIII) are French or English; and still harder to ascribe unsigned bindings from 1800 onwards (and most bindings in big English libraries are unsigned) to any particular binder. The only safe method of attribution seems to me to be tickets, stamps, or notes by the original owner (e.g., Wodhull, Heber, Drury, etc., etc.). Otherwise it is better to make one's own guess, but to keep it to oneself. One will be wrong, at least, as often as one is right.

After these preliminary remarks I propose to pass to a consideration of the work of Charles Lewis, undoubtedly for twenty years after 1810 the leading figure in London bookbinding.

CHARLES LEWIS

The particulars regarding his origin and early career are summarised in BS/ HOWE/LBB. p. 58. We unfortunately do not know the exact dates between which he was working at 4 Middle Scotland Yard and at 7 Denmark Ct., Strand, respectively, nor when he moved to 29 Duke St., though this later move was not later than 1817. The first binding by him which can be definitely dated is of 1812 (see H. M. Nixon, "English Bookbindings X" in the *Book Collector*, Summer, 1954). No binding definitely emanating from Scotland Yard is at present known. Ovid's *Epistles* (BM. 17157) has been rebound and only the Scotland Yard ticket has survived. A similar ticket was on the russia binding of Leland's *Itinerary* (No. 1190 in Quaritch's Cat. 93/1888), but present whereabouts are unknown. I have a typical Heringesque binding in green morocco on the 2nd edition of Scott's *Lady of the Lake*, 1810, which bears the ticket "Bd by/C. L./7 D.C." and may well be contemporary.

The volume dated 1812 (BM. G. 6479) described by Mr. Nixon is charming and has all the naïvety which one would expect from so early a performance. It is, however, not entirely original in conception, when compared with C. Hering's binding on *A True Report . . . Capt. Frobisher*, 1577, referred to above, which is almost certainly earlier.

An early dated (in Heber's handwriting) specimen is of 1818, and cost £2 14s. to bind. It is on J. Yates's *Hould of Humilitie* (1582: BM. C. 57. c. 15); olive green straight-grained morocco gilt, ornamentation of straight and curved lines on spine, sides, and inside edge; blind-stamped on inside covers "Bound by C. Lewis". Its execution has still some of the gaucherie and all the charm of youth.

Another binding which may be roughly contemporary with the preceding is that in my own collection on Dibdin's dedication copy of the 1814 Brunet's *Manuel du Libraire*. It is bound in golden olive green straight-grained morocco in imitation of the so-called "Duodo" or Marguerite de Valois bindings (see Plate XIII). The tools and tooling are of astonishing virtuosity and I venture to feel that the general effect is perhaps superior in a way to the original "Duodos".

Another group of Lewis bindings which I find of great excellence may be exemplified by the plain lines and sparse extra toolings on Caesar, *Opera* (1469: BM. G. 9181) in olive green straight-grained morocco.

Perhaps the most frequent type of binding used by Lewis for the very influential patrons of his Duke St. premises is that which combined straight lines on the back and sides with very heavy "Aldine" leaf tools in the corners and panels. This style, which was sometimes combined with similar decoration round a white vellum centre on the inner covers, and on other occasions with a highly decorative all-morocco doublure, was to become an almost universal style used by many prominent English and even continental binders until well into the 1830s. A typical example is the dark blue straight-grained morocco gilt binding on *Valerius Maximus*, (Mainz, 1471: BM. G. 9153). The fine tools and the heavy tools often changed from the inner to the outer sides, and vice-versa.

Apart from the above larger classes, it is almost impossible to say if Lewis had a middle-period style, and what it was. He had a large staff (well over twenty), but he obviously managed to control them till 1830, before which date no binding of bad execution, though many of doubtful taste, seems to have left his workshop. He never seems to have hesitated at flagrant imitation (e.g., of Mackinlay's square corners on the edges of a dark blue straight-grained morocco gilt binding on Ulpian's *Commentaries on Demosthenes* (Aldus 1527: BM. G. 8514), or at spoiling a good mixture of straight lines and Grolieresque motives on the covers by an over-elaborate doublure. Again, he spoilt a pure "Payne" side with a single line and a not bad "near-Payne" back on A. Politian, *Misc.* (Florence, 1489: BM. G. 8674) by most elaborate doublures, at least half of which are covered by minute dentelle and filigree work.

I do not propose to deal with the latest phase of "Lewis" binding, covering the imitations of mid-eighteenth-century French bindings and mostly executed in red or green paste-grain morocco (or sheep). I feel that they were executed during a period when C. Lewis was losing control of the business and when Bedford, his foreman, the arch-imitator of all and every style, was gaining control. It would be of great assistance if we could trace the earliest date of the C. Lewis green skiver "Duke St." label, which I also find in bad taste and definitely post-1830.

On the other hand, it would not be fair to forget that Lewis left a number of competent successors who still kept alive the tradition of his best work such as Clarke, Murton, C. Smith, Wilson, etc. Moreover, the bad taste of the later Lewis "pastiches" may be principally due to the patrons who liked and insisted on having them.

A NOTE ON MATERIALS

MOROCCO

Throughout the period, morocco and, to a lesser extent, physically but not artistically speaking, vellum were the materials on which binders lavished their best skill. Both before 1780 and still about 1790–95 they in the main used for their finest work the fine-grained smooth morocco skins, mostly of red colour, which had been typical of the previous period. This type of morocco was used for the bindings executed for Hollis and Hanway, and also by Baumgarten and a number of anonymous binders. By about 1772, however, as may be seen from the signed bindings by Payne and Wier in the Storer Bequest at Eton College, the use of heavy straight-grained morocco was well introduced and tended gradually to predominate more and more for the finest work. The colours mostly used were red, blue, black, citron, green (apple and olive), and purple (very rarely). About 1835 straight grain was gradually replaced by hard- (or circular) grained morocco which distinguishes the bindings of Mackenzie, Bedford, and Wright, or by paste-grained morocco (of bad wearing quality) often used by Charles Lewis in his later period for his imitations of French eighteenth-century bindings.

SKIVER

Bright, highly polished skiver, mostly maroon in colour, was employed on annuals, almanacks, and albums from about 1830. First examples are perhaps due to T. Gosden and then to Remnant and Edmonds, who, according to Arnett, introduced this style of binding about 1829. For its method of application see below under "Tools".

VELLUM

It seems legitimate to argue that the bindings with designs on the undersurface of transparent vellum produced by the Edwards family, though to some extent executed in London, emanated even more from Halifax, whence they originated and where the bulk of them continued to be produced. Frye, the other main producer of similar bindings,* though probably at a later date, was also domiciled outside London, in fact primarily at Halifax. He was an excellent binder in various styles, but was no doubt inspired by Edwards.

It is, however, to be remembered that besides the above and the ordinary "vellum" binder, whose business was essentially utilitarian, quite a number of West End binders used vellum for bindings of the highest artistic rank, among them Kalthoeber, Staggemeier, C. Hering, de Caumont, and Hayday. By far the finest collection known to me is in the Quin Bequest in the Library of Trinity College, Dublin. The main part of the spine and sides of such bindings showed the natural vellum surface, but the decoration was carried out mainly in fine gold tooling consisting of "greek" surrounds and scroll-work, both floral and allegorical. The general effect was heightened by parts of the surrounds and interstices of the designs having the vellum delicately stained, preferably light blue or green, or, apparently for colours where staining was unsatisfactory, with morocco appliqués. In some cases black or blue ruling was also added on the sides.

RUSSIA

Throughout the period, this material, despite its bad wearing qualities, was much favoured, especially for large, not to say weighty, volumes. As far, however, as I have been able to note, this material underwent no great technical or artistic development during the period. In original and unspoilt condition, it is full of dignity and charm.

CALF

Progress on this material between 1780–1840 I find frankly disappointing, especially when I compare it with the astonishing variety of the calf used in France from about 1820, and even earlier in Spain. Some advance was no doubt made

---

* They are perhaps "on" and not "under" the vellum, otherwise infringement of the Edwards patent would appear to have been involved.

from a technical point of view in the production of marbled calf, especially of contrasting colours used, for example, by Dillon of Chelsea. There were also interesting, if sporadic, experiments made (largely outside London) in such directions as etching, painting, etc., on calf (which will be dealt with elsewhere), but which really represent a variation in treatment rather than in the material itself.

CLOTH

The use of this material for edition binding probably started about 1823, but I do not propose to deal specifically with it. My reasons are that the use of cloth only became generalised between 1830 and 1840, which latter I have taken as my closing date, and that it is more intimately connected with mechanical than with hand binding.

SILK

Although silk makes a very occasional appearance as a binding material in the earlier half of our period (see Schweder in the Alphabetical List; and also Holl, of Worcester, ref. CR/BB. p. 91), it plays no role except possibly between 1825–40, when it was, though rarely, used as an intermediate between cloth and leather for edition binding on annuals, almanacks, etc., without ever obtaining the perfection achieved in the use of the material in France by such publishers as Lefuel, Janet, etc.

VELVET

Though this material was much used in earlier times for church and luxury bindings, it was during our period employed even less than silk. If used by Richard Dymott, just before the period with which we are dealing, no specimens seem to have survived. Brassington ascribed considerable use of velvet to Charles Lewis, but no such bindings by him have been identified. It appears to have crept back towards 1830–40, but mainly as a background for heavy gilding or metalwork. Cut or stamped velvet, as used on the Continent from about 1830, does not seem to occur in Great Britain.

SILVER AND OTHER METAL WORK, TORTOISE-SHELL, WOOD, ETC.

Although all these materials were used on the Continent for book-covers during the period, practically no examples seem to occur in this country. The only exceptions which occur to me are the use of metal clasps, locks, and corners. Also worthy of note is the very elaborate ormolu cover (over velvet) on the Duke of Sussex's L.P. copy of Ackerman's *Westminster Abbey, 1812* (now shown in the Abbey itself). The work is most elaborate and for technical reasons it may have

PLATE III DAWSON & LEWIS $(10'' \times 13\frac{1}{4}'')$

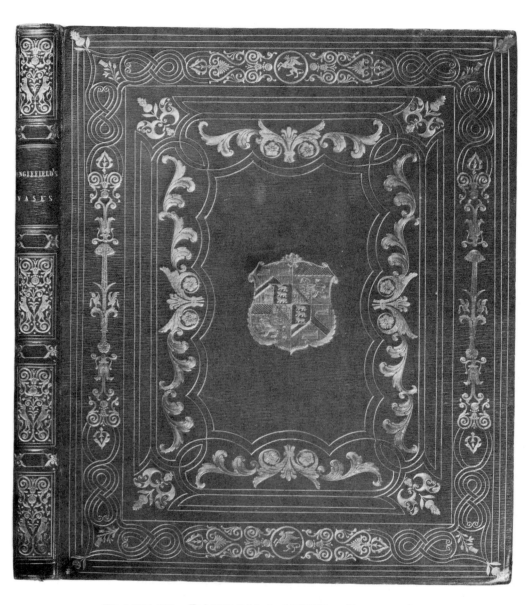

PLATE IV   DAWSON & LEWIS   ($9\frac{1}{2}'' \times 11\frac{3}{4}''$)

been bound soon after publication, though in taste it might well date twenty years later.

TOOLS

A feature during the period, and even as early as 1765, was the re-emergence and perfectioning of fine bookbinders' tools. Though the famous firm, or rather family, of toolmakers named Timbury make their first appearance about 1785, it is apparent from about 1765 and possibly earlier that a degree of finesse was reappearing after the doldrums which succeeded the brilliant 1660–1700 period. Furthermore original forms were being evolved for Hollis and Hanway, and possibly Pingo may have been among the designers of tools which had a distinctly "new look". Baumgarten may have contributed to the movement and so also may Robert Adam, who possibly designed the tools for his *Ruins of Diocletian* bindings, and J. Stuart, who may have done the same for his *Antiquities of Athens*. Payne certainly used and possibly designed quite original tools for his decorated style of bindings, and Wier was probably responsible for the limited range of brilliant tools used on his MacCarthy period bindings.

An important influence may well have been the steady influx of binders and journeymen from Scotland, bringing with them a knowledge of the fine workmanship prevalent there and also at least an acquaintance with that of Dublin. In both these two countries binding was then (pre-1780) well ahead of that done in London. The tools, now at Windsor Castle, used in George III's bindery are well worth study. By 1835 Joseph Morris & Co. boasted that they possessed 20,000 bookbinders' tools, a fact that is not astonishing in view of the facility, noted elsewhere, with which bookbinders imitated each others' tools.

THE USE OF LARGE BLOCKS

English binders never used large blocks as extensively as they were employed in France, where the production of "cathedral" plates covering almost the whole of the sides and even the spines of bindings became a commonplace from about 1825. English specimens of the process are comparatively rare. I recall a blind-stamped English binding of the sort signed by Remnant and Edmonds on Tombleson's *Rhine* which with typical neo-gothic incongruity exhibited on the sides two views of York Minster which were no doubt thought to be "near enough" to Cologne Cathedral.

More common are the formalised neo-gothic or neo-classical bindings by Hering (J.?), from about 1812, and a little later by Dawson and Lewis (who had already produced somewhat similar bindings built up by single tools) embodying the use of whole blocks or large tools, with the aim no doubt of greater speed and with an eye on a gift-book public.

Between 1825–35 the use of engraved plates, largely founded on the illustration of the volumes within the bindings, tended to be used as the principal or even the sole element of the decoration of the sides and spines on books destined for the gift or semi-luxury trades. Typical examples can be seen on Lady Blessington's or R. J. Turner's *Annuals,* and more elaborate and larger ones on such books as *Beauties of the Bosphorus,* etc., etc.

The plates were generally engraved by a series of talented artists, often of German origin, and approximated closely to those used about the same date in France and elsewhere on the Continent both on leather and more commonly on cloth bindings.

Having dealt with a class and style of bindings which is essentially international, I may perhaps refer here to a style of binding (for "binding" and not "casing" it appears to be) which seems to be indigenous and not to have spread abroad, though somewhat similar productions are to be found in the "souvenir" books or containers to be found in Germany, for valentines, amateur poems, and the like. In England these first appear about 1825, and proved of wide acceptance till about 1845. The material employed was a highly polished skiver (see "Materials") and appears at first on the popular bindings for Walton's *Angler* and *Lives.* These bindings had at least a superficial individuality. Later they assumed a conventionalised "Midsummer Night's Dream" appearance, which, although represented by a limited number of plates, embodied a fineness of detail which would not discredit a seal-engraver. The plates covering the whole of the back and sides of volumes, running up to the conventional scrap-album size, were evidently applied with skill and under considerable pressure. Fine examples occur on L. B. Sheridan's *Comic Offering Almanacks* (see Plate V).

EXCEPTIONAL METHODS OF DECORATION

(1) ETRUSCAN STYLE AND OTHER ACID-BITTEN METHODS

These seem in the main to be of provincial origin. The best known are no doubt those produced by the Edwards family of Halifax, though they may have produced similar bindings in London. At least one such binding by Charles Hering is known, and two apparently "Edwards" bindings in the Rylands Library carry Staggemeier and Welcher tickets.

(II) LINE AND WASH DRAWINGS

These are by no means uncommon, but again seem mostly to have originated in the provinces. The principal *signed* examples seem to have been done by Scott of Carlisle, but there are interesting unidentified specimens, either embodying mythological scenes, or views of gothic buildings. The designs appear to have been drawn in monochrome wash on the calf surface and then, possibly after being in some way "fixed", to have been preserved by a form of high varnishing. The designs are usually surrounded by straight black lines, finished at the angles with gilt roundels, which gives them a family resemblance. Genre drawings, etc., a more elaborate form of the above, also appear to be of provincial origin. The only specimens known to me are noted in CR/BB. pp. 63, 107, under Downes, and Lee & Co.

(III) VERNIS-MARTIN

Though this process, originating from coach-decoration, was not uncommonly applied to bindings of the late eighteenth and early nineteenth centuries in France, I believe that the only known English example is in my own collection, showing two plaques on the sides of a typical late eighteenth-century binding in red morocco on the 2nd edition (1789) of William Gilpin's *Observations on the River Wye*. The plaques are Gilpinesque in subject but do not correspond to any of the plates in the volume (see Plate XXXV).

Bindings on the Vernis-Martin system do not seem to reappear in this country till about 1840–50, when they took on an oriental or "tartan" aspect.

(IV) BINDINGS WITH COLOURED LACQUER INCRUSTATIONS

This class of binding, though uncommon, is well known on the Continent from about 1830 on almanacks, gift books, etc.; but the only English producer appears to be J. S. Evans (q.v.), who seems to have acquired his knowledge of the process by somewhat devious means.

(V) GOTHIC EFFECTS PRODUCED BY INDIVIDUAL TOOLS

Specimen tools in the gothic manner can be found at Windsor Castle among those formerly employed in George III's Buckingham Palace Bindery. Examples of such gothic handwork by Walther, MacKinlay, Mackenzie, Dawson and Lewis, and Lubbock (of Newcastle) are extant and of charming effect.

(VI) SINGLE AND DOUBLE FORE-EDGE PAINTINGS

Whether the revival of the art can be solely attributed to the Edwards of Halifax family, there seems no doubt that they brought it to a degree of perfection which led to a surprising and indeed confusing host of imitators, many of whom are still active to-day.

(VII) EDGE-GILDING, GAUFFERING AND STAINING

An interesting series of processes, which to some extent represent a revival of old-time practices, are to be found in the employment of one or more of the above separately, or in combination, on the closed as opposed to the "fanned" edges. A binding (in my own collection and possibly originally Mrs. Piozzi's copy) on the Baskerville *Paradise Lost* of 1760 combines all three. The "shell" binding on Admiral Keppel's *Box* and the Rutherford *Cicero* "Fasces" binding show gilt printing and staining, and a Sowler binding (CR/BB. p. 153) gauffering and gilding. The effects are varied and pleasing.

The processes are usually applied by one or other mechanical device, but I know of cases where water-colour has been used, with or without gauffering. In the case of a binding (probably about 1825) on W. Hayley's *Life of George Romney*, 1809, the edges are decorated in various water-colours and the interstices filled with gauffering on the gilt. In another case of a contemporary morocco and calf binding on R. Phillip's *Sylva Florifera*, 2 Volumes, 1825, the edges are decorated with a charming water-colour pattern of roses, pansies, and convolvuli.

PLATE V   DE LA RUE & Co   (4″ × 6¼″)

PLATE VI   EVANS, J. S. $(5\frac{3}{4}'' \times 8\frac{3}{4}'')$

MISCELLANEOUS REFERENCES

ABB/CBS.	"British Signed Bindings in the Abbey Collection", *Proc. Cambridge Bibl. Soc.,* Vol. I, 1948–51, pp. 270–9.
AE/BML.	A. Esdaile, *The British Museum Library*, London, 1946.
AE/COLL.	Collection of A. Ehrman.
AE/COLL/LAB.	Bookbinders' tickets in possession of A. Ehrman.
AE/f.	Information communicated by A. Ehrman.
AE/HEAL/LAB.	Bookbinders' tickets, etc., in the Heal Collection, per A. Ehrman.
BB.	*The Bookbinder*, 1888–90.
BR/BM.	*British Bookmaker*, 1891.
BS/DPB/1726/75	Bib/Soc., *Dictionary of Booksellers and Printers (1726–75)*, Oxford, 1950.
BS/HOWE/LBB.	Bib/Soc., E. Howe, *London Bookbinders (1648–1815)*, Oxford, 1950.
BS/HOWE/LBB/ADD.	Additions to the above recorded by H. M. Nixon.
CR/BB.	C. Ramsden, *U.K. Bookbinders outside London (1780–1840)*, London, 1954.
F.S.C.	Freeman of Stationers' Company.
GROLIER	Grolier, *Guide du Bibliophile*, Vol. I, 1946–48; Vol. II, 1949–51, Paris.
HOB/ABB.	G. D. Hobson, *English bindings in the J. R. Abbey Collection*, London, 1940.
JBO/AE.	List of binders, communicated by J. B. Oldham to A. Ehrman.
LAB/JONES	Collection of bookbinders' tickets, etc., lent to H. M. Nixon in July, 1951.
LAB/KNA.	Bookbinders' tickets in R. J. Knaster Collection.
LAB/PEARSON	Collection of bookbinders' tickets, lent by Dr. J. Sidney Pearson per H. M. Nixon, July, 1951.
LBB/HOWE	E. Howe, *The London Bookbinders (1780–1806)*, London, 1950.
MUNBY	(I) List of signed British bindings in the Collection of A. N. L. Munby, November, 1951.

MUNBY—*contd.*	..	(II) "Collecting English Signed Bindings", autumn number of the *Book Collector*, 1953.
		(III) Various personal communications.
O.C.	..	Author's own Collection.
OLD/SH. ..	..	J. B. Oldham, *Bindings in Shrewsbury College Library*, Oxford, 1943.
P/LABEL ..	..	Album of bookbinders' tickets, lent by Ivor Poole, December, 1950. Dates are those given in the album.
SCH/S. de R/IV.	..	*British, etc., Bindings in the Schiff Collection*, Vol. IV, Paris, 1935.
SLB.	..	E. Howe and J. Child, *Society of London Bookbinders, (1780–1951)*, London, 1952.
TIMP/42. ..	..	Timperley's *Encyclopaedia*, London, 1842.
WH/CAT. ..	..	Sale Catalogue of Private Collection of Francis Wheeler, Giraud-Badin, 1932.
WSM/KS/NEW.	..	Information communicated by Dr. W. S. Mitchell.
,, /A.	..	Article by W. S. Mitchell in *Durham University Journal*, December, 1953.
,, /54.	..	*British Signed Bindings in King's College, Newcastle-upon-Tyne*, 1954.

E.D.	..	Possible earliest date of working.
L.D.	..	,, latest ,, ,, ,,
BB.	..	Bookbinder.
BEP/WM. ..	..	Watermark on binder's endpaper(s).
BS.	..	Bookseller.
PR.	..	Printer.
ST.	..	Stationer.

LONDON DIRECTORIES CONSULTED

Goss,★

page

63	KENT/DIR/83	..	Kent's Directory	1783
69	AND/90	..	Andrew's London Directory	1790
72	BRI/DIR/91	..	Universal British Directory	1791 (or 1790)
82	,, ,, /98	..	,, ,, ,, Vol V	1798
77	BOY/94	..	Boyle's General London Guide	1794
89	HOLD/02/04	..	Holden's Triennial Directory	1802–3–4
92	,, /05/07	..	,, ,, ,,	1805–6–7
97	,, /11	..	,, Annual ,,	1811
108	,, /22/24	..	,, Triennial ,,	1822–3–4
103	JOHN/17	..	Johnstone's London Directory	1817
104	,, /18	..	,, ,, ,,	1818
102	PO/DIR/17	..	Post Office Directory	1817
118	,, ,, /28	..	,, ,, ,,	1828
122	,, ,, /31	..	,, ,, ,,	1831
132	,, ,, /39	..	,, ,, ,,	1839
134	,, ,, /40	..	,, ,, ,,	1840
111	PIG/DIR/23	..	Pigot's London Directory	1823–24
113	,, ,, /24	..	,, ,, ,,	1824
118	,, ,, /28	..	,, ,, ,,	1828
123	,, ,, /32	..	,, ,, ,,	1832
128	,, ,, /36	..	,, ,, ,,	1836
131	,, ,, /38	..	,, ,, ,,	1838
106	ROB/DIR/20	..	Robson's London Directory	1820
107	,, ,, /21	..	,, ,, ,,	1821
110	,, ,, /22	..	,, ,, ,,	1822
116	,, ,, /26/7	..	,, ,, ,,	1826/7
120	,, ,, /29	..	,, ,, ,,	1829
121	,, ,, /30	..	,, ,, ,,	1830
123	,, ,, /32	..	,, ,, ,,	1832
124	,, ,, /33	..	,, ,, ,,	1833
127	,, ,, /35	..	,, ,, ,,	1835

★ Goss, C. W. F., *London Directories (1627–1853)*, London, 1932.

COWIE'S BOOKBINDER'S MANUAL

LIST 28	..	Cowie's *Bookbinder's Manual*			1828 (1st ed.)
COWIE/29	..	,,	,,	,,	1829 (2nd ed.)
,, /31	..	,,	,,	,,	1831 (3rd ed.)
,, /32	..	,,	,,	,,	1832 (4th ed.)
,, /7	..	,,	,,	,,	ca. 1840 (7th & new ed.)

All editions of this Manual are extremely scarce. For the 1st edition of 1828 I have retained the reference used by Howe. For the 1829, 1831, and 1832 editions I have used the abbreviations COWIE/29, etc.; and for the seventh edition I have used COWIE/7. I have been unable to locate 5th and 6th editions. (Further reference to this Manual will be found in the Introduction.)

ADAMS, *Bartholomew*
(BS/HOWE/LBB. p. 1).

ADAMS, G.
Add.: 22 Sidmouth St., Cromer St.
Refs.: PIG/DIR/23.

ADAMS, *Thomas*
    ,,   ,,   *Frederick* (32).
    ,,   *Thomas* (ca. 40).
Add.: 39 Cleveland St., Fitzroy Sq.
(24): 5 Talbot Ct., Gracechurch
St. (32): 32 Lime St., Leadenhall
St. (36): 14 Little Tower St.
(Thomas) (ca. 40).
Refs.: COWIE/31: 32: PIG/DIR/24:
32: 36: 38: ROB/DIR/32: 35: PO/
DIR/40: COWIE/7.

ADLARD, *John*
(see Adlard & Lycett).
Add.: 35 Villiers St., Strand.
Refs.: COWIE/29: 31: PIG/DIR/32:
36: 38: ROB/DIR/29: 32: 35: 40:
PO/DIR/40: COWIE/7: SLB. pp.
109 & 128.
O.C.: Dickson: *Dry Rot.* 37.
f.m.g., Lewis style, with urns on
sides. The publishers were J. &
C. Adlard, Bartholomew Close,
but the binding is blind-stamped
"Bd. by J. Adlard." (?) Admitted
as F.S.C. on 6.8.1822.

ADLARD & LYCETT
(see Adlard, John).
Add.: 27 Nelson St., City Rd. (?):
35 Villiers St., Strand (28).
Refs.: PIG/DIR/28: AE/COLL/LAB.

AGG, *James* (? E.D. 23)
Add.: 34 Shoemakers Row, Black-
friars (28): 21 Paternoster Row,
St. Paul's (31): 2 Johnson's Ct.,
Fleet St. (36): No. 9 (40): 116
Fleet St. (ca. 40).
Refs.: PIG/DIR/28: 32: 36: COWIE/
31: 32: ROB/DIR/32: 35: 40: PO/
DIR/40: COWIE/7. According to
Bell's *Monthly Messenger* of
21.9.23, Agg was then a board-
binder to the trade.

AITKEN
(BS/HOWE/LBB. p. 1).
Initials of partners were at one time
"F. & I."
(BS/HOWE/LBB/ADD).

AITKEN, *Charles James*
Add.: 2 Langley St., Long Acre:
4 George St., Adelphi (36):
4 York Bldgs., Adelphi (ca. 40).
Refs.: COWIE/31: 32: PIG/DIR/32:
36: 38: ROB/DIR/32: 35: 40: PO/
DIR/39: 40: COWIE/7.

AITKEN, *F. A.*
Refs.: Huth Sale No. 648.

AITKEN, *John*
Add.: 6 Woburn Ct., Bloomsbury:
49 Gt. Wild St., Lincolns Inn
Fields (40).
Refs.: PIG/DIR/30: PO/DIR/40: Huth
Sale No. 3681: BM. C. 25. c. 17.

AITKIN & WHITE
(BS/HOWE/LBB. p. 1).

AKED, *Joseph*
Add.: 16 Devereux Ct., Strand:
1 Palgrave Place, Strand (ca. 40).
Refs.: PIG/DIR/36: 38: ROB/DIR/40:
COWIE/7.

ALDUS, *John*
Add.: 14 New St. Sq.: 16 Devereux
Ct., Strand (40).
Refs.: PIG/DIR/36: 38: PO/DIR/40.

ALLAWAY, *John*
(BS/HOWE/LBB. p. 1).   (BS. &).
Refs.: ROB/DIR/20: 22: AE/COLL/LAB:
LAB/PEARSON.

ALLCHIN, *Francis*
(BS/HOWE/LBB. p. 2).
Add.: 22 Warwick Sq.
Refs.: HOLD/02/04.

ALLCHIN, *Thomas*
(BS/HOWE/LBB. p. 2).

ALLEN, *Mrs. Ann*
(BB.'s Toolmaker).
Add.: 25 New St., Cloth Fair.
Refs.: PO/DIR/40.

ALLEN, *Benjamin William*
(& ST.).
Add.: 30 Ebury St., Pimlico.
Refs.: PIG/DIR/32: 36: ROB/DIR/40
(as "ST., etc.").

ALLEN, *C.*
(BB.'s Toolmaker).
Add.: 81 Gt. Portland St.
Refs.: PO/DIR/40.

ALLEN, *George*
(& ST.).
Add.: 111 London Wall.
Refs.: PIG/DIR/32: 36.

ALLEN, *John and/or James*
(Vellum Binder).
Add.: 20 King St., Borough.
Refs.: ROB/DIR/20 (James): 22 (J.):
PIG/DIR/24: 28: (John).

ALLEN, *William*
(Book Edgegilder).
Add.: 4 Coxes Ct., Aldersgate St.
Refs.: ROB/DIR/40.

ALLEN, *William*
(BB.'s Toolmaker: Plow-knives).
Add.: 27 Gt. St. Andrew St., Seven
Dials.
Refs.: PO/DIR/40: COWIE/7.

ALMOND, *George*
Add.: 3 St. James' Market (28):
125 Jermyn St. (31).
Refs.: COWIE/31: 32: PIG/DIR/28:
32: ROB/DIR/32: 35.

ALSWORTH, *William*
Add.: near Lambeth Church: 19
High St., Lambeth (ca. 40).
Refs.: COWIE/29: 31: COWIE/7.

AMOUX, *John*
(& BS.).
Add.: 34 Newington Causeway,
West.
Refs.: PIG/DIR/23.

AMYON (or Anyon) & HOLLINGS
Add.: 17 Charles St., Covent
Garden.
Refs.: PO/DIR/28: 31.

ANDERSON, *Eliz.*
Add.: Tyson (or Tysson) St.,
Whitechapel.
Refs.: COWIE/29: 31: PIG/DIR/32.

ANDERSON, *James*
(BS/HOWE/LBB. p. 2).

ANDERSON, *John*
(BS/HOWE/LBB. p. 2).

ANDERSON, *John*
(BS/HOWE/LBB. pp. 2/3).

ANDERSON, *John*
Add.: 13 Turk St., Bethnall Green.
Refs.: PIG/DIR/24.

ANDERSON, *Robert*
Add.: 27 Maiden Lane, Covent
Garden.
Refs.: COWIE/29: 31: PIG/DIR/24:
28: ROB/DIR/29.

ANDERSON, *William*
(Vellum Binder).
Add.: 4 St. Benet's Pl., Grace-
church St.
Refs.: COWIE/29: 31: 32: PIG/DIR/
28: 32: ROB/DIR/32: 35: 40: PO/
DIR/40: COWIE/7.

ANDERSON & BRETT
(See Brett).
Add.: 3 Nag's Head Ct., Grace-
church St.
Refs.: JOHN/17: ROB/DIR/20.

ANDREWS, *William Thomas*
(BS. &).
Add.: 356 Strand: 24 Holywell St.,
Strand (36).
Refs.: COWIE/29: 31: PIG/DIR/23:
24: 28: 36: 38: ROB/DIR/20: 22:
35.

ANNEREAU, *Isaac*
(BS/HOWE/LBB. p. 3).
Add.: 9 Gt. Suffolk St., Borough
(20): Borough Rd. (29).
Refs.: COWIE/29: 31: ROB/DIR/20:
SLB. p. 90/1.

ANNIS, *Joseph*
   ,,   *James* (32)
  Add.: Kennington Cross (28):
    Vauxhall (29): 13 Gt. Park St.
    (32).
  Refs.: COWIE/29: 31: PIG/DIR/32.

ANSDELL, *Samuel*
  Add.: 11 Adams St. West, Portman
    Sq.
  Refs.: PIG/DIR/36: 38: PO/DIR/40.

ANTT, *Samuel*
  (BS. &).
  Add.: Waterloo Rd., Lambeth.
  Refs.: ROB/DIR/35.

ANYON & HOLLINGS
  (See Hollings, James).
  Add.: 17 Charles St., Long Acre.
  Refs.: ROB/DIR/29.

APPLEBEE, *William*
  (& ST.).
  Add.: 157 Upper Thames St.
  Refs.: PIG/DIR/32.

APPLEBY, *Henry*
  (BB.'s Toolcutter).
  Add.: 33 & 36½ Charles St., Hatton
    Garden.
  Refs.: PIG/DIR/32: 36.

APPLETON
  (BS/HOWE/LBB. p. 3).

APPLETON, *James*
  (BS/HOWE/LBB. p. 3).

Add.: Appleton Pl., Walworth
  Common (28).
Refs.: PIG/DIR/28.

ARMITAGE, *William*
  Add.: 20 Fann St., Goswell Road:
    36 Threadneedle St. (ca. 40).
  Refs.: COWIE/31: 32: PIG/DIR/32:
    COWIE/7.

ARMSTRONG, *Thomas*
  (See Fairbairn &).
  BS/HOWE/LBB. p. 3).
  Add.: 11 & (later) 23 Villiers St.
  Refs.: COWIE/28: 29: 31: PIG/DIR/
    28: 32: 36: 38: ROB/DIR/29: 32:
    35: 40: PO/DIR/40.
  O.C.: Northwick's *Ancient Coins*:
    26: 3/4 m.g.: vermicular linen
    sides: label "Bd. by/TA/23/V.S.,
    Strand."

ARMSTRONG, *Thomas*
  (Nephew of above).
  (BS/HOWE/LBB. p. 3).
  Refs.: SLB. passim.

ARMSTRONG, *W.*
  (BS/HOWE/LBB. p. 3).
  Refs.: HOLD/11 gives two **W.**
    Armstrongs, both ST., working
    at 14 Smithfield Bars, and at 38
    High Holborn respectively.

ARNOTT, *John*
  ,,   *William* (? 28).
  Add.: 3 Belle Sauvage Yd., Ludgate

PLATE VII   FAIRBAIRN & ARMSTRONG $(8\frac{3}{4}'' \times 12'')$

PLATE VIII   HAIGH $(3\frac{1}{2}'' \times 6'')$

Hill (20): 4 Carthusian Ct., Aldersgate (24): 6 Shoemaker Lane (28) 39 St. Andrew's Hill (38).

Refs.: COWIE/29: 31: PIG/DIR/24: 32: 36: 38: ROB/DIR/20: 22: 29: 32: 35: 40: PO/DIR/40: COWIE/7: John A. was admitted a F.S.C. by redemption on 7.4.1818.

ARNOUX, *John*
(& Vellum Binder in 29)
Add.: 21 Garden Row, London Rd. (20): 27 Bridgehouse Place, Newington Causeway (28): No. 37 (29).
Refs.: COWIE/29: 31: PIG/DIR/24: 28: ROB/DIR/20: 29.

ASHER, *A.*
Add.: 83 Aldersgate St.
Refs.: PIG/DIR/32.

ASHEW, *George*
(BS/HOWE/LBB. p. 4).

ASHKETTLE, *W.*
Add.: 3 Greystoke Place.
Refs.: PIG/DIR/32.

ASHLEY, *James*
(& BS. & ST.).
Add.: 37 Haymarket.
Refs.: PO/DIR/40.

ASHMAN, *Thomas*
,, *George*
Add.: 5 Tabernacle Sq., Finsbury (28): 6 Bridgwater Sq. (36): 3 Cherry Tree Ct., Aldersgate St. (40).
Refs.: PIG/DIR/28: 36: 38: ROB/DIR/40: PO/DIR/40: SLB. pp. 47 & 49.

ASPERNE, *James*
(Bookseller, patronised J. Lovejoy: probably only ordered bindings on commission).
Add.: Bible, Crown & Constitution, 32 Cornhill.
Refs.: PO/DIR/17: HOLD/11: The Bible and Crown figures on his ticket.

ASTLE, *Thomas*
,, *Mary* (35)
,, *Jos. Thomas* (36)
,, *G.* (38)
,, *& Sons* (40)
,, *& Co.* (ca. 40)
Add.: 7 Talbot Ct., Gracechurch St. (24): Salters Hall Ct. (28): 4 Artichoke Row, Mile End Rd. (36): 2 Cloak Lane, Cheapside (35/6): 80 Coleman St. (ca. 40).
Refs.: COWIE/29: 31: PIG/DIR/24: 28: 32: 36: 38: ROB/DIR/20: 22: 29: 32: 35: 40: PO/DIR/31: 40: COWIE/7.

ATKINS, *William* ("*Harmony*")
(BS/HOWE/LBB. p. 4).

AULT, *James*
  Add.: 5 Bishop Place, Fulham Rd.
  Refs.: PIG/DIR/32.

AUSTIN(G), *Henry J.*
  Add.: 35 Warwick Lane (36): 25
  Castle St. Falcon St. (40).
  Refs.: PIG/DIR/36: 38: ROB/DIR/40:
  PO/DIR/40.

AXELBY, *William*
  (BS/HOWE/LBB. p. 4).

BACON, *John*
  Add.: 7 Upper Ebury St., Pimlico.
  Refs.: PIG/DIR/32.

BAILEY, *George*
  Add.: 15 Red Lion St., Holborn
  (28): 7 Duke St., W. Smithfield
  (36).
  Refs.: PIG/DIR/28: 32: 36: 38:
  ROB/DIR/35: 40: PO/DIR/40.

BAIN, *Alexander*
  (& Toolcutter: 38).
  Add.: 90 Hatton Garden (36): 30
  Brook St., Holborn (40).
  Refs.: PIG/DIR/36: 38: ROB/DIR/40.

BAIRD
  (BS/HOWE/LBB. p. 5).

BAKER, *John*
  Add.: 11 Monkwell St., Wood St.:
  15 Bath St., Newgate St. (ca. 40:
  no initial).
  Refs.: PIG/DIR/28: COWIE/7.

BALL, *George*
  Add.: 6 Smart's Bldgs.: 20 Little
  Carter Lane (ca. 40).
  Refs.: PIG/DIR/32: 36: COWIE/7 (no
  initial).

BALL, *Joseph*
  (Toolcutter).
  Add.: 10 Charles St., Goswell Rd.
  Refs.: PIG/DIR/36.

BALLARD, *Thomas*
  (BS/HOWE/LBB. p. 6).

BALLARD, *William*
  (BS/HOWE/LBB. p. 6).

BANFIELD, *Thomas*
  (BS/HOWE/LBB. p. 6).

BARDET & BOYLAN
  E.D.: ? 35.
  Refs.: Huth Sale No. 7670: BM.:
  11403 a. 23: is a full st. gr. mor.
  binding signed at base of spine.
  The sides are in the Clark/Lewis
  tradition; the spine in the early
  Bedford style.

BARFORD, *Charles*
  Add.: 11 Clarendon Sq., Somers
  Town (35): 27 Poland St., Oxford
  St. (36).
  Refs.: ROB/DIR/35: 40: PIG/DIR/36:
  38: PO/DIR/40: COWIE/7.

BARLING, *William/Mary/George*
(BS/HOWE/LBB. p. 7).
Refs.: HOLD/11 (M) : PIG/DIR/32 :
(? Mary or George) : see also
Handcock, I.

BARNES, *Thomas*
(BS/HOWE/LBB. p. 7).
(BS., ST. &).
Add.: No. 9 Piccadilly East (02).
Refs.: HOLD/02/04:11 : PO/DIR/17.

BARNFATHER, *T.* (or ? J.)
Add.: Cooper's Ct., Gt. Windmill
St.
Refs.: COWIE/31 : 32 : ROB/DIR/32.

BARRATT, *William*
(BS. & ST. in 20).
Add.: 21 Portugal St., Lincolns Inn
Fields.
Refs.: COWIE/29 : 31 : PIG/DIR/24 :
28 : 32 : 36 : 38 : ROB/DIR/20 : 22 :
29 : 35 : 40 : PO/DIR/40 : COWIE/7.

BARRETT, *John*
Add.: 3 Boston St., Hackney Rd.
Refs.: PIG/DIR/36 : 38.

BARRON, *Richard*
(Vellum Binder).
Add.: 20 Gt. Bell Alley.
Refs.: PIG/DIR/28.

BARRY, *Sarah*
(PR. & BS. in 20).
Add.: 2 Bridge St., Westminster.
Refs.: ROB/DIR/20 : 22.

BARRY, *Walter Edward*
(BS/HOWE/LBB. p. 7).
Add.: No. 2 Bridge St. (02).
Refs.: HOLD/02/04.

BARRY, *William*
(BS/HOWE/LBB. p. 7).
Refs.: COWIE/29 : 31 (still at Bridge
St., Westminster). The Bishops-
gate St. address mentioned in BS/
HOWE/LBB is probably his private
address.

BARTLETT, *C. S.*
Add.: 8 Athol Place, Manchester Sq.
Refs.: ROB/DIR/40.

BARTON, *Elizabeth. Widow*
(BS/HOWE/LBB. p. 8).
Refs.: PIG/DIR/24.

BARTON, *Joseph*
(BS/HOWE/LBB. p. 8).

BARTON, *William*
(BS/HOWE/LBB. p. 8).
Refs.: COWIE/29 : 31 : PIG/DIR/28 (at
11 Lovell's Ct.) : ROB/DIR/29.

BASS, *Robert Henry*
Add.: 23 Paul St., Finsbury.
Refs.: PIG/DIR/28.

BATCHELOR, *Joseph and/or John*
Add.: 6 Johnson's Ct., 165 Fleet St.
(28) : 112 Fetter Lane (29).

Refs.: COWIE/29: 31: PIG/DIR/28:
32: 38: ROB/DIR/29: 32: 35: 40:
PO/DIR/40: COWIE/7.

BATE, *Absalom*
(& Vellum Binder).
Add.: 4 Goldsmith St., Gough Sq.
Refs.: COWIE/29: 31: PIG/DIR/24:
28: 32: 36: 38: ROB/DIR/20: 22:
29: 32: 35: 40: PO/DIR/40. Apprenticed to Mary Flavell and
admitted a F.S.C. on 11.4.20.

BATE, *James*
(BS/HOWE/LBB. pp. 8 & XXXIV).

BATEMAN, *Thomas*
Add.: Little Ct., Leicester Sq. (28):
14 Goodge St., Tottenham Ct.
Rd. (29): No. 37 (29): 36
Tottenham St., Fitzroy Sq. (?
LAB/JONES).
Refs.: COWIE/29: 31: PIG/DIR/28:
32: 36: 38: ROB/DIR/29: 32: 40:
COWIE/7.

BATEMAN & SON
Add.: 81 Devonshire St., Queen's
Sq.
Refs.: AE/HEAL/LAB.

BATES, *Henry*
(Bookclasp Makers).
Add.: 35 Noble St., Cheapside.
Refs.: COWIE/29: 31: PIG/DIR/23.

BATTEN, *David*
(Publisher).

Add.: Clapham Common.
Refs.: LAB/KNA. (ca. 25).
O.C. Impey, E. B.: German
Poetry, 2 vol.: 1840. f. ch. g.:
broad doublures: silk tabis.
Stamped "Bd. by B., C."

BAUMGARTEN, *John*
(BS/HOWE/LBB. pp. 8/10 & XXXIV).
Add.: Duchy Lane, Strand.
Refs.: Dibdin's *Bibl. Tour*, II, p.
412, & *N.E. & S. Tour*, p. 1052.
O.C. Fournier: *Traités, sur . . .
l'Imprimerie*, n.d: (but individual
parts dated 1758–63): f. red
morocco g. (see Plate I): authenticated by M. Wodhull's note
dated 3.2.1774, giving cost as 7/6
for sewing and 7/6 for binding by
Baumgarten. Euripides: *Hecuba
& Iphigenia*: 1524: Wodhull Cat.
1024): f. mottled c. g.; in the
Manchester University Library is
similarly authenticated. The
Burdett-Coutts First Folio, now
in the Fogger-Shakespeare Library, is said in the Lee Census, to
be rebound by Baumgarten, but
the F.S. Library cannot confirm.
Mr. A. N. L. Munby, on p. 271
of the *Book Collector*, Vol. 1, No.
4, gives hints as to some further
probable examples. Mr. Muir,
and the author have bindings in
morocco & calf respectively with
the strap & ribbon tool (shown in
Plate I) on the spine, which can be

PLATE IX   HAYDAY   (6½″ × 10″)

PLATE X   HERING, C. $(5\frac{1}{2}'' \times 8\frac{1}{2}'')$

attributed to Baumgarten with considerable certainty.

BAUMGARTEN & KALTHOEBER
(BS/HOWE/LBB. p. 9).

BAWDEN, *Thomas*
(BS. &).
Add.: 43 Museum St.
Refs.: PIG/DIR/23.

BAXTER, *Elizabeth/John/George*
(Clasp Maker and sometimes BB.).
(BS/HOWE/LBB. p. 10).
Add.: (see below).
Refs.: COWIE/31: 32: where two Baxters are mentioned, one at Queen's Square, Aldersgate St., and the other at Ivy Lane, where Howe first notes the family in 1802. COWIE/29 only mentions the one at Queen's Sq. HOLD/11 (same address as HOLD/09 in HOWE). ROB/DIR/29 gives *Thomas* Baxter at 5 Queen's Sq., Aldersgate St.

BAXTER, *Hector*
Add.: Belle Sauvage Yd., Ludgate Hill (28): 4 Ivy Lane, Newgate St. (32): 49 Little Britain (35): 49 Bartholomew Close (36).
Refs.: PIG/DIR/28: 32: 36: 38: ROB/DIR/35: 40: PO/DIR/40: COWIE/7.

BAYLEY, *John*
Add.: Kensington Gravel Pits.
Refs.: PIG/DIR/32. A "John Bayley" was apprenticed to James Black and became a F.S.C. on 6.3.21.

BEADON, *Abraham*
Add.: 41 or 42 Gloucester St., Red Lion Square.
Refs.: COWIE/29: 31: PIG/DIR/32: 36: 38: ROB/DIR/29: 32: 40: COWIE/7.

BEAMS, *W.*
COWIE/7.

BEAMS, *W.*
(Vellum Binder).
Add.: 78 St. Martin's Lane.
Refs.: COWIE/31: 32: PIG/DIR/32: ROB/DIR/31: 32.

BEAN, *John*
Add.: 25 Warwick Lane, Newgate St. (22): 8 Lovell's Court, Paternoster Row (24): 3 Amen Corner, Paternoster Row (31).
Refs.: COWIE/29: 31: PIG/DIR/24: 32: 36: ROB/DIR/22: 32: 35.

BEARD, *Frederick*
(BB.'s Toolcutter).
Add.: 24 Hyde St., Bloomsbury (17): 41 Brunswick Pl., St. John St. Rd. & 1 Seckford St.,

Clerkenwell (40): 20 Exmouth St. (ca. 40).
Refs.: PO/DIR/17: 40: ROB/DIR/20: 22: 40: COWIE/7.

BECKLEY, *Edward* & LEWIS
(BS/HOWE/LBB. p. 10).
Refs.: PIG/DIR/24: COWIE/29: 31: (B. only in each case): HOLD/11: PO/DIR/17: ROB/DIR/20: 22: 32: (B. & L.).

BEDFORD, *Francis*
b. 1800. d. 1884.
Refs.: BB., Vol. I, p. 55: & Vol. VI, p. 77: AE/COLL/LAB: HOB/ABB. Vol. IV, No. 115. Though Bedford was prominent before 1840, he does not seem to have set up on his own till 1841, when he left the firm of Charles Lewis. He had been the latter's foreman for many years and appears to have exercised a predominating influence for a considerable time before Lewis's death in 1836. (See Plate XIII).

BEESON, *William*
(ST. &).
Add.: Constable Row, Mile End Rd.
Refs.: PIG/DIR/32.

BEETLESTONE, *George*
(PR. in 40).

Add.: 68 Freeschool St., Horselydown.
Refs.: PIG/DIR/36: ROB/DIR/40.

BELL, *John*
(BS/HOWE/LBB. p. 10 & SLB. passim).
E.D.: ? 1768.
Add.: near Exeter Change, Strand (63): 133 Strand (83).
Refs.: BS/DPB/1726/75. p. 22: KENT/DIR/83. Lord Riddell in his *First Edition Club Cat. of J. Bell*, confirms that no *signed* bindings by Bell have come to his notice.

BELL & *Son* (38)
  „   *Thomas* (40).
Add.: 21 Laurence Pountney Lane, Cannon St.
Refs.: PIG/DIR/38: ROB/DIR/40: PO/DIR/40: COWIE/7.

BEND (or BIND), *H.*
Add.: 5 Ave Maria Lane.
Refs.: COWIE/31: 32: ROB/DIR/32.

BENDEHAN
(ST., BB., etc.).
Add.: 101 Whitechapel Rd.
Refs.: HOLD/11.

BENEDICT, *Francis I & II/Charles*
(BS/HOWE/LBB. p. 10). (& BS.).
Add.: 38 Arundel St. (32): 1 Southampton Bldgs., Chancery Lane (36).

Refs.: HOLD/11: COWIE/29: PIG/
DIR/20: 24: 32: 36: ROB/DIR/20:
22: 32: 35.

O.C.: *Cabinet de L. Bonaparte*,
n.d.: f.m.g.: oval green ticket,
address round (since sold):
Douce's *Illust^ns of Shakespeare*,
2 vol. 07, f.m.g. (blue labels
without address).

The first Benedict was Francis
Lucas and the second, who died
Dec. 1862, Francis Benjamin
(BB. VOL. III, No. 20, p. 172).
The latter was admitted a F.S.C.
on 4.5.1824.

BENEDICT & WILLIAMS

(Presumably the successors of
Charles, who must have retired
between 1838 & 40).

Add.: 1 Southampton Bldgs.,
Chancery Lane.

Refs.: ROB/DIR/40.

BENGOUGH, *John*

„　　　*Mary Ann* (38).

Add.: 20 Bartholomew Close (28):
No. 19 (29): 7 Albion Bldgs.,
Bartholomew Close (38).

Refs.: COWIE/29: 31: PIG/DIR/28:
32: 36: 38 (M.A.): ROB/DIR/29:
32: 35: 40: PO/DIR/40.

BENSON, *Thomas*

(ST. in 40).

Add.: King's Rd., Gray's Inn.

Refs.: PIG/DIR/38: ROB/DIR/40.

BENTLEY, *John William*

Add.: 27 Poland St., Oxford St.

Refs.: COWIE/31: ROB/DIR/29: 32:
35: PIG/DIR/32.

BERRESFORD, *Jesse James*

(BS/HOWE/LBB. p. 11).

Add.: 26 Fleet St. (ca. 15).

Refs.: COWIE/28: 29: 31.

O.C.: *Account of Corporation of
London Dinners to Emperor of
Russia and Duke of Wellington*.
Red mor. with B.'s label with
Blue Coat Boy and City of
London Arms.

BERRESFORD, *William I & II*

(BS/HOWE/LBB. p. 11).

Add.: Pinner Ct., Gray's Inn (?
W. II).

Refs.: ROB/DIR/20.

BERRESFORD, *William (? III)*

Add.: 102 Fetter Lane (32): 7
Norwich Ct., Fetter Lane (36).

Refs.: PIG/DIR/32: 36.

BERRY, *Cornelius*

(& ST.).

Add.: 18 Sweeting Alley.

Refs.: JOHN/17: was probably a
F.S.C. about then, as his son, and
apprentice of the same name, was
admitted 6.7.1824.

BERRY, *Margaret*

Add.: 3 Ingram's Ct., Fenchurch St.

Refs.: AND/90.

BESANT, *Charles*
Add.: 2 Marshall St., Golden Sq.
Refs.: COWIE/29: 31: PIG/DIR/28:
32: 36: 38: ROB/DIR/29: 32: 35:
40: PO/DIR/40.

BEST, *Thomas*
(BS/HOWE/LBB. p. 11).
Refs.: COWIE/29: HOLD/11: PIG/
DIR/24: 28: 32: ROB/DIR/22: 29:
32: 35.

BEVAN, *Charles Stanley*
Add.: 1 Chapel Court, S. Audley
St.: No. 5 (ca. 40).
Refs.: COWIE/29: 31: PIG/DIR/28
(Charles *J*): 32: 36: 38: ROB/DIR/
29: 40: PO/DIR/40: COWIE/7.

BEVERSTOCK, *John*
(BS/HOWE/LBB. p. 11/12).

BEWS(B)Y, *James*
Add.: 5 Bishops Court, Old Bailey.
Refs.: COWIE/29: 31: ROB/DIR/20.

BICKERS, *James*
„   *Henry* (? 32).
Add.: 21 Noel St., Soho.
Refs.: COWIE/31: 32: PIG/DIR/32:
ROB/DIR/32 (James): 35 (J).

BICKERSTAFF, *Robert*
b. 1758. d. 18.12.35.
(Primarily a BS.).
Add.: 210 Strand.
Refs.: TIMP/42, p. 942, who says he

was apprenticed to Macfarlane in
Shoe Lane, but was a bookseller
1797/1818: HOLD/11 (BS., etc.).

BIELEFELD, *Samuel August*
(BS/HOWE/LBB. p. 12).
Refs.: LAB/JONES.   No. 4 Prince's
St.

BIRCH, *Robert*
(ST. &).
Add.: 35 Little Eastcheap.
Refs.: HOLD/11.

BIRCH, *Thomas*
(BS/HOWE/LBB. p. 12).
„   *Frances* (32).
Add.: 9 Brown's Buildings, St.
Mary Axe.
Refs.: COWIE/29: 31: ROB/DIR/20:
PIG/DIR/24: 32 (F. at No. 8).

BIRD, *Charles*
(BS/HOWE/LBB. p. 12).
Refs.: AE/COLL.

BIRD, *Henry*
(BS/HOWE/LBB. pp. 12/13).
Refs.: ROB/DIR/35: 40 (which describes him as Bookbinders' Stationer).

BIRD, *John II*
d. Aug. 8, 1804, see Gentleman's
Magazine, 1804, p. 794.
(BS/HOWE/LBB. p. 12).

BIRD, *John III*
(BS/HOWE/LBB. p. 12).
Add.: 52 Hatton Garden.
Refs.: COWIE/29: PO/DIR/17: 40:
PIG/DIR/24: 28, 32: 36: 38: ROB/
DIR/20: 22: 29: 32: 35: 40.
(Label Stamped on Vol. XI of
Religious Tracts, dispensed by
S.P.C.K., dated 1818 and bound
in calf in their usual style with
the Society's blind stamp. Nice
oval ticket on individual ½ calf
bdg., ca. 22, seen at Foyle's).

BIRD, *John Henry*
(BS/HOWE/LBB. p. 13).

BIRNIE, *Collin*
(BS. &).
Add.: 14 Maiden Lane, Covent
Garden.
Refs.: ROB/DIR/20: 22.

BISSAGAR, *George*
(BB.'s Toolmakers).
Add.: Strand, near Adelphi
Theatre: 47 Bunhill Row (29):
7 Bartholomew Close (32).
Refs.: COWIE/29: 31: ROB/DIR/29:
PIG/DIR/32.

BLACK, *Alexander*
(BS/HOWE/LBB. p. 14).

BLACK, *James*
(BS/HOWE/LBB. p. 13/4).
Add.: 9 York St., Covent Garden.

Refs.: HOLD/11: ? Weber: Fore-
edge Painting p. 80: BM. G.
6213: *Churchyardes' Choice,* 1579.
Handsome dark blue st. gr. mor.,
richly gilt spine, sides and
dentelles. Ticket "Bd by/JB/9/
YS/C.G.".

BLACK, *Jas. & Son*
(BS/HOWE/LBB. p. 14).
    ,,   & Co. 40.
Add.: 2 Tavistock Sq. & 9 York St.
Refs.: PO/DIR/17: 40.

BLACK, *Robert*
(BS/HOWE/LBB. p. 13 & BS/HOWE/
LBB/ADD).
(BS/DBR/1726/75 gives him about
1775 as "Alexander & Robert").
The Moss Sale binding is now in
Ld. Rothschild's Collection.
Engraved trade card or ticket
(3½" × 2½") with Masonic em-
blems in J. Sidney Pearson col-
lection "Robert Black/BB and/
BS/in George Yard, Gt. Tower
Hill/London/N.B. Paperhanging
for Exportation/B. Clowes,
Sculp. Gutter Lane." See also
Quaritch Cat.: 1889/98: Hoe:
176 Bindings, No. 131.

BLACKBURN, *J.*
(ST. &).
Add.: 32 Knightsbridge.
Refs.: ROB/DIR/20: 22 (BS. only).

BLACKLEY, *Matthew*
Add.: 27 N. Audley St.
Refs.: PIG/DIR/38 : ROB/DIR/40 : (No. 24 : ST).

BLESSED
(BS/HOWE/LBB. p. 14).

BLEWIT, *John*
(BS/HOWE/LBB. p. 14).

BLEWIT, *William*
(BS/HOWE/LBB. p. 14).
Refs.: HOLD/11 (5 Crown Ct., Warwick Lane).

BLUMFIELD, *George*
Add.: 22 Wells St., Cripplegate.
Refs.: PIG/DIR/32 : COWIE/7.

BODENHAM, *M.*
Add.: 32 Angel St., St. Mary-le-Grand.
Refs.: COWIE/29 : 31 : ROB/20 : 22 : PIG/DIR/24.

BOHN, *John* (*Henry* : see A. N. L. Munby : Phillips Studies III, p. 92).
(BS/HOWE/LBB. p. 14).
Refs.: HOLD/11 : LAB/JONES : WSM/ KC/NEW/54 p. 5.
O.C.: Lavater: *Essays*, 5 vol. 1789/98. Lent to BM., Aug. 54 : (a similar binding sold at Sotheby's in 1953 bore J. B.'s ticket.)

BOLDEN, *William/Elizabeth*
(BS/HOWE/LBB. p. 14/5).
  „ *Fernal* (32).
Add.: *16* St. Peter's Hill (28) : 7 Bell St., Doctors' Commons (32) (Fernal).
Refs.: COWIE/29 : 31 : PIG/DIR/28 : 32 (F) : ROB/DIR/20 : 29 :32 : 35.

BOLTON, *Charlt.* (? *Charlotte*)
Add.: 42 Whisker St., Clerkenwell.
Refs.: PIG/DIR/32.

BOND, *C.*
Add.: 21 Cambridge Rd., Whitechapel.
Refs.: COWIE/29 : 31 : ROB/DIR/29.

BONE, *William*
(& Book Edgegilder).
Add.: 12 Albemarle St., Clerkenwell (31) : 3 Broadway, Blackfriars (36) : 76 Fleet St. (ca. 40).
Refs.: COWIE/31 : 32 : ROB/DIR/32 : 35 : 40 : PIG/DIR/32 : 36 : 38 : PO/ DIR/40 : SLB./passim : COWIE/7 (no initial).

BONNEY, *John*
(BS/HOWE/LBB. p. 15).

BOOBYER, *William*
Add.: Norfolk Pl., Chelsea.
Refs.: PIG/DIR/32.

BOOTH, *William*
     (BS., BB. & ST.).
  ,,   *John*
  E.D.: May have been working as
    early as 1779.
  Add.: Duke St., Portland Place
    (95): 32 Duke St., Manchester
    Sq. (32).
  Refs.: PO/DIR/40.
    O.C.: Hume: *Dialogues*, 2nd Ed.
    1779: ? cont. tree calf, red label
    "BS. & B.": Dubreuil, J: *Practical
    Perspective*, 7th ed. n.d. (ca. 1795)
    white label "'BS., B., & ST.'".
    LAB/PEARSON: LAB/JONES: AE/
    HEAL/LAB: Billhead (28).

BOUCHER, *J.*
  (Bookclasp Maker).
  Add.: 7 Queen Sq.
  Refs.: PIG/DIR/23.

BOUNDEN, *Joshua*
  Add.: 19 Mortimer St., Cavendish
    Sq.
  Refs.: COWIE/29: 31: ROB/DIR/20.

BOUNEBY, *James*
  Add.: 2 Red Lion St., Spitalfields.
  Refs.: JOHN/17.

BOWDEN, *Thomas*
  Add.: 43 Museum St.
  Refs.: COWIE/29: 31: ROB/DIR/20:
    22: PIG/DIR/24.

BOWDERY & KERBY
  (BS. &).
  Add.: 190 Oxford St.
  Refs.: HOLD/11: PIG/DIR/23: 28.
    O.C.: Chag. mor. on Gold-
    smith's *Works*, 35 (Ticket gives
    the firm's name only).

BOWMAN, *James*
  Add.: 4 Sussex Pl., Bermondsey
    Wall.
  Refs.: PIG/DIR/36.

BOWRON, *George*
  (& ST.).
  Add.: 11 or 24 Dartmouth St.,
    Westminster: 213 Oxford St.
    (ca. 35).
  Refs.: COWIE/29: 31: PIG/DIR/32:
    36: 38: ROB/DIR/29: 35: 40: PO/
    DIR/40. The Oxford St. address
    was seen on a $\frac{1}{2}$ mor. binding on a
    vol. of Italian Costumes at Marks
    (Sept. 52). Apprenticed to W.
    Searle, he was made a F.S.C. on
    6.2.27.

BOYER, *N.*
  (See Hayday).
  E.D.: 26 ?
  Add.: 4 Poland St., W.
  Refs.: ROB/DIR/35: PIG/DIR/36.
    B.M.C. 46. p. 33. A magnificent
    light brown fully gilt pol. mor.,
    with doublure in coloured mor.
    of Kings of Spades and Hearts on
    Hoyle's *Games*, 1826.

BOYS, *John*
(BS/HOWE/LBB. p. 16).
Add.: *12* Ivy Lane (91).
Refs.: BRI/DIR/91.

BRADFORD, *Jos.*
(& ST.).
Add.: 87 Hoxton Old Town.
Refs.: PIG/DIR/32.

BRADSTREET'S
Refs.: Huth Sale No. 2054.

BRAHAM, *M.*
(& ST.).
Add.: 88 Pleasant Pl., Kingsland
Rd.
Refs.: PIG/DIR/36.

BRAIN, *Robert*
Add.: 15 Maidenhead Ct., Alders-
gate St.
Refs.: PIG/DIR/36.

BRANCH, *John*
Add.: 14 Pleasant Row, King's
Cross.

BRASS
Add.: 3 Staining Lane, Wood St.
Refs.: COWIE/29: 31.

BREAKWELL, *William*
(BS/HOWE/LBB. p. XXXIV).
Add.: 20 Queen St., Golden Sq.
Refs.: PIG/DIR/24: ROB/DIR/20: 22:
29.

BREN, *Thomas*
Add.: 18 Union St. East, Spital-
fields.
Refs.: ROB/DIR/40.

BRETT & ANDERSON (24)
(see Anderson & Brett).
  „   *William.*
  „   *Sarah* (36).
(Vellum Binder).
Add.: 3 or 5 Nag's Head Ct.,
Gracechurch St.
Refs.: COWIE/29: 31: PIG/DIR/24:
28: 32: 36: 38: ROB/DIR/22: 29:
32: 35: 40: PO/DIR/40.

BRIGGS
E.D. ? 30.
Add.: 23 Piccadilly.
Refs.: Ticket seen at Libris, Feb.
1952. "Made by/B/23 P" on
handsome st. gr. mor. album
with gilt lock.

BRIGHTWELL, *John*
(BS/HOWE/LBB. p. 16).

BROOKE, *Richard*
(BS/HOWE/LBB. p. 104).
(BB.'s Toolcutter).

BROOKS, *Henry*
(BS., ST. &).
Add.: 87 New Bond St.
Refs.: PO/DIR/40.

BROOKS, *I.* or *J.*
(ST., BS. &).
(BS/HOWE/LBB. p. 16).
Add.: 3 John St. (ca. 10): 421
Oxford St. (? 20).
Refs.: ROB/DIR/20: 22. See Saw-
yer's Cat. 210/1952. No. 376.
Red mor. gilt on Johnson &
Chalmers: *English Poets*, 21 vol.
1810. Ticket: "Bd. by/I. Brooks
/3 John St. (erased)/421 (added
in ink) Oxford St.". According
to P. Dobell Cat. 143/No. 413, a
J. Brooks was binding at 8 Baker
St., Portman Sq., ca. 1836.

BROWN, *James*
Add.: 10 Macclesfield St., Soho.
Refs.: PIG/DIR/28.

BROWN, *John*
(BS/HOWE/LBB. p. 17).

BROWN, *Joseph*
Add.: Old St. Rd.
Refs.: COWIE/29: 31: PIG/DIR/28.

BROWN, *S.*
Add.: 72 Old St. Rd.
Refs.: ROB/DIR/29.

BROWN, *Samuel Daniel*
(BS/HOWE/LBB. p. 17).

BROWN, *Sarah*
(& ST.).
Add.: 15 Charles Square, Hoxton.

Refs.: COWIE/31: 32: PIG/DIR/32:
ROB/DIR/32.

BROWN, *Thomas Francis*
(Vellum Binder).
Add.: 22 New Union St.: 22
London Wall (35).
Refs.: PIG/DIR/22: ROB/DIR/35.

BROWN, *William*
Add.: 28 Windmill St., Finsbury
Refs.: PIG/DIR/36.

BROWNING, *John*
Add.: 1 Ivy Lane, Newgate St.
Refs.: ROB/DIR/40.

BROWNING, *Hannah*
(BS/HOWE/LBB. p. 17).

BRUCE, *Joseph*
(& ST.).
Add.: 9 Sweeting's Alley.
Refs.: JOHN/17: F.S.C. by 1815.

BRUCE, *Thomas*
Add.: 15 Granby St., Waterloo Rd.
Refs.: PIG/DIR/36.

BRYANT, *Edmund*
Add.: 21 Whitehorse Yard, Drury
Lane.
Refs.: PIG/DIR/32: 38: ROB/DIR/35.

BUCHANAN, *Jock*
(See SLB. p. 36).

BUICK or BULCK, *Robert*
  Add.: 1 Orange Ct., Orange St.,
  Leicester Sq.: 28 Litchfield St.
  (35): No. 23 (36): No 7 (40).
  Refs.: COWIE/29: 31: PIG/DIR/28:
  36: 38: ROB/DIR/29: 35: 40:
  COWIE/7.

BULL, *J.*
  (Bookclasp maker).
  Add.: 1 Fleet Market.
  Refs.: COWIE/29: 31: PIG/DIR/23.

BULL, *B. E.*
  Add.: 25 New Quebec St., Portman
  Sq.
  Refs.: ROB/DIR/35.

BULL, *F.*
  Add.: 17 Bartholomew Terrace,
  St. Luke's.
  Refs.: ROB/DIR/40.

BULLOCK, *William*
  Add.: 35 Clerkenwell Close.
  Refs.: COWIE/29: 31: PIG/DIR/28:
  RON/DIR/29.

BULLWINKLE, *Joseph*
  (Vellum Binder in 40 & Edge-
  gilder).
  Add.: 4 Church Lane, Whitehall
  (28): 5 Cullum St., City (36).
  Refs.: PIG/DIR/28: 32: 36: 38: ROB/
  DIR/40: PO/DIR/40: COWIE/7.
  Apprenticed to Edward Heath, he
  was made a F.S.C. on 7.12.30.

BUNCE, *John*
  Add.: 13 Denmark Ct., Strand.
  Refs.: HOLD/11.

BUNNEY, *W.*
  (Vellum Binders).
  Add.: 9 St. Pancras Lane, Queen St.
  Refs.: COWIE/31: 32: PIG/DIR/32:
  ROB/DIR/32: 35.

BUNTING, *William*
  Add.: 7 East Harding St., Gough
  Sq.
  Refs.: ROB/DIR/40. His name,
  "Bunting, Binder" figures on the
  spine of original cloth binding on
  Dickens' *Oliver Twist*, 3 vols., 38,
  sold at Sotheby's, 13.10.53, lot
  317.

BURCH
  (BS/HOWE/LBB. p. 17).

BURGESS, *Charles*
  Add.: 33 Walter Lane, Fleet St.
  Refs.: PO/DIR/40.

BURN, *J.*
  (BS/HOWE/LBB. p. 18).
  Add.: 12 Kirby St., Hatton Garden
  (40) (as vellum binder).
  Refs.: PO/DIR/40. There is an I.
  Burn in ROB/DIR/20 at 39 Kirby
  St.

BURN *Family*
(BS/HOWE/LBB. p. 18).
,, T. & Son. (28). (Also vellum
binder ca. 32).
,, T. & Sons (38).
,, T. (40).
Refs.: BR/BM/40/p. 13 says Thomas
Burn came from Newcastle-on-
Tyne and started in London in
Middle Row, Holborn in 1781.
COWIE/29: PO/DIR/17: 40: JOHN/
17: PIG/DIR/24: 32: 36: 38: ROB/
DIR/22: 29: 32: 35: 40: COWIE/7:
LAB/PEARSON/:
O.C.: Ticket, taken from *German
New Testament*, 1825, published
by B. & F.B.S., rough sheep with
their blindstamp on side.

BURN, *William*
Add.: 12 Kirby St., Hatton
Garden.
Refs.: ROB/DIR/35: There was a W.
Burn at No. 37, according to
ROB/DIR/20. Apprenticed to
Thomas B. and admitted a F.S.C.
on 7.9.1819.

BURNETT, *Thomas*
(BS/HOWE/LBB. p. 18).
d. 1820.
Refs.: SLB./p. 52/3 & 56: LBB/HOWE
p. 77.

BURNS
Add.: 27 Portman St., Portman Sq.
Refs.: Ticket on ¾ m.g. with
figured cloth sides, apparently ca.
1835, on H. Cave's *Picturesque
Buildings of York*, 1810, 2 Parts
in 1. (O.C.)

BURSLEM, *James*
(ST. &).
Add.: 13 Gt. Surrey St., Black-
friars Rd.
Refs.: JOHN/17.

BURT(T), *Thomas*
,, ,, & Sons (ca. 40).
(Claspmakers).
Add.: Southampton St., Clerken-
well (29): 45 Northampton St.,
Clerkenwell (23 & 32).
Refs.: COWIE/29: 31: ROB/DIR/32:
35: 40: PIG/DIR/23: 36: 38: PO/
DIR/40: COWIE/7.

BURTON, *Robert*
(BS/HOWE/LBB. p. 18).

BURTON, *S.*
(BS/HOWE/LBB. p. 18).

BUSH, *Robert*
Add.: Church St., Hackney: ? 15
Jewry St., Aldgate (ca. 40).
Refs.: PIG/DIR/32: ROB/DIR/35: PO/
DIR/40: COWIE/7 (no initial).

BUSHTON, *William*
Add.: 13 Middle Row, Blooms-
bury.
Refs.: JOHN/17.

BUSS, *George*
(BS/HOWE/LBB. p. 18).
Add.: 5 Plough Ct., Fetter Lane
(11): 2 Dorrington St., Clerken-
well (17): 25 Little Sutton St.,
Goswell Rd. (32).
Refs.: HOLD/11: COWIE/29: 31:
JOHN/17: ROB/DIR/20: 22: PIG/
DIR/24: 28: 32: 36.

BUSS, *John*
Add.: 2 King's Head Ct., Fetter
Lane.
Refs.: PIG/DIR/32.

BUTLER, *Jane*
(BS. &).
Add.: 80 S. Audley St.
Refs.: ROB/DIR/29.

BY, *Charles*
  „ *& Son* (32).
Add.: 85 Quadrant, Regent St.
(28): 2 Rathbone Place (31).
Refs.: COWIE/31: 32: PIG/DIR/28:
32: ROB/DIR/32.

BYERS, *Robert*
Add.: 84 Margaret St., Cavendish
Sq. (31): 12 Cleveland St.,
Fitzroy Sq. (38).
Refs.: COWIE/31: 32: PIG/DIR/32:
36: 38: ROB/DIR/32: 35: 40.

BYWORTH, *George*
(ST. &.: Vellum Binder ca. 32).
Add.: 16 Duke St., West Smithfield.

Refs.: COWIE/29: 31: PIG/DIR/32:
36: 38: ROB/DIR/29: 32: 35: 40.

CALVERT, *John*
Add.: 5 Hart St., Covent Garden.
Refs.: PIG/DIR/36.

CAMERFOOT
Add.: Angel Ct., Strand.
Refs.: COWIE/29: 31.

CAMP, *A. M.*
(BS/HOWE/LBB. p. 19).
Refs.: ROB/DIR/20: 22.

CAMP, *Doffinby Duhest, Davy, or*
David
(BS/HOWE/LBB. p. 19).
Refs.: HOLD/11: PO/DIR/17: ROB/
DIR/20: 22: JOHN/17 (David, ST.
&).

CAMP, *Eliza.*
Add.: 21 Bridgwater Sq. (32):
28 Milton St., Cripplegate (36).
Refs.: PIG/DIR/32: 36.

CAMP, *James M.*
(BS/HOWE/LBB. p. 19).

CAMP, *John*
(BS/HOWE/LBB. p. 19).

CAMP, *Thomas*
(BS/HOWE/LBB. p. 19).
Add.: 21 Barbican (24): 16/17
Staining Lane, Wood St. (28).

Refs.: COWIE/29 : PIG/DIR/24 : 28 :
32 : PO/DIR/31 : ROB/DIR/29 : 32.

CAMP, *William*
(BS/HOWE/LBB. p. 19).
Add.: 21 Bridgwater Sq. (29).
Refs.: COWIE/29 : ROB/DIR/29 : PO/
DIR/31.

CAMPBELL, *Charles S.*
Add.: 16 Albion Bldgs., Bartholo-
mew Close.
Refs.: PIG/DIR/38.

CAMPBELL, *James*
(BS/HOWE/LBB. pp. 19/20 &
XXXIV).

CANDAR, *J.*
Add.: Marsh Pl., Lambeth.
Refs.: COWIE/29 : 31 : ROB/DIR/29.

CANHAM, *John*
(& ST.).
Add.: 21 Gloucester St., Queen Sq.
Refs.: PIG/DIR/36 : 38 : ROB/DIR/40 :
PO/DIR/40.

CAPES, *Thomas*
(BS/HOWE/LBB. p. 20).

CARPENTER, *James*
(BS/HOWE/LBB. p. 20)
,,   *James & Thomas*
Add.: 4 Wardrobe Terrace, Doc-
tors' Commons.

Refs.: COWIE/29 : PIG/DIR/24 : 28 :
32 : 36 : 38 : ROB/DIR/20 : 22 : 29 :
32 : 35 : 40 : PO/DIR/40 : COWIE/7.

CARPENTER, *John*
(BS/HOWE/LBB. p. 20).

CARPENTER, *William*
Add.: 41 Brewer St. (24) : 4 Bed-
ford Ct., Covent Garden (28).
Refs.: PIG/DIR/24 : 28.

CARPENTER & CO.
E.D. ? 00.
Add.: 14 Old Bond St.
Refs.: O.C.:   Label "Bd by/C &
Co/14 O.B.S." on 2 vol. Tasso:
Gerusaleme Lib. 1778: bd. white
vellum.

CAPRON, *W.*
Add.: 4 Provost St., Hoxton.
Refs.: COWIE/29 : 31 : ROB/DIR/29.

CARPUE, *Joseph Francis*
Add.: 26/26 Duke St., Lincolns Inn
Fields (24) : 20 Old Compton St.
(35) : No. 18 (40).
Refs.: COWIE/29 : PIG/DIR/24 : 28 :
32 : 36 : 38 : ROB/DIR/22 : 29 : 32 :
35 : 40 : PO/DIR/40.

CARR, *Thomas*
(BS/HOWE/LBB. p. 20).

CARR & CO.
(& ST.).
Add.: 19 Duke St., St. James'.
Refs.: JOHN/17.

CARTER, *James*
   ,,   *John* (28).
Add.: 2 Bell Yard, Doctors' Commons (91): 16 Gresse St., Tottenham Ct. Rd. (22).
Refs.: BRI/DIR/91: COWIE/29: 31: PIG/DIR/24: 28: ROB/DIR/22.

CARY, *Richard*
Add.: 9 Prospect Pl., Cambridge Heath.
Refs.: PIG/DIR/36.

CASSON, *William Robert*
(Vellum Binder).
Add.: 8 Bath St., Newgate St.
Refs.: COWIE/31: 32: PIG/DIR/32: ROB/DIR/32: 35.

CATERER, *Henry*
Add.: 4 New Bridge St., Vauxhall.
Refs.: PIG/DIR/32.

CATMAN, *H.*
(Vellum Binder).
Add.: 3 Pell St., Ratcliff Highway.
Refs.: PIG/DIR/24.

CATMUR, *Henry*
(Vellum Binder: BS. & ST. in 1828).
Add.: 14 Ship Alley, Wellclose Sq.: 46 Bethnal Green Rd. (36).
Refs.: PIG/DIR/28: 36: COWIE/7.

CAUMONT, *Comte de*
(BS/HOWE/LBB. p. 20).
Refs.: See CR/BB p. 49. I have since acquired 3 "Models" in f.c.g., with the Frith St. label, which support Mr. Ehrman's theory that the Count was a skilful imitator of contemporary binders in different styles. BB. VOL. III p. 2 states that his account book with Frith St. ticket was then (ca. 1890) in the possession of M. Ferdinand Grimont. (See Plate II.)

CAWTHORN, *G.*
(etc., etc.).
Add.: 132 Strand.
Refs.: O.C.: *Idler*: mottled calf, 1799. Elaborate Ticket: BS., BB., ST., PR. & Publisher, etc.

CEDY, *Bennett*
Add.: 16 Little Warner St., Clerkenwell.
Refs.: COWIE/29: 31: ROB/DIR/29

CHAPMAN, *James*
(BS/HOWE/LBB. p. 21).

CHAPPELL, *C.*
E.D.: ? 30.
Add.: 3 Brecknock Rd., N.
Refs.: LAB/KNA (ca. 30).

CHAPPLE, *Clement*
(B.S., etc.).
Add.: 66 Pall Mall.
Refs.: HOLD/11: BM. G. 17721/3.
Full calf on: Dr. Trusler: *Modern Times*, 1785. Ticket "Bd. by/ C.C/at his Circulating Library/ P.M.".

CHIPP, *Benjamin*
(BS/HOWE/LBB. p. 21).
Add.: 22 Ivy Lane, Newgate St.
Refs.: COWIE/29: 31: PIG/DIR/24.

CHIPP, *Margaret*
„ *Mary* (35).
„ *M. & Son* (37).
Add.: 1 Ivy Lane, Newgate: 2 Amen Corner, St. Paul's (36).
Refs.: PIG/DIR/28: 32: 36: 38: ROB/ DIR/29: 35 (Mary): 40: PO/DIR/ 40.

CHIPP, *Thomas*
(BS/HOWE/LBB. p. 21).

CHIRM, *Sylvanus*
(BS/HOWE/LBB. pp. 21 & XXXIV).

CHISMAN, *J.*
(BS., ST. &).
Add.: 42 Albany St., Regent's Park.
Refs.: PO/DIR/40.

CHRISTIE, *James*
(BS. &).

Add.: 190 High Holborn.
Refs.: HOLD/11.

CHRISTIE, *Thomas*
Add.: 14 Chalcroft Terrace, New Cut.
Refs.: PIG/DIR/28.

CHRISTIE, *William*
Add.: 9 & 10 New North St., Red Lion Sq.
Refs.: COWIE/31: 32: PIG/DIR/32: 36: 38: ROB/DIR/32: 35: 40: PO/ DIR/40.

CHURTON
E.D.: ? 30.
Refs.: O.C.: *Ste. Bible*, 1710, f.c.g. signed in blind "Bound by Churton" (style of J. Mackenzie).

CLAPHAM, *Samuel*
Add.: 1 Medway St., Westminster.
Refs.: PIG/DIR/38.

CLARK, *Andrew*
(BS/HOWE/LBB. p. 21).

CLARK, *W.*
„ *Caroline* (36).
Add.: 7 Upper Marylebone St.
Refs.: COWIE/29: 31: ROB/DIR/29: PIG/DIR/32: 36 (Caroline): BM. C. 21. e. 15.

CLARKE
There were several binders of this name active in London during the

first half of the nineteenth century. They are not very easy to distinguish, nor is it known what relationship, if any, exists among them.

(I) CLARK, J., mentioned without any address in the 1808 *"Corrected List of Prices as agreed by the Booksellers and Bookbinders of London and Westminster"* (see BS/HOWE/LBB. pp. XIX and 22).

(II) CLARKE, CHARLES, at 14 or 15 Frith St. between about 1810–20.
  Refs.: HOLD/11 : JOHN/17 : 18 : ROB/DIR/20 : BM. G. 8.

(III) CLARKE, JOHN. One of the best and most prolific of the London binders of the period. He figures in all the directories from about 1821 up to the end of our period and even beyond. He was first at No. 1 Meard St., Soho (ROB/DIR/22), but in 38 appears to have moved to 61 Frith St. (see PIG/DIR/38 and COWIE/7). He is probably the binder who in 1841 joined up with Bedford. The partnership lasted till 1850, after which Clarke carried on alone till 1859 (see BS/HOWE/LBB. p. 22). Specimens of his work occur frequently.

(IV) CLARKE, JOHN. Appears at 25 Dean St. between 1838 and 42, when the firm apparently became Clarke & Weemys at 13 Charles St., Hatton Garden.

CLARKE, *W.*
  (BS. &).

Add.: 92 South Side, Royal Exchange.
Refs.: ROB/DIR/20 : 22.

CLARKE & WEEMYS
  (see Clarke IV above).
  Add.: 13 Charles St., Hatton Garden.
  Refs.: LAB/KNA/ PIG/DIR/42.

CLAXSTON
  (BS/HOWE/LBB. p. 22).

CLEAVER
  (BB., BS., ST., etc.).
  Add.: 30 King St., Portman Sq.
  Refs.: LAB/JONES ("Bound by").

CLEMENT, *William*
  (ST. &).
  Add.: 192 Strand.
  Refs.: ROB/DIR/20.

CLOSE, *John/Hannah/John Samuel*
  (BS/HOWE/LBB. p. 22).

CLOUT, *H. F.*
  „ *William Frederick* (32).
  Add.: 30 Duke St., Bloomsbury.
  Refs.: COWIE/29 : 31 : PIG/DIR/28 : 32 : 36 : 38 : ROB/DIR/29 : 32 : 35 : PO/DIR/40.

CLYDE
  Add.: 9 Newman St.
  Refs.: COWIE/7.
  O.C.: *Poultry Yard*: by P.

PLATE XI   HERING, C. $(4\frac{1}{4}'' \times 6\frac{1}{4}'')$

PLATE XII   HERING, C. $(2\frac{3}{4}'' \times 4\frac{3}{4}'')$

Boswell, Glasgow, 40. The 39 and 41 Editions in my O.C. are in exactly similar bindings, of Victorian "gothic" style, signed by Hering at the same address. HOE, Cat. II, No. 1488, reports a green mor. bdg. on Greene's *Works*, 31.

COBB, *Joseph*
  Add.: 203 Sloane St., Chelsea.
  Refs.: COWIE/29: 31: ROB/DIR/29: PIG/DIR/36.

COGHLAN, *J.*
  (BS. &).
  Ca. 1780.
  Add.: Duke St., Grosvenor Sq.
  Refs.: Though primarily a bookseller, there is a red mor. large octavo binding in Lord Rothschild's Collection on Barbaudt's *Sacred Hymns*, etc., London, 1766, said to have been the French Ambassador's copy and with bookplate with the Wilson arms. It has "Coghlan" at the head of spine, and "Binder" at the base of spine. (Information supplied by M. Craig, April 53.)

COLE, *Robert and/or Richard*
  (There may have been two Coles).
  (& Book Edgegilder in 1838).
  Add.: 40 Little Britain (29: 5 Queen's Sq., Aldersgate St. (31): 5 Queen's Ct., Aldersgate St. (40):

3 Keen's Row, Walworth Rd. (ca. 40).
  Refs.: COWIE/29: 31: 32: PIG/DIR/ 32: 36: 38: ROB/DIR/29: 32: 35: 40: COWIE/7. Richard Claude Cole was apprenticed to George Kitcat and admitted as F.S.C. in Feb. 1817.

COLLETT, *Thomas Henry*
  Add.: 84 Edgware Road.
  Refs.: PIG/DIR/36: 38.

COLLIER, *George*
  (BS/HOWE/LBB. p. 23).
  „   „   *& Son* (40).
  Add.: 24 Duke St., Smithfield (20): 72 Hatton Garden: *and* 4½/5 Cross St. (32): (PO/DIR/40 lists C, G. & Son at the first address, and C, G. at the second).
  Refs.: COWIE/29: PIG/DIR/24: 28: 32: 36: 38: ROB/DIR/20: 22: 29: 32: 35: 40: PO/DIR/40: COWIE/7: LAB/JONES.
  O.C.: *Picturesque Tour*, 16, stamped calf.

COLLINS & TAYLOR
  Add.: Oxendale (or Oxenden) St., Haymarket.
  Refs.: COWIE/29: 31: 32: PIG/DIR/ 32: ROB/DIR/32.

COLLINS, *Goulding*
  Add.: 26 Crown Ct., Little Russell St.: 26 Martlett Ct., Bow St.

(36): 2 Gloucester St., Queen's Sq. (48).

Refs.: ROB/DIR/35: 40: PIG/DIR/36: 38: PO/DIR/40.

COLLINS, *Henry George*
(Vellum Binder in 35).

Add.: 87 Queen's St., Cheapside: No. 3 (38).

Refs.: ROB/DIR/35: PIG/DIR/38. Gave himself as a BB. in registering a son, Henry Edward, on 15.3.35, as born to his wife Matilda, on 5.2.35. (Harl. Soc. 44 St. Pancras, Soper Lane.)

COLLINS & COOK
(ST. &).

Add.: 10 Bishopsgate St. Without.

Refs.: PIG/DIR/32.

COLLYER, *Joseph*

Add.: 28 Shoemaker Row, Blackfriars.

Refs.: ROB/DIR/22: PIG/DIR/24: A Joseph Collyer was a F.S.C. by 1810. His son George Clayton C. was admitted a F.S.C. on 3.8.1817. A Joseph C. Jr. apprenticed to J.C. and then to John Smith, was made a F.S.C. on 4.12.28.

COLNAGHI, *Son & Co.*

E.D.: 18 ?

Add.: Pall Mall St.

Refs.: Impressed in gilt on inside edge of a russia binding on an 1818 publication, seen at Marks late 1951.

COLTHARD, *T.*

Add.: 42 Berwick St., Soho: 39 Upper John St., Tottenham Ct. Rd. (38): 22 Cleveland St., Middlesex Hosp. (40).

Refs.: COWIE/29: 31: PIG/DIR/28: 32: 36: 38: ROB/DIR/29: 32: 35: 40: PO/DIR/40.

COMERFORD, *Richard*

Add.: 11 Angel Ct., 335 Strand.

Refs.: PIG/DIR/28.

CONDIE, *James*

Add.: 5 Southampton Bldgs., Holborn: No. 46 (28).

Refs.: COWIE/29: 31: PIG/DIR/24: 28: ROB/DIR/22: 29.

CONSTABLE, *George/John*
(BS/HOWE/LBB. p. 23).

Add.: 4 James St., Haymarket: 68 Prince's St., Leicester Sq. (29) (John).

Refs.: HOLD/11: COWIE/29: 31: PIG/DIR/24: 28: 32: ROB/DIR/20: 22: 29 (G): 32. JOHN/17 gives him as Henry.

COOK, *Bertha*
(BS/HOWE/LBB. p. 23).

COOK, *James*
(BS/HOWE/LBB. p. 24).

COOK, *Livett*
(BS. in 40).
Add.: 1 Maiden Lane, Covent Gdn.
Refs.: COWIE/29: 31: PIG/DIR/24: 28:
32: 36: 38: ROB/DIR/22: 29: 40.
O.C.: Nice olive mor. gilt bdg.
in Lewis style, on *Maria Stuarta
Innocens* 1627, signed "Bound by
L. Cook".

COOK, *Matthias*
Add.: 9 Little Britain.
Refs.: AND/90.

COOK, *William*
(BS/HOWE/LBB. p. 24).
Refs.: HOLD/11: BS/DPB/1726/75:
p. 60.

COOKE, *G.*
E.D.: ? 05.
Add.: 1 Dunstan's Hill, Tower St.
Refs.: O.C.: Ticket "GC/1 D.H.,
T.S./Books in all languages./
Every description of binding/
Executed with elegance" on *Views
in North Britain*, 1805, ½ mor. gr.

COOKE, *James*
Add.: 9 Well-yard, Little Britain.
Refs.: HOLD/11.

COONEY, *Thomas*
Add.: 5 Angel Ct., 336 Strand.
Refs.: PIG/DIR/36.

COOPER
(BS/HOWE/LBB. p. 25).

COOPER, *George*
Add.: 25 Jewin Ct.
Refs.: ROB/DIR/40.

COOPER, *Joseph*
Add.: 20 Houndsditch.
Refs.: HOLD/11.

COPE, *George A.*
Add.: High Row, Knightsbridge
(29): 4 York St., New Rd.,
Chelsea (32).
Refs.: COWIE/29: 31: 32: PIG/DIR/
32: 36: 38: ROB/DIR/32: 35: 40:
PO/DIR/40.

COPE, *William*
(Vellum Binder).
Add.: 88 St. Martin's Lane: No. 85
(ca. 40).
Refs.: PO/DIR/40: COWIE/7.

CORDEVAL, *Louis (Cordaval or
Cordavau)*
(BS/HOWE/LBB. p. 25).
Possibly a French Emigré and a
relation of "Courteval", the well-
know Paris binder.
Add.: 57 Chandos St.
Refs.: BM. 2. p. 2, 3 & 11 (No.
"17"). Oxydised orange label,
similar to those used by Kalthoeber, figured on a calf binding
on an undescribed item in Sotheby
Sale, 5.11.51, dating about 1810/
15. Name read "Cordavau".

CORFIELD, *Joseph*
(Book Edge gilder and Marbler).
Add.: 17 St. John's Lane: 44 Kirby
St. (ca. 40).
Refs.: PIG/DIR/36: 38 (also listed as
BB.): ROB/DIR/40: PO/DIR/40:
COWIE/7.

CORNIE or CORMIE, *William*
Add.: 36 Union Row, New Kent
Road: 6 Love Lane (28).
Refs.: PIG/DIR/28: COWIE/29/31: On
24.8.28 he registered the birth of
a son, Henry, b. 8.5.28, by his
wife Elizabeth. (Harleian Soc.
LXV, St. Mary, Aldermanbury.)

COSGRAVE, *John*
Add.: 4 King's Head Court, St.
Martin's-le-Grand.
Refs.: PIG/DIR/28.

COUCHMAN, *Edward*
(& ST. & PR.).
Add.: 10 Throgmorton St.
Refs.: O.C.: Ticket on Shelley:
Queen Mab, 22: f.m.g. "E.C./
BB., ST./& PR./10 T.S/London/
& Machine Ruling". Surround:
"Account Books/made on an im-
proved/principle." Apprenticed
to Stephen Couchman, and ad-
mitted as F.S.C. on 4.3.1817..

COURT, *David Thomas*
Add.: 37 Dorset St., Portman Sq.
Refs.: PIG/DIR/32.

COURT, *Richard*
Add.: 42 Primrose Hill (28): 1
Angel Ct., Skinner St. (29).
Refs.: COWIE/29: 31: 32: PIG/DIR/
28: 32: ROB/DIR/29: 32: 35.

COURTHOPE & BAYLY
Add.: 33 Rotherhithe St.
Refs.: PIG/DIR/38.

COURTIER, *Charles*
(& ST.).
Add.: 22 Commerical Rd., Lam-
beth (31): 3 Bouverie St., Fleet
St. (40).
Refs.: COWIE/31: 32: ROB/DIR/32:
35: 40: PIG/DIR/32: 36.

COURTNEY, *W.*
Add.: 3 St. George's Pl.
Refs.: ROB/DIR/35.

COWIE & STRANGE
Add.: 24 Fetter Lane.
Refs.: ROB/DIR/29.

COX, *Davis*
(BS/HOWE/LBB. p. 25).
,, *James* (31).
Add.: Old Exchange (various Nos.
from 1824).
Refs.: COWIE/29: 31: 32: PIG/DIR/
24: 28: 32: 36: ROB/DIR/22: 29:
32: 35.

COX, *Ebenezer*
(BB.'s Toolmaker).

PLATE XIII HERING & BEDFORD $(8\frac{3}{4}'' \times 11\frac{1}{4}'')$

PLATE XIV   JOHNSON $(8'' \times 10\frac{1}{4}'')$

Add.: 31 Brooke St., Holborn.
Refs.: PO/DIR/40.

COXHEAD (? *Joseph*)
Add.: New Round Ct., Strand:
Strand (11): 249 High Holborn
(23).
Refs.: HOLD/11 (Jos. BS.): PIG/
DIR/23. Ticket on Vol. I (1799)
of M. Park's *Travels*, Sotheby
30.7.51/192. "J. Coxhead, Book-
binder, Successor to Messrs.
Wolters, etc." (q.v.).

CRAIG, *William/A.*
(BS/HOWE/LBB. p. 26).

CRAWFORD, *Alexander*
(BS/HOWE/LBB. p. 26).
Add.: 18 Peerless Row, City Rd.:
18 Pool Terrace, Bath St., City
Rd. (36).
Refs.: HOLD/11 : COWIE/29 : 31 : PIG/
DIR/24 : 28 : 32 : 36 : 38 : ROB/DIR/
22 : 32 : 35 : 40 : PO/DIR/40 :
COWIE/7.

CRAWFORD, *A.*,
Add.: 6 Provost St., Hoxton.
Refs.: ROB/DIR/29.

CRAWFORD, *Henry*
Add.: 1 & 3 Queen's Head Passage,
Newgate St.: 3 Amen Corner
(38).
Refs.: PIG/DIR/32 : 36 : 38 : ROB/DIR/
32.

CRAWFORD, *James*
Add.: 44 Great Chart St., Hoxton
(38): 13 Somerset Pl., Hoxton
(40).
Refs.: PIG/DIR/38 : ROB/DIR/40.

CRAWFORD, *William*
(BS/HOWE/LBB. p. 26).
Add.: 16 Peerless Row, City Rd.:
16 Pool Terrace, Bath St. (32).
Refs.: PIG/DIR/24 : 28 : 32 : 36 : 38 :
ROB/DIR/22 : 32 : 35 : PO/DIR/40 :
COWIE/7.

CRAWFORD, *W., Jr.*
(& BS.).
Add.: 124 Cheapside.
Refs.: O.C.: Moore: *Lalla Rookh*,
'20. f. blond m.g.

CRENAN, *John*
(BS/HOWE/LBB. p. 27).

CRESWICK, *W.*
Add.: 5 John St., Oxford St.
Refs.: Blank paper album, bd.
plain cloth, ca. 30, Alister Matthews' Cat. 43, No. 457. Ticket:
"Bd. by, etc." seen on calf
binding on an 1828 work.

CREW & SPENCER
E.D.: ? 30.
Add.: 27 Lamb's Conduit St.
Refs.: LAB/JONES ("Bound & sold
by"): ABB/CBS.

CRISP, *James*
    (& ST.).
  ,,   *& Son* (ca. 40).
  Add.: 18 Noel St., Wardour St.:
    44 Newman St. (35): No. 54
    (40).
  Refs.: COWIE/31: 32: ROB/DIR/29:
    32: 35: 40: PIG/DIR/32: 36: 38:
    PO/DIR/40: COWIE/7.

CROSS, *Thomas*
  Add.: 3/4 Bartlett's Bldgs., Holborn
    Hill: 6 King's Head Ct., Holborn
    Hill (40).
  Refs.: COWIE/29: 31: PIG/DIR/28:
    32: 36: 38: ROB/DIR/29: 32: 35:
    40: SLB./p. 103: WSM/KC/NEW/
    54. p. 9.

CROUCH, *George*
    (& BS.).
  Add.: 15 Charles St., Long Acre
    (22): 9 Tottenham Ct., New Rd.
    (28): 10 Greystoke Place (32):
    1 Crown St., Water St. (36):
    5 Tudor St., Blackfriars (40).
  Refs.: COWIE/29: 31: PIG/DIR/24:
    28: 32: 36: 38: ROB/DIR/22: 40:
    PO/DIR/40.

CROWTHER, *Ann*
    (BS/HOWE/LBB. p. 27).

CULLOCK, *Henry*
  Add.: 8 Albion Bldgs.
  Refs.: ROB/DIR/20.

CULLUM, *William*
    (BS/HOWE/LBB. p. 27).

CULLUM, *William Knight*
    (BS/HOWE/LBB. p. 27).

CURTIS, *Edward*
    (& ST.).
  Add.: 6 Church St., Lambeth(?):
    19 Dartmouth St., West (20).
  Refs.: ROB/DIR/20.

CURTIS, *Samuel*
  Add.: Dartmouth St., Westminster
    (29): 28 Milton St., City (38).
  Refs.: COWIE/29: 31: PIG/DIR/38:
    ROB/DIR/40: PO/DIR/40: COWIE/7:
    LAB/JONES.

CURTIS, *Thomas*
    (BS/HOWE/LBB. p. 28).
  Add.: 9 Clare St., Drury Lane: 7
    Yeates Corner, Carey St. (32).
  Refs.: COWIE/29: 31: PIG/DIR/24:
    32: ROB/DIR/20: 22.

CUSHION, *George*
  Add.: 15 Frith St., Soho.
  Refs.: PIG/DIR/24.

CUSTANCE, *James*
    (Vellum Binder).
  Add.: 39 Margaret St. East, Spa-
    fields.
  Refs.: COWIE/31: 32: ROB/DIR/32:
    35.

DAFFORD, *John*
   ,,   *& Son*
(BB.'s Press Maker).
Add.: 88 Whitecross St., St. Luke's:
   22 Gt. Mitchell St. (ca. 40).
Refs.: COWIE/29: 31: COWIE/7.

DAFFORN & SON
(& ST.).
Add.: 22 Mitchell St., St. James'.
Refs.: PO/DIR/40.

DAIKERS, *James*
(Vellum Binder).
Add.: 34 Gt. Tower St.
Refs.: COWIE/31: 32: ROB/DIR/32:
35.

DAINTREE, *Thomas*
(PR. & in 40).
Add.: 7 Ebenezer Place, Lambeth
   (32): 7 Paradise St., Lambeth
   (38).
Refs.: PIG/DIR/32: 38: ROB/DIR/40.

DALTON, *J.*
   ,,   *George Edward*
     (BS/HOWE/LBB. p. 28).
   ,,   *Harriet* (29).
Add.: 8 Gt. Mary's Bldgs.: 14a
   Bear Yard, Lincolns Inn Fields
   (ca. 40).
Refs.: HOLD/11: COWIE/29: 31:
   PIG/DIR/24: 38: ROB/DIR/22: 29
   (H): COWIE/7.

DARTNALL, *Richard*
   (BS/HOWE/LBB. p. 29).
   ,,   *Mrs.* (?)

DAVIES, *Daniel*
Refs.: JOHN/17.

DAVIES, *David*
Add.: 27 Villiers St., Strand: 8
   George St. (29).
Refs.: COWIE/29: 31: PIG/DIR/24:
   38: ROB/DIR/22: 29 (G. St.): 32
   (No. 3).

DAVIES, *George*
Add.: 3/4 Warwick Sq., Newgate
   St.: 3 White Hart St., Newgate
   Mkt. (36).
Refs.: COWIE/31: 32: PIG/DIR/28:
   32: 36: 38: ROB/DIR/29: 35: 40:
   PO/DIR/31: 40.

DAVIES, *Thomas*
Add.: 117 Minories.
Refs.: PIG/DIR/32.

DAVIES, *Watkin*
Add.: 41 St. Andrew's Hill (28):
   24 Addle Hill (32).
Refs.: PIG/DIR/28: 32.

DAVIES, *William*
Add.: 88 Pleasant Row, Kingsland
   Rd.
Refs.: PIG/DIR/32.

DAVIS, *Mrs.*
Add.: 33 Dorset St., Spitalfields.
Refs.: PO/DIR/40.

DAVIS, *J.*
,,   & *Porter* (36).
,,   & *Co.* (40).
(BS. &).
Add.: 104 Sloane St.
Refs.: ROB/DIR/32: PIG/DIR/36:
COWIE/7.

DAVIS, *John*
(BB.'s marbled papers).
(BS/HOWE/LBB. p. 104).

DAVIS, *(Robert ?)*
(BS/HOWE/LBB. p. 29).
Refs.: COWIE/29: 31: ROB/DIR/22.

DAVIS, *William*
E.D.: 07 ?
Add.: 15 Southampton Row.
Refs.: Ticket seen Feb. 1952 at
Fisher & Sperr on Mason's 2
vol. Ed. of T. Gray. The label
indicated that he was primarily a
bookseller and stationer, but mentions that he did bookbinding "to
pattern".

DAVI(E)S & POWELL
(Bookclasp Makers).
Add.: 7 Queen Sq., Bartholomew
Close.
Refs.: COWIE/29: 31: PIG/DIR/28:
36: 38: ROB/DIR/29: 32: 35: 40:
PO/DIR/40.

DAVISON
Add.: 16 Albion Bldgs., Bartholomew Close: 11 Jewin Crescent:
16 A.B. & 18 J.C. (35).
Refs.: COWIE/29: 31: ROB/DIR:32:
35: 40: PIG/DIR/36: 38: PO/DIR/
40: COWIE/7: LAB/KNA (4).

DAW
Add.: Salters Hill Ct., Cannon St.
Refs.: COWIE/29: 31.

DAW, *J. J.*
(Vellum Binder & Gilder).
Add.: 5 Oxford Ct., Cannon St.:
14 Sherburn Lane (24).
Refs.: JOHN/17: PIG/DIR/24.

DAW, *John*
(Vellum Binder in 35).
Add.: 1 St. Thomas Apostle Ct.,
Clock Lane.
Refs.: PIG/DIR/32: ROB/DIR/35.

DAWKINS, *John D.*
(BS/HOWE/LBB. p. 29).
,,   *C. J.* (35).
Add.: 89 Bartholomew Close: 4
Princes St., Barbican (35).
Refs.: COWIE/29: 31: PIG/DIR/24:
28: 32: ROB/DIR/20: 29: 35.

DAWS, *W.*
(& BS. & ST.).
Add.: 18 Commerce Pl., Brixton
Rd.
Refs.: PO/DIR/40.

DAWSON, *Henry*
Add.: 41 Frith St., Soho.
Refs.: PIG/DIR/36.

DAWSON, *Thomas*
Add.: 31 Brooke St., Holborn (29):
16 High Holborn (32): 27 New
North St., Red Lion Sq. (36).
Refs.: COWIE 29: 31: ROB/DIR/29:
PIG/DIR/28: 32: 36: 38.

DAWSON & LEWIS
Add.: 5 Richmond's Bldgs., Dean
St., Soho.
Refs.: COWIE/29: 31: JOHN/17:
PIG/DIR/24: 32: ROB/DIR/20: 22:
29: SCH/S. de R/IV. 49.
O.C.: Moses: *Vases*. 19: olive
m.g. Etruscan decor[s]: (Arms:
Ponsonby & Shaftesbury): (tic-
ket): Cockburn's *Swiss Scenery*,
20, f.m.g. (ticket): Milton: *Poems*,
4 vol. 16, f.m.g. (ticket) "Sold by/
Rodwell & Martin/46 New Bond
St./Bound by/D & L/ R.B/
Soho.": Britton: *Winchester*,
17, blue m.g. gothic decor[s],
largely hand-tooled: (ticket)
(Arms of Ponsonby & Shaftes-
bury). (See Plates III and IV.)

DAY
BS/HOWE/LBB. p. 29).

DAY, *William*
(BB.'s Toolcutter).
Add.: 6 Staple Inn Bldgs. (36):

12 Middle Row, Holborn (38):
No. 1 (40).
Refs.: PIG/DIR/36: 38: ROB/DIR/40.

DEAN, *Richard*
Add.: 2 Bartholomew Terrace, City
Rd.
Refs.: COWIE/29: 31: PIG/DIR/28:
ROB/DIR/29.

DE LA ROCHE, *Henri*
Add.: 5 King St., Portman Sq.
Refs.: HOLD/11.

DE LA RUE, *Thomas*
Refs.: SLB. p. 132. This firm produced a number of fine albums,
annuals, etc., stamped on the
backs and sides with very finely
executed blind imprints, which
form a section of bookbinding
technique which is deserving of
close and specialised study. (See
Plate V). There is a magnificent specimen of such binding on
the New Testament, printed in
gold, published (n.d.) and signed
on spine by D. L. R., Cornish
and Rock., in the Rylands
Library (Sp. 21, 117).

DEMONSEAU, *Joseph/Jane*
(BS/HOWE/LBB. p. 29).

DENMEAD
Add.: 7 Adams Place, Borough.
Refs.: COWIE/29: 31: ROB/DIR/29.

DESCHLEIN, *Frederick*
(BS/HOWE/LBB. p. 30).
Add.: 20 Duke Ct., St. Martin's
Lane. (BM. G. 4379).
Refs.: HOLD/11: SCH. S. de R. IV/
No. 39: Took over Kalthoeber's
business about 1813 and died ten
years later. His bindings are not
common.

DICKINS, *Charles*
(Bookclasp Makers).
Add.: Jacob's Well Ct., Barbican
(29): 2 Golden Lion Ct., Aldersgate St. (36): 7 New St. (ca. 40).
Refs.: COWIE/29: 31: PIG/DIR/36:
38: COWIE/7.

DILLON, *Robert (of Chelsea)*
(BS/HOWE/LBB. p. 30).
Add.: 21 Queen St., Golden Sq.
(11).
Refs.: HOLD/11.
O.C.: Roscoe: *Lorenzo de Medici*,
2 vol. 97: f.m.g. Yellow label
"Bd by/D/C". Aristoteles: *De
Poetica*, 94, same label, but
white: calf gilt., tree calf sides
with olive green surrounds.

DIPPIE
Add.: Zoar St., Gravel Lane.
Refs.: COWIE/29: 31.

DIXON, *Charles*
Add.: 10 Bull's Head Ct., Newgate
St.
Refs.: ROB/DIR/32.

DOBBINS, *Benjamin*
(BS/HOWE/LBB. p. 30).

DOBSON, *Joseph*
Add.: 21 Warwick Lane, City.
Refs.: PIG/DIR/36: 38.

DONNISON, *John*
Add.: 9 White Hart Ct., Bishops-
gate St. & 26 Liverpool St.: L.S.
only (32).
Refs.: COWIE/29: 31: ROB/DIR/29:
PIG/DIR/32: 36: Apprenticed to
John Seear and admitted a F.S.C.
6.6.20.

DORE, *George*
(BS. & 35).
Add.: 27 Galway St., St. Luke's
(32): 9 Upper North Place,
G.I. Rd. (35).
Refs.: PIG/DIR/32: ROB/DIR/35.

DORRINGTON, *Samuel*
Add.: 8 George St., Adelphi.
Refs.: COWIE/31: 32: PIG/DIR/32:
ROB/DIR/32.

DOUGLAS, *Thomas*
(BS/HOWE/LBB. p. 31).
Refs.: AND/90.

DOUGLAS, *Joseph*
(BS/HOWE/LBB. p. 31).

60

DOWSE, *James*
    Add.: 106 Great Guildford St.
      Borough.
    Refs.: PIG/DIR/38.

DREW, *John*
    (BS/HOWE/LBB. p. 31).

DRURY, *H.*
    E.D.: 22 ?
    Refs.: Juvenal : *Satyrae.* MSS.
      1471 : Firmin-Didot Sale 1881,
      No. 8 : gilding by C. Lewis.

DRYER, *Benjamin*
    (& BS.).
    Add.: 17 Duke St., W. Smithfield.
    Refs.: COWIE/29 : 31 : PIG/DIR/28 :
      ROB/DIR/29.

DUDLEY, *Thos.*
    (& Book and Card Edgegilders).
    Add.: Friar St. & 1 Printer St.,
      Blackfriars.
    Refs.: COWIE/29 : 31 : ROB/DIR/29.

DUGGIN, *William*
    Add.: 14 Clarendon Sq.
    Refs.: PIG/DIR/32.

DUTHIE, *Thomas*
    (BS/HOWE/LBB. p. 32).
    Add.: 6 Dyers Bldgs., Holborn (29).
      8 Wine Office Ct., Fleet St. (32).

Refs.: COWIE/29 : 31 : PIG/DIR/32 :
    36 : ROB/DIR/29.

DYKE, *Gilbert*
    Add.: 277 Whitechapel Rd.
    Refs.: PIG/DIR/36. (Hollings Cat.
      253/No. 213 mentions the ticket
      of T. Dykes on a ½ c.g. binding
      ca. 1837).

DYMOTT, *Richard/Mary*
    (BS. & to the Duke of Gloucester).
    (BS/HOWE/LBB. p. 31).
    Add.: Opposite Somerset House,
      Strand.
    Refs.: BS/DPB/1726/75. (Note :
      Richard died in 1779, but his
      widow bound into my period.)

EARLE, *William*
    Add.: 25 Frith St., Soho.
    Refs.: AND/90.

EAST, *Edward*
    (BS/HOWE/LBB. p. 32).

ECKFORD, *Joseph*
    (BS/HOWE/LBB. p. 32).

EDDINGTON
    (BS/HOWE/LBB. p. 32).

EDGAR, *William*
    Add.: 14 Edmund St., King's
      Cross.
    Refs.: PIG/DIR/32.

EDGEL(L)ER, *William*
　Add.: 1 New Inn Passage, Clare
　　Mkt.: 41 Hemlock Ct., Lincolns
　　Inn Fields (40): 7 Houghton St.,
　　C.M. (ca. 40).
　Refs.: PIG/DIR/38: ROB/DIR/40: 41:
　　42: COWIE/7.

EDMONDS, *George*
　(BS. & 35).
　Add.: 26 Hosier Lane, Smithfield
　　(32): 24 King's St., Holborn (35).
　Refs.: PIG/DIR/32: ROB/DIR/35.

EDMONDS, *Jacob*
　(see Remnant & Edmonds, ca. 31).
　Refs.: SLB. p. 68.

EDWARDS family (*of Halifax and
　　London*)
　Refs.: BS/HOWE/LBB. p. 33. The
　　best account of the binding
　　activities of this famous family is
　　to be found in Mr. T. W.
　　Hanson's article in No. 6 (1948)
　　of the *Book Handbook*. The
　　firm was founded by William
　　Edwards in Halifax about 1755,
　　and they seem to have been pro-
　　ducing well by 1780 all their three
　　specialities, i.e., fore-edge paint-
　　ings, calf bindings in the "Etrus-
　　can" style, and decorated vellum
　　bindings. James, William's
　　second son, came to London in
　　1784, and it was there that on Jan.
　　28th, 1785, he was granted a

patent (No. 1462 Patent Office)
for the Edwards "under the
vellum-painting" process. Thereafter this class of binding seems to
have been regularly produced
both in the London and Halifax
workshops, though the patent
was eventually transferred by
James to his younger brother
Thomas, who continued to work
in Halifax till 1826. All three of
the Edwards specialities appear to
have found imitators, but none of
them up to the standard of the
originals. (See Plate XXIX.)

EDWARDS, *W.*
　(Bookedge Lockmaker).
　Add.: 49 Goswell Rd.: 2 Jewin St.,
　　Aldersgate (& at Birmingham).
　Refs.: ROB/DIR/40: PO/DIR/40.

EEDY
　Add.: 37 Tavistock St.
　Refs.: Huth Sale No. 2064, 3183:
　　COWIE/7: W. H. Crawford Sale
　　1891/2343: green mor.

EELES, *Thomas Robert*
　　　" 　& *Son* (ca. 40).
　Add.: 54 Exmouth St., Spa Fields:
　　22 Cursitor St. (ca. 40).
　Refs.: PIG/DIR/36: COWIE/7.

EGLETON, *Abraham Charles*
　Add.: 90½ Holborn Hill & 5 Gold-
　　smith Row, Gough Sq. (40).

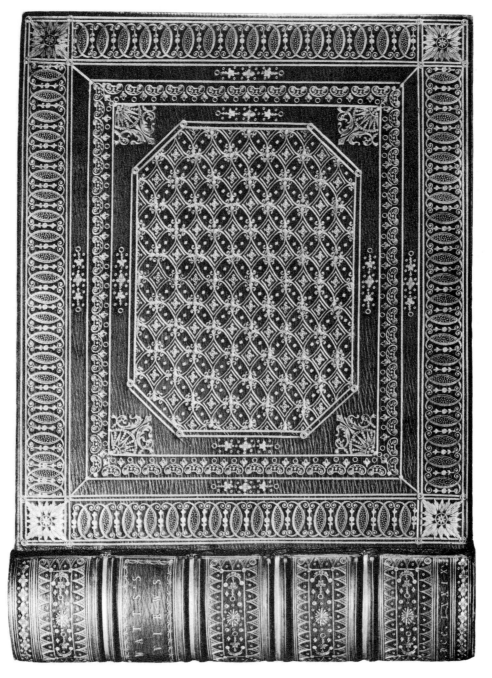

PLATE XV   KALTHOEBER   (11" × 8½")

PLATE XVI   KALTHOEBER   *(11½″ × 14″)*

Refs.: ROB/DIR/40: PO/DIR/40: COWIE/7.

EGLETON, *Abraham Charles*
(see BS/HOWE/LBB. p. 33).
Add.: 16 St. John Lane, Clerkenwell (29): 29 Turnmill St., Clerkenwell (32.A.): 38 New St. Sq., Shoe Lane (32.C.): 17 Queen St. (ca. 40).
Refs.: COWIE/29: 31: PIG/DIR/32: ROB/DIR/29: 32: COWIE/7. From the record of his Freedom of the Stationers' Co. on 3.4.10, where he is given as the son of Stephen, he was probably Abraham's brother, rather than his son.

EGLETON, *Andrew*
Add.: 4 Brownlow St., High Holborn.
Refs.: HOLD/11.

ELKINS, *Valentine*
(BS. &).
Add.: 8 Baker St., Portman Sq.
Refs.: ROB/DIR/32: 35. I have in my O.C. an excellent hard-grain mor. gt. binding on the 1633 Elzevir *Greek Testament*. The work is in the plain, early Bedford style. Blind-stamped "Bound by, etc."

ELKINS, *William*
(& BS. & ST.).
Add.: 170 Oxford St.
Refs.: LAB/JONES.

ELLIOTT, *Charles*
(Binder to the British Museum).
E.D.: 73. L.D. 13.
Refs.: AE/BML. p. 337 (Son of Thomas Elliott: see BS/HOWE/LBB. p. 34).

ELLIOTT, *J.*
(BS/HOWE/LBB. p. 33).

ELLIOTT, *William*
(BS/HOWE/LBB. p. 34).
Add.: 51 Stanhope St.
Refs.: HOLD/11: COWIE/29: 31: ROB/DIR/20: 22: PIG/DIR/24.

ELLIOTT, *William*
(BS/HOWE/LBB. p. 34).
Add.: 3 Warwick Lane.
Refs.: ROB/DIR/20: 22: PIG/DIR/24.

ELLIS, *George*
,,   & Bone (35).
,,   J. (35).
Add.: 5 Knightrider Ct. (32): 1 Ivy Lane (32 *E. & B.*): 3 Chapter House Ct. (32 *G. & J.*).
Refs.: COWIE/31: 32: PIG/DIR/32: 36: ROB/DIR/32: 35. George was freed by redemption in 1832.

ELLISON, *Thomas Jones*
(BS/HOWE/LBB. p. 34).
,,   T. J. Jr. (36).
Add.: 27 Water Lane, Fleet St. (36): 17 Ave Maria Lane (40).

Refs.: COWIE/29 : 31 : PIG/DIR/28 : 32 : 36 (Jr.) : 38 : ROB/DIR/20 : 40 : COWIE/7.

ELSWORTH, *John*
  Add.: 2 Meredith St., Clerkenwell.
  Refs.: ROB/DIR/35.

EMERY, *William*
  Add.: 5 Windmill St., Lambeth.
  Refs.: COWIE/29 : 31 : ROB/DIR/20.

ENGLER, *Gustav*
  Add.: 9 Foley Place.
  Refs.: PIG/DIR/32.

ENTWISLE, *John*
  Add.: 30 Earl St., Finsbury.
  Refs.: COWIE/29 : 31 : ROB/DIR/29 : 32 : PIG/DIR/32 : LAB/JONES.

ESQUILLANT, *Frederick Caius*
  (ST. in 40).
  Add.: 346 Oxford St.
  Refs.: Label O.C.: PIG/DIR/36 : ROB/DIR/40.

EVANS, *Joseph*
  Add.: 26 Queen St., Golden Sq.
  Refs.: COWIE/29 : 31 : ROB/DIR/20 : PIG/DIR/28 : 32.

EVANS, *Joseph Stuart*
  (& Vellum Binder).
  Add.: 57 Berners St. (31) : 64 Berwick St. (35).
  Refs.: COWIE/31 : 32 : PIG/DIR/32 :

36 : ROB/DIR/32 : 35 : 40 : COWIE/7. Athett's *Bibliopegia* 1335. pp. 121/2 ascribes to him a process for illuminated binding borrowed from the French. I have an excellent specimen in my O.C. on the *Book of Gems*. 1836 (see Plate VI).

EWING, *James*
  Add.: 8 Oxford Arms Passage.
  Refs.: PIG/DIR/36.

EWING, *Matthew*
  (BS/HOWE/LBB. p. 34).
  Refs.: COWIE/29 : 31 : PIG/DIR/24 : 28 : 32 : 36 : 38 : ROB/DIR/22 : 29 : 32 : 35 : 40 : PO/DIR/40 : COWIE/7. O.C.: Cheap calf bdg. on Worsley's *Rules for ... French Language*, 14 : an early example of trade binding for school use; running blindstamp ornament on sides near spine with name "*EWING*" in sloped capitals.

EWINS, *Samuel*
  (& Bible warehouse).
  Add.: 17/18 Duke St., W. Smithfield : 10 Lambeth Hill, Upper Thames St. (ca. 40).
  Refs.: PIG/DIR/32 : COWIE/7.

EWSTERS, *Sam*
  (Vellum BB.).
  Add.: 9 Aldersgate St.
  Refs.: HOLD/11.

EXLEY, *D. & Co.*
Add.: 10 Red Lion Ct., Fleet St.
Refs.: PO/DIR/40.

FAIRBAIRN, *Robert*
(BS/HOWE/LBB. pp. 3 & 35).
Add.: 10 Duke St., Adelphi: No.
23 (ca. 36).
Refs.: COWIE/29: PIG/DIR/28: 32:
36: 38: ROB/DIR/29: 32: 35: 40:
PO/DIR/40: KNA/LAB.

FAIRBAIRN, *Thomas*
(BS/HOWE/LBB. p. 3 (under Armstrong) & p. 35: also SLB.,
passim.)
d.1800.
Refs.: He appears to have never
risen above the rank of Finisher.

FAIRBAIRN & ARMSTRONG
(BS/HOWE/LBB. pp. 3 & 35).
Refs.: ROB/DIR/20: 22: PIG/DIR/24.
Huth Sale No. 1935.
O.C.: *Capta Constantinopli*, Paris,
23: f.m.g., with black overlays on
sides and spine. (See Plate VII.)
The roll on the sides was used by
Staggemeier (see SCH/S. de R/
IV. 23) and the date makes the
attribution to F. & A. probable.
Other bindings by F. & A. are
No. 2268 in Hoe Sale IV and No.
1698 in W. H. Crawford Sale
1891. See also Rylands Library,
R. 4745 from the Rev. T.
Williams Collection.

FAIRBROTHER, *William*
Add.: 3 Shoemaker Row, Black-
friars.
Refs.: PIG/DIR/28.

FARGHER & LINDNER
„   *Benjamin* (08).
(Also see Lindner).
(BS/HOWE/LBB. pp. 35 & 60).
E.D. ? 02: (Probably worked
together till 08, after which date
each listed separately: their joint
address seems to have been Exeter
Ct., Strand.)
Refs.: COWIE/29: PIG/DIR/28: ROB/
DIR/20(F): 35.
O.C.: Cowper's *Poems*, 02: 2 vol.
f.m.g.: oval ticket: Aeschines:
Orationes. 01, f.m.g.: oblong
ticket: WH/CAT. 146: ascribes
their tools to R. Payne and
says they may have been his
disciples. For other specimens
see BM. G. 10482 & g. 236. k. 24.

FARNES, *J.*
(BS., ST. &).
Add.: 62 Cable St., Wellclose Sq.
Refs.: ROB/DIR/20.

FARQUHAR, *William*
(Journeyman Bookbinder).
(see S.L.B. pp. 73/74 & 107).

FARRELL, *Robert*
Add.: 8 Gt. Mays Bldgs., St.
Martin's Lane: 13 Newcastle St.,
Strand (38).

Refs.: ROB/DIR/35: 38: PIG/DIR/38: PO/DIR/40.

FAULDER, *Robert*
(& BS.).
(see Rodwell, J.).
Add.: 42 New Bond St. (90): No. 46 (11).
Refs.: AND/90: HOLD/11.

FAULKNER, *Henry*
(BS/HOWE/LBB. p. 35 & SLB. p. 57).
Add.: Heath Cock Ct., Strand (? 15): George Ct., Adelphi (? 25).
Refs.: Benger's Cat. 9/71.
The above dated addresses are taken from Quaritch Cat. 93/ Nos. 1132 & 3.

FAULKNER, *John*
(BS/HOWE/LBB. p. 35 & SLB. pp. 53, 56/7).
Refs.: JOHN/17: PIG/DIR/28: 32: Red mor. bdg., worn on exterior, fine interior broad dentelles, high decorated, silk endpapers & ticket (Sotheby Sale 25.11.52, No. 334). There is also a nice blue mor. bdg. with the Queen St. ticket in the Christie Bequest at Manchester University. An earlier John Faulkner was binding in 1790 at 9 Abchurch Lane (see AND/90).

FAULKNER, *Thomas William, Sr.*
(BS/HOWE/LBB. p. 35 & SLB. passim.).
Refs.: ABB/CBS/LAB. (Green St.).

FAULKNER, *Thomas William* (?) *Jr.*
(BS. &).
Add.: 1 Paradise Row, Chelsea.
Refs.: HOLD/11: LIST/29: ROB/DIR/ 20: 22: BS.): 32: 35: PIG/DIR/32: 36.

FEARMAN, *William*
(BS/HOWE/LBB. p. 36).

FEATHERSTONE, *Richard*
Add.: 60 Baldwin's Gdns.
Refs.: PIG/DIR/32.

FELLOWES, *William*
Add.: 21 Bread St. Hill (35): 4 Amen Corner (38).
Refs.: ROB/DIR/35: PIG/DIR/36: 38: PO/DIR/40: COWIE/7.

FERGUSSON, *Jock*
(SLB. pp. 73/4).
Refs.: Though a famous character, he never appears to have risen above being a journeyman.

FERRALL, *Roger*
Add.: 8 Gt. May's Bldgs., St. Martin's Lane.
Refs.: PIG/DIR/36.

PLATE XVII   LEISHMAN $(8\frac{1}{2}'' \times 10\frac{1}{2}'')$

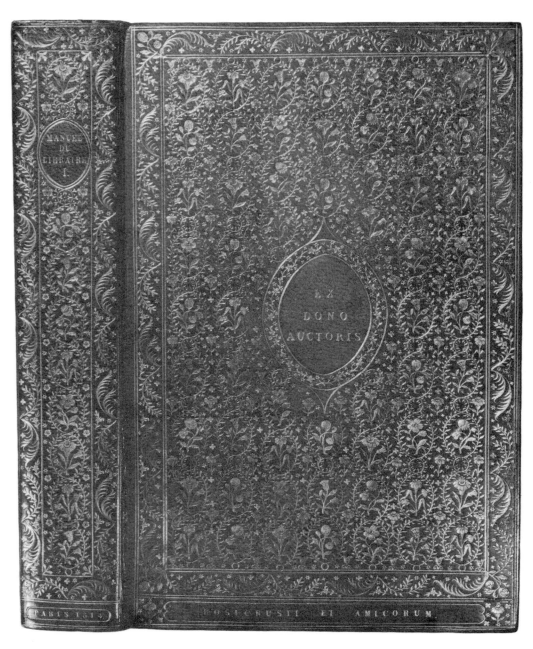

PLATE XVIII   LEWIS, C.   ($6'' \times 9\frac{1}{4}''$)

FEUQUIERE
Refs.: BB., VOL. III, p. 3, refers to a French emigré of this name having been a London bookbinder.

FIENNES, *Morrice*
(BS/HOWE/LBB. p. 36).

FINCH, *William*
(BS/HOWE/LBB. p. 36).
Refs.: COWIE/29: 31.

FIN(D)LAY, *David*
Add.: 4 Upper James St., Golden Sq.
Refs.: PIG/DIR/24: ROB/DIR/20: 22.

FINLAY, *T.*
Add.: 60 Poland St. (22): 36 Broad St., Grosvenor Sq. (31).
Refs.: COWIE/29: 31: PIG/DIR/24: 28: ROB/DIR/22: 29: ABB/CBS: HUTH/SALE/No. 1825.

FINNEY, *David*
(BS/HOWE/LBB. p. 36).

FISH, *Filby*
Add.: 3 Denzell St., Clare Market.
Refs.: PIG/DIR/32.

FISHER, *James*
(BS/HOWE/LBB. p. 36).

FISHER, *James William*
Add.: 8 Redcross Sq. (36): 26 New Union St., Little Moorfields (40).
Refs.: PIG/DIR/36: PO/DIR/40.

FISHER, *Thomas*
(& print seller in 40).
Add.: 1 Hanway St., Oxford St. No. 19 (ca. 40).
Refs.: COWIE/31: 32: PIG/DIR/32: 36: 38: ROB/DIR/32: 35: 40: PO/DIR/40: COWIE/7: He may be the binder from Chester who was employed by the Bishop of London & at Westminster Abbey. (BR./BM./VOL. IV. 41/5.)

FITZGERALD, *Charlotte*
Add.: 87 Charlotte St., Rathbone St.
Refs.: PIG/DIR/32.

FLACK, *Edward*
Add.: 15 Cobourg Pl., Borough Rd.
Refs.: PIG/DIR/38: PO/DIR/40.

FLACK, *James (or J.C.)/M.*
(BS/HOWE/LBB. p. 36).
Refs.: HOLD/11.

FLAVELL, *William/Mary (also S., & John William)*
(BS/HOWE/LBB. p. 36).

FLEET, *Robert (or Richard)*
(BS/HOWE/LBB. p. 36).
(Vellum Binder & Needle-maker.)
„ *Thomas* (? date).
Add.: 3 & 8 Aldersgate St.
Refs.: COWIE/29: 31: JOHN/17: PIG/DIR/24: 32: ROB/DIR/20: 22

(both Richard) 32 : 35 : PO/DIR/17 : 40.

FLETCHER
Add. : West St., Smithfield.
Refs. : COWIE/29 : 31.

FLIGHT, *Charles*
(& ST.).
Add. : 9 Gt. Suffolk St.
Refs. : JOHN/17.

FLINT, *Thomas*
(BS. &).
„ *Mrs. Ann* (40).
E.D. ? 23.
Add. : 28 Burlington Arcade (29).
Refs. : ROB/DIR/29 : PO/DIR/40.
Boerner's Cat. XXI/181, which describes a green morocco binding on S. Johnson's *Rasselas*, 1823, with ticket.

FLOOD, *Luke*
(BS/HOWE/LBB. p. 37).

FORD, *George*
(BS/HOWE/LBB. p. 37).
Add. : 47 St. John St. (91).
Refs. : BRI/DIR/91 : HOLD/11.

FORD, *George*
Add. : 76 Little Britain.
Refs. : PIG/DIR/32.

FORD, *James*
(Booklock Mfrs.).

Add. : 6 Monkwell St., Cripplegate.
Refs. : ROB/DIR/35 : PO/DIR/40.

FORD, *Joseph*
Add. : 40 Charles St., City Rd.
Refs. : COWIE/31 : 32 : PIG/DIR/32 : 36 : ROB/DIR/32 : 35.

FORD, *James*
(Bookclasp Makers).
„ *J. B. H.* (40).
Add. : 14 Fell St., Wood St. (20) : 15 Philip Lane, London Wall (22) : 2 Doby Ct., Monkwell St. (23) : No. 1 (31) : 6 Monkwell St. (36).
Refs. : COWIE/29 : 31 : PIG/DIR/23 : 28 : 36 : 38 : ROB/DIR/20 : 22 : 40 : PO/DIR/31.

FORD, *William*
(& BS. & ST. in 40).
Add. : 60 & 69 Wood St., Cheapside.
Refs. : ROB/DIR/20 : 22 : PIG/DIR/32 : 38 : PO/DIR/40 : COWIE/7.

FORSTER, *James*
Add. : 2 Nelson Pl., City Rd.
Refs. : PIG/DIR/28 : 32.

FOSBROOKE, *Leonard*
Add. : 34 Shoemakers Row, Broadway, City.
Refs. : PIG/DIR/36.

FOUCHEE, *James*
(BS/HOWE/LBB. p. 37).

68

FOUNTAIN, *Henry*
  Add.: 41 Ogle St., Gt. Titchfield St.
  Refs.: PIG/DIR/36.

FOWLER, *Benjamin*
  Add.: 9 Shire Lane.
  Refs.: PIG/DIR/32.

FOWLER, *George*
  Add.: 2 Blossom St., Norton Folgate.
  Refs.: ROB/DIR/20.

FOWLER, *George William*
  (BS/HOWE/LBB. p. 37).

FRANCIS, *James*
  Add.: 4 Chapter House Ct., St. Paul's.
  Refs.: ROB/DIR/32.

FRANCIS, *James*
  (BS. &).
  Add.: 2 Bridge St., Lambeth.
  Refs.: PO/DIR/17.

FRANCIS, *James*
  Add.: 50 Hatfield St., Blackfriars.
  Refs.: COWIE/29: 31: PIG/DIR/28: ROB/DIR/29.

FRANCIS, *John*
  (BB.'s Toolcutters).
  Add.: 5 Dean St., Holborn: 10 Hatton Gdn. (ca. 40).
  Refs.: COWIE/29: 31: PIG/DIR/32: 36: 38: ROB/DIR/40: COWIE/7.

FRANKS & CLEAVER
  (BB.'s Toolcutter).
  (BS/HOWE/LBB. p. 104).

FRASER
  E.D. 28 ?
  Add.: Regent St.
  Refs.: Munby Coll. (? 28).
    O.C.: Scott: *Marmion*: 35. f.m.g. publisher's binding type.

FRASER, *George*
      d. 24.
      (BS/HOWE/LBB. p. 38: also SLB. passim.).
    ,,   & *Son* (17).
    ,,   & *Co.* (32).
    ,,   *James* (38).
  (See also Thomas, infra.)
  Add.: F. & Son were at No. 84 St. Martin's Lane about 1817.
  Refs.: COWIE/29: 31: JOHN/17: PIG/DIR/24: 28: 32: 36: 38: ROB/DIR/20: 22: 29: 32: 35: 40: PO/DIR/40.

FRASER, *James*
  (BS/HOWE/LBB. p. 38 & p. XXXIV: also SLB. passim).

FRASER, *Thomas*
  Add.: 84 St. Martin's Lane.
  Refs.: PO/DIR/31.

FREETH, *Charles*
  Add.: 31 Seymour Place.
  Refs.: ROB/DIR/22: PIG/DIR/24.

FREGO, *Thomas*
    Add.: 22 Poland St.
    Refs.: ROB/DIR/35.

FREMONT, *Harriet & Ann*
    Add.: 30 Brown's Lane, Spital-
    fields.
    Refs.: ROB/DIR/35.

FRENCH, *John*
    (BS/HOWE/LBB. p. 39).

FRITH, *Michael*
    (BS/HOWE/LBB. p. 39).

FRYER, *J.*
    (& BS.).
    Add.: 15 Gower St. North, New
    Rd.
    Refs.: PO/DIR/40.

FRY, *Edmund*
    Add.: 73 Houndsditch.
    Refs.: ROB/DIR/35.
    Apparently a F.S.C. by 1816.

FULLER, *S. & T.*
    Add.: 34 Rathbone Place.
    Refs.: Tickets seen at Fletcher
    (about 1840). Another ticket
    seen at Dawson's on folio album
    in maroon mor. gilt with
    elaborate broad inside borders
    and yellow silk endpapers about
    1830/5.

GABRIEL, *E.*
    (ST., BS. &).
    Add.: 111 Fore St., Cripplegate.
    Refs.: HOLD/11.

GALABIN
    (see Henington).

GALABIN, *Septimus Barry*
    (b. 1780. d. 19.9.12: ST. &:
    youngest son of John William
    Galabin.)
    Refs.: TIMP/42. p. 894.

GALE, *Henry*
    E.D.: ? 20.
    Add.: 16 Goswell Rd.
    Refs.: LAB/JONES ("Bound by"):
    LAB/KNA (ca. 26): PIG/DIR/36: 38:
    COWIE/7.

GANDAR, *John*
    ,,   *Egerton & Gandar* (38)
    ,,   *J.* (40).
    Add.: 28 King St., Goswell Rd.:
    44 Theobalds Rd. (31): 9 Prince
    St., Red Lion Sq. (38).
    Refs.: COWIE/31: 32: PIG/DIR/28:
    32: 38: ROB/DIR/32: 40: PO/DIR/
    40.

GARDINER, *G.*
    Add.: 6 Cross St., Blackfriars Rd.
    Refs.: PIG/DIR/28.

GARDINER, *Richard*
    (BS/HOWE/LBB. p. 40).

GARDNER, *John*
(BS/HOWE/LBB. p. 40).

GARDNER, *Sarah*
Add.: 44 Aldermanbury.
Refs.: AND/90.

GARRARD, *Thomas*
(ST. &).
Add.: 174 Ratcliff Highway.
Refs.: ROB/DIR/20: 22.

GARROD, *Samuel*
(Bookbinder to the Duke of Kent
in 1817).
(& BS.).
Add.: 30 Paddington St.: 88 High
St., Marylebone (28): 7 Notting-
ham St., Marylebone (29): 27
South St., Manchester Sq. (31):
36 Upper York St., Portman Sq.
(38).
Refs.: JOHN/17: COWIE/29: 31: 32:
PIG/DIR/24: 28: 32: 38: ROB/DIR/
20: 22: (BS., ST. &): 29: 32: 35:
PO/DIR/31.

GARROD, *Samuel, Jr.*
Add.: 8 Ridinghouse Lane.
Refs.: PIG/DIR/32.

GAUNT
Add.: Bond St., Borough Rd.
Refs.: COWIE/29: 31.

GEORGE, *James*
Add.: 8 West St., Hackney.
Refs.: PIG/DIR/32.

GEORGE, *Joshua* (35).
    „   *Joseph* (38).
Add.: Red Lion St., Holborn (29):
79 Berwick St. (35): 102 Dean
St., Soho (38).
Refs.: COWIE/29: 31: PIG/DIR/38:
ROB/DIR/35: 40: PO/DIR/40.

GHISLIN, *James*
Add.: Braziers Bldgs., Fleet Mar-
ket: Bleeding Heart Yd., Hatton
Yd.
Refs.: COWIE/29: 31: ROB/DIR/29.

GIBBS, *George*
Add.: 9 St. Martin's Churchyard.
Refs.: PIG/DIR/28.

GIBBS, *J. T.*
    „   *J.* (40)
    (& ST.).
Add.: 11 Gt. May's Bldgs., St.
Martin's Lane: 8 Gt. Newport St.
(ca. 40).
Refs.:   PIG/DIR/38:   PO/DIR/40:
COWIE/7.

GIBSON, *George*
Add.: 8 West St., Hackney (32):
108 Drummond St., Somerstown
(36).
Refs.: PIG/DIR/32: 36: 38: ROB/DIR/
40.

GILL, *James Henry*
Add.: 5 Hunt's Ct., St. Martin's
Lane.
Refs.: PIG/DIR/28.

GILMOUR
  E.D.: 13 (?)
  Forbes, J., *Oriental Memoirs*: 2 Vol.
  13. f.m.g. & doublures. Michel-
  more. Cat. 37, Part I, p. 16,
  signed on doublure "Gilmour
  Bibliopegist". A notable binding.
  (May be the Salisbury binder
  who bound for Lord Lansdowne)

GILSON, *George*
  (Vellum Binder).
  Add.: White Lion Ct., Birchin
  Lane.
  Refs.: ROB/DIR/35.

GLADDING, *John*
  Add.: 20 City Rd.
  Refs.: PIG/DIR/38 : ROB/DIR/40.

GLADDING, *R.*
  Add.: 97/8 Whitechapel Rd.
  Refs.: ROB/DIR/40.

GLAISHER, *George*
  Add.: 3 Petty's Ct., Oxford St. (32) :
  23 Nassau St., Goodge St. (38).
  Refs.: PIG/DIR/32 : 36 : 38 : ROB/DIR/
  40 : PO/DIR/40 : COWIE/7.

GLAISHER (*or Glaister*)
  „ *John* (20).
  „ *James* (24).
  „ *Mary* (32).
  Add.: 7 Charterhouse St.

Refs.: COWIE/29 : 31 : PIG/DIR/24 :
  28 : 32 : 38 : ROB/DIR/20 : 22 : 29 :
  32 : 35.

GLAISHER, *William*
  (Apparently a relative of James).
  Add.: 7 Charterhouse St.
  Refs.: PIG/DIR/36.

GLANVIL
  Add.: Wormwood St., Bishops-
  gate.
  Refs.: COWIE/29 : 31 : ROB/DIR/22.

GODARD & KELLY
  Add.: 15 Gower Place (? date) :
  8 Cromer St., Judd St.
  Refs.: LAB/KNA : PIG/DIR/32.

GODWIN, *William*
  Add.: 10 Knightsbridge.
  Refs.: PIG/DIR/32.

GOOD, *Susannah & Son*
  (ST. &).
  Add.: 63 Bishopsgate Without.
  Refs.: PIG/DIR/32.

GOODING, *Philip*
  (BB.'s Toolmakers).
  Add.: 16 Commercial Pl., City
  Rd. (28) : Edward St., Blackfriars
  Rd. (29).
  Refs.: COWIE/29 : 31 : PIG/DIR/28 :
  32.

GOODMAN, *Christopher*
  (BS/HOWE/LBB. p. 41).

GOODWIN, *Edward*
      (BB., BS. & Vellum
      BB).
   „   *William Thomas* (36).
Add.: 2 New St. Hill, Shoe Lane
   (23): 2 Shoe Lane (28): 1 Ann's
   Place, Westminster Rd. (36):
   15 Shoe Lane (ca. 40).
Refs.: COWIE/29: 31: PIG/DIR/23:
   28:32:36: (as William Thomas):
   ROB/DIR/29: 32: 35: COWIE/7.

GOSDEN, *Thomas*
      (BS/HOWE/LBB. p. 41).
   „   *Henry T.* (40).
Add.: 1 New Inn Bldgs., Wych St.
   (36).
Refs.: HOLD/11: JOHN/17: COWIE/
   29: 31: PIG/DIR/36: 38: ROB/DIR/
   20: 22: PO/DIR/40: SLB. p. 132.
   O.C.: Montague: *Disquisition*:
   26: f.m.g. (W.M. on E.P. 1829)
   is a curious production with
   unusual tooling on spine and
   sides.

GOTELEE   Hounslow
   (BS. etc.).
Refs.: LAB/JONES ("Bound by").

GOUGH, *Henry*
   (Binder to H.R.H. Duke of Sussex:
   see label in Munby Collection).
Add.: 48 Northampton St., Clerkenwell (17): 142 St. John's St.
   Rd., Clerkenwell (28): No. 43
   (32).

Refs.: COWIE/29: 31: JOHN/17:
   PIG/DIR/28: 32: ROB/DIR/20: 32:
   35. W. H. Crawford Sale 1891/
   No. 1634 is stated to be "repaired
   by Gough."

GOUGH
   Add.: Maidenhead Ct., Aldersgate
   St.
   Refs.: COWIE/29: 31.

GOYDER, *Joseph*
   Add.: Tothill St., Westminster.
   Refs.: COWIE/29: 31: ROB/DIR/20.

GRAHAM, *James*
      (BS/HOWE/LBB. p. 41).
   Add.: *19* Bartholomew Close (11).
   Refs.: HOLD/11: PIG/DIR/24: 28:
   32: ROB/DIR/20: 22.

GRAHAM, *John*
   Refs.: JOHN/17.

GRAHAM, *Matthew J.*
   Add.: 4 Gee St., Goswell Rd.
   Refs.: COWIE/31: 32: PIG/DIR/32:
   ROB/DIR/32.

GRAHAM, *William*
   (SLB. pp. 14 & 16).
   Refs.: I cannot trace that he ever
   became a master-binder.

GRANT, *John*
   Add.: 3 Ave Maria Lane.
   Refs.: ROB/DIR/20: PIG/DIR/24.

GRANT & Co.
(BS. in 40).
Add.: 7 Wellington St., Strand.
Refs.: PIG/DIR/38: ROB/DIR/40.

GRAVES
(BS/HOWE/LBB. p. 41).

GRAVES, *Arthur*
(Publisher in 1840).
Add.: 10 Gerrard St., Soho (35):
9 King William St., Strand (38).
Refs.: PIG/DIR/36: 38: ROB/DIR/35:
40: PO/DIR/40. Signature seen
on a book dated 1820 at Marks in
1949. The binding may be rather
later.

GRAY/GRAY & BUNCE
(BS/HOWE/LBB. p. 41).
Refs.: Same as G. Gray, 113
Swallow St. (?) who signed a tree
calf binding on 1802 work in
Sotheby Sale 4.2.53, No. 564:
Hodgson Sale 9/54/5, No. 433
first item had a label "Bd. by
G.G./G.L.C./New B.S." on a
1803 work.

GRAY, *William*
Add.: 34 Stanhope St., Clare
Market (20): Apollo Ct., Fleet
St. (32).
Refs.: COWIE/29: 31: PIG/DIR/24:
28: 32: ROB/DIR/20: 22.

GRAY, *Son* & FELL
(BS. &).
Add.: 60 Piccadilly.
Refs.: PIG/DIR/23: 28: 32.

GRAYSON, *Richard*
(BS/HOWE/LBB. p. 41).

GREEN, *Rowland*
(BS. &).
Add.: 27 Barbican.
Refs.: ROB/DIR/35.

GREENING, *W.*
E.D.: ? post 40.
Add.: 183 Fleet St.
Refs.: LAB/JONES.

GREENLAND, *James*
Add.: 2 Charles St., Somerstown.
Refs.: PIG/DIR/32: 36: ROB/DIR/35.

GREIG, *Alexander*
(BS/HOWE/LBB. p. 42 & SLB. p. 46).

GRELLIER, *Henry*
(& ST. in 1838).
Add.: 19 Church St., Soho (28):
23 Gerrard St., Soho (29).
Refs.: COWIE/29: 31: PIG/DIR/28:
32: 38: ROB/DIR/29: 32: 35: 40:
PO/DIR/40.

GRIFFITH
Add.: 8 Baker St.
Refs.: Ticket on *France Illustrated*
n.d.: "Bd. by G., BS. & ST., 8

BS.". The binding in trade mor. in the Bedford style appeared to me to be an "edition" binding, and I doubt if it was executed by Griffith.

GRIMSHAW, *Job*
    „   & SPANTON (38).
    „   & CO. (40).
Add.: 4 Sion College Gdn., Aldermanbury.
Refs.: PIG/DIR/36: 38: ROB/DIR/35: 40: PO/DIR/4.

GRIMSHAW & HUNT
Add.: 6 Staple Inn Bldgs.
Refs.: COWIE/29: 31: 32.

GRIMSHAW & HURST
Add.: 35 Brooke St., Holborn: Kyle Inn Bldgs. (32).
Refs.: COWIE/31: ROB/DIR/29: 32: PIG/DIR/32.

GRIX, *George*
Add.: 10 James St., St. Luke's.
Refs.: PIG/DIR/32.

GROVE, *Charles Kay*
Add.: 2 Leathersellers Bldgs.
Refs.: PIG/DIR/36.

GROVE, *Percy*
Add.: 3 Mitre Ct., St. Paul's.
Refs.: PIG/DIR/28.

GROVER, *Henry*
Refs.: On 6.6.24 he registered the birth of a daughter, Anne, by his wife, Ann, and gave his address as BB. of Aldermanbury. (Harl. Soc. LXV).

GUY, *Edward*
(BB.'s Toolcutter & Claspmaker).
Add.: 37 Bedford St., Commercial Rd.: 4 Harp Lane, Shoe Lane (ca. 40).
Refs.: PIG/DIR/32: COWIE/7.

GWYNNE, *James*
(BS/HOWE/LBB. p. 42).

GYDE, *Charles*
Add.: 10 Upper Rosamon St., Clerkenwell: 7½ Red Lion Ct., Fleet St. (ca. 40).
Refs.: ROB/DIR/35: PIG/DIR/36: COWIE/7.

HAIGH, *James*
(Ornamental (*sic*) Bookbinder).
Add.: 25 Poland St.
Refs.: JOHN/17.

HAIGH, *Thomas*
(BS/HOWE/LBB. p. 42).
Add.: 25 Poland St., Oxford St. (20).

Refs.: COWIE/29★ : AE/COLL/Stamp. ROB/DIR/20 : 22.

O.C.: *Bible*, f.m.g.: presentation label shows it was bound before 1.1.19 : binder's name stamped on last leaf (see Plate VIII).

★ If this entry is correct, there is some difficulty in reconciling it with the failure of Haigh, reported before April 1825, see BS/HOWE/LBB. p. 3, under Armstrong, Thomas.

HALE, G.
Add.: 28 Webb's County Terrace, New Kent Rd.
Refs.: PIG/DIR/38.

HALL, *A. & W.*
E.D.: ? post 40.
Add.: Cambridge Terrace, Camden Town.
Refs.: LAB/JONES.

HALL, *James*
(BS/HOWE/LBB. p. 42).

HALL, *J. E.*
(Gilder and Marbler).
Add.: 15½ Peerless Row, City Rd.: 7 Warwick Sq., City (ca. 40).
Refs.: PO/DIR/40 : COWIE/7.

HAMLET, *Thomas*
Add.: 6 Gravel Lane, Southwark.
Refs.: COWIE/31 : 32 : ROB/DIR/32.

HAMPSON
(BB.'s Pressmaker).
Add.: Long Lane, Smithfield (32): 47 Old Bailey (ca. 40).
Refs.: COWIE/32 : 7.

HANAWELL
Add.: Philanthropic Reform, London Rd.
Refs.: COWIE/29 : 31.

HANCOCK
E.D.: ca. 1838.
Refs.: SLB./p. 120: where the view is expressed that they may be edition-binders for publishers: may be the same as W. Hancock (q.v.).

HANCOCK, *A*
(BS/HOWE/LBB. p. 42).
Add.: 3 Warwick Sq., Warwick Lane (11).
Refs.: HOLD/11.

HANCOCK, *T.*
(BS/HOWE/LBB. p. 43).
Refs.: BRI/DIR/98 (v) in Livery List and as HANDCOCK & BARLING, BS. & BB. in Trade Section at 30 Warwick Lane. (BS/HOWE/LBB/ADD).

HANCOCK, *W.*
(India-rubber Binder).
Add.: Glasshouse Yard, Aldersgate St.

Refs.: PIG/DIR/38: patented his process in 1836 (BR./BM./IV/39
p. 19).

HANDS, *John*
(BS/HOWE/LBB. p. 43).
Refs.: There was a John HAND
[sic] (ST. & BB.) in 1790 at 2
Little Newport St. (AND/90).

HANSON, *James*
(BS/HOWE/LBB. p. 43).

HARDESTY, *Robert*
    „   „   *George* (28).
Add.: 20 Bury St., Bloomsbury
(22): 47 Hampden St., Somers-
town (28).
Refs.: COWIE/29: 31: ROB/DIR/22:
PIG/DIR/24: 28 (R.G.).

HARDING, *John*
Add.: 3 Long Lane, Smithfield.
Refs.: PIG/DIR/36.

HARDING, *Richard*
Add.: 11 Duke St., Lincoln's Inn
Fields (38): 5 New North St.,
Red Lion Sq. (40): 23 East St.
R.L.S. (ca. 40).
Refs.: PIG/DIR/38: ROB/DIR/40:
COWIE/7.

HARDING, *Robert*
Add.: 26 Dorset Crescent, New
North Rd.
Refs.: ROB/DIR/35.

HARDING & LEPARD
Add.: 4 Pall Mall East.
Refs.: ROB/DIR/35.

HARDISTY, *Robt. G.*
(? see Hardesty, R.G.).
Add.: 2 Little Vine St., Piccadilly.
Refs.: PIG/DIR/28.

HARGREAVES, *John*
Add.: 1 Ivy Lane, Newgate St.:
21 Warwick St., City (ca. 40).
Refs.: PIG/DIR/38: PO/DIR/40:
COWIE/7.

HARLEY, *Thomas*
Add.: 86 Britannia St., City Rd.
Refs.: COWIE/29: 31: PIG/DIR/28:
32: 36: ROB/DIR/29: 32: 35: 41:
42.

HARLOW, *William*
(Probably never more than a
finisher).
Refs.: SLB./p. 47.

HARMOOD, *Joseph*
(BS/HOWE/LBB. p. 43).
Add.: 3 Newington Causeway (11).
Refs.: HOLD/11.

HARRINGTON
(Vellum Binder).
Add.: Belle Sauvage Yard, Ludgate
Hill.
Refs.: COWIE/29: 31.

HARRIS, *John*
(BS. &).
Add.: 47 Brandon St., Walworth
New Town.
Refs.: PIG/DIR/28.

HARRIS, *John*
(Vellum Binder).
Add.: 4 New Park St., Southwark.
Refs.: COWIE/31: 32: PIG/DIR/32:
ROB/DIR/32: 35.

HARRIS, *William*
(BS. &).
Add.: 98 High St., Shadwell.
Refs.: HOLD/11: ROB/DIR/20: 22 (E).

HART, *Charles*
Add.: 12 Robert St., Grosvenor Sq.
Refs.: ROB/DIR/35.

HART, *Henry*
(BS/HOWE/LBB. p. 43).

HARVIG, *J.*
Add.: 76 Drury Lane.
Refs.: PIG/DIR/28.

HARWOOD, *John*
Add.: 6 Kennington Lane: 28
Fenchurch St. (22).
Refs.: COWIE/29: 31: ROB/DIR/20:
22 (ST. & BS.).

HASLAM, *George*
Add.: Printer's St., Blackfriars (28):
Huish Ct., Blackfriars (29).

Refs.: COWIE/29: 31: PIG/DIR/28:
ROB/DIR/29.

HATCHARD, *William*
Add.: 24 New St., Brompton.
Refs.: COWIE/31: 32: PIG/DIR/32:
36: 38: ROB/DIR/32: 35: 40:
COWIE/7.

HATTON, *Richard*
Add.: 5 John St., Gt. Surrey St.:
24 Gt. New St., Fetter Lane
(ca. 40).
Refs.: PIG/DIR/32: COWIE/7.

HAWKINS, *James*
(BS/HOWE/LBB. p. 44).

HAWKINS, *William*
Add.: 11 Berwick St., Soho.
Refs.: COWIE/31: 32: PIG/DIR/32:
ROB/DIR/32.

HAY, *J.*
(& PR.) (? see next entry).
Add.: 22 Worcester St., Southwark.
Refs.: HOLD/11.

HAY, *Joseph*
Add.: 114 Long Lane, Bermondsey.
Refs.: COWIE/29: 31: PIG/DIR/28:
32: 36: ROB/DIR/29: 32: 35:
PO/DIR/40.

HAYDAY, *James* (often spelt *Heyday*)
It is by no means easy to follow the
peregrinations of this important binder, who probably worked as late as

1859: the following facts appear to be fairly certain:

(*a*) By 1828 he was working with N. Boyer, a distinguished binder, who may have worked on his own for a year or two previous.

(*b*) He appears as "Heyday" in COWIE/29: 31 at 31 Little Queen St., Lincolns Inn Fields.

(*c*) In ROB/DIR/29 he figures as "& Co.".

(*d*) By PIG/DIR/38 the "& Co." is dropped.

(*e*) By ROB/DIR/40 there is J.H. at George Yd., Lincolns Inn Fields, though the PO/DIR/40 gives the old address.

(*f*) By 40, Hayday & Co. was also established at Oxford (see HOLLO-WAY, of Brighton).

Add.: 18 Gloucester St., Queen St. (26): 31 Little Queen St., L.I.F. (29).

Refs.: COWIE/29: 31: PIG/DIR/28 (H. & B.): 32: 36: 38 (*No.* "& Co."): ROB/DIR/29 ("& Co."): 32: 35: 40: PO/DIR/40: COWIE/7: SLB./p. 109: 119.

O.C.: Billing: *Wounds of Christ*, 1814, f.m.g.: Bewick: *British Birds*: 2 vol. 04: f. vellum g. (see Plate IX).

HAYDAY & BOYER
(see Hayday: & Boyer).
Add.: 18 Gloucester St., Queen St.
Refs.: PIG/DIR/28.

HAYES, *John*
(BS/HOWE/LBB. p. 44).
Add.: 4 Bartlett's Bldgs.
Refs.: HOLD/11.

HAYES, *John*
(Gilder and Marbler in 38).
Add.: 34 Greenhill's Rents (36): 3 Seckford St., Clerkenwell (40).
Refs.: PIG/DIR/36: 38: ROB/DIR/40: PO/DIR/40.

HAYES, *Mary*
(Possibly widow of John Hayes of same address).
Add.: 4 Bartlett's Bldgs., Holborn.
Refs.: ROB/DIR/20: 22: PIG/DIR/24.

HAYS, *Alfred*
Add.: 13 Gt. Castle St., Oxford St.
Refs.: PIG/DIR/38: ROB/DIR/40 (where he is given as manufacturing stationer to the trade).

HEALEY, *John*
(BS/HOWE/LBB. p. 45).

HEARD, *J.*
(BS/HOWE/LBB. p. 45).
Refs.: COWIE/29: 31.

HEARN & STAPLES
(BB.'s Toolcutter).
Add.: 8 Tavistock Row, Covent Gdn.
Refs.: PIG/DIR/32.

HEARNE
  (BS., BB. & ST.).
  E.D.: 05 (?)
  Add.: 81 Strand.
  Refs.: WH/CAT. 147: AE/f/LAB:
  Label, seen at Marks (late 1951)
  styles him as "BS., BB., & ST.".

HEATH, *Charles*
  (BS/HOWE/LBB. p. 45).
  Add.: 21 Warwick Lane (91).
  Refs.: BRI/DIR/91.

HEATH, *Edward*
  (BS/HOWE/LBB. p. 45).
  Add.: 78 Wood St., Cheapside.
  Refs.: COWIE/29: 31 (though decd.
  1821/22): PO/DIR/17: ROB/DIR/20:
  22 (James).

HEBERT & MANN
  (see MANN, *Robert*).
  Add.: 111 Fleet St.
  Refs.: ROB/DIR/20.

HEDGES, *Augustin/Thomas*
  (BS/HOWE/LBB. O. 45).

HELT, *George John*
  (BS. & 32).
  Add.: 40 London Rd., Southwark
  No. 90 (32).
  Refs.: COWIE/29: 31: PIG/DIR/28:
  32: 36: ROB/DIR/29: 32: 35.

HENBROUGH, *T.*
  Add.: 14 Cleveland St.
  Refs.: ROB/DIR/35.

HENBROUGH, *Thomas H.*
  Add.: 52 Goodge St.
  Refs.: ROB/DIR/35.

HEN(N)INGTON, *Bernard*
                (BS/HOWE/LBB. p.
                  46).
                (& ST.).
      ,,   & *Son* (32).
      ,,   & *Galabin*
      ,,   ,,   & *Co.*
                        (36).
  Add.: 2 Ingram Ct., Fenchurch St.
  (24): 168 Fenchurch St. & 2
  Ingram Ct. (? date): 142 F.S.
  (36).
  Refs.: PIG/24: 32: 36: Labels:
  MUNBY/COLL: LAB/KNA: O.C.:
  Green label, last (36) name
  and address: W. Irwing *History
  of Columbus*: 4 vol. 1828: st. gr.
  c. g.: label "Bd. by/H./I.C/.F.S.".
  WSM/KC/NEW/54/p. 13.

HENRY, *Charles*
  Add.: 10 St. Martin's Lane.
  Refs.: HOLD/11.

HERBERT, *John William*
  Add.: 13 Angel Ct., Strand: 35
  Brydges St., Covent Gdn.
  Refs.: PIG/DIR/32: ROB/DIR/35.

HERBERT, *Thomas*
(BB.'s Toolcutter).
(BS/HOWE/LBB. p. 104).

HERDSFIELD, *George*
(BS/HOWE/LBB. p. XXXIV).

HERING, *Charles, Sr.*
d. 09, or 12.
(BS/HOWE/LBB. p. 46).
Refs.: See early tickets reproduced
in WH/CAT. 1932. Actually there
are two forms of the "B" ticket,
one reading "Bound by/C.
HERING" and the other
"BOUND BY/C. Hering". Ac-
cording to SCH/S. de R/IV, Nos. 31
and 34, there exist two variants
of the latter.
O.C.: Curious calf g. bdg. on
Baxter's *Apparitions*, 1691 (see
Plate XI), with earliest "A"
ticket at *10* St. Martin (*sic*) *St.*
General Etruscan facture with
circles in corners of gilt two-line
broad panels, and black blind
stamped floral design between
them. The centres of sides are
mottle-grained with standing
devil silhouette in the centre, and
in corners two skulls, owl and
crowned head on crossed swords.
The back is heavily restored.
O.C.: *Aristotelis de Poetica*: 1794,
L.P., st. gr. mor., double spine
bands in Walther's style, also
bears earliest ticket and the bind-

ing may well be contemporary.
Apparently bound before Hering
became Payne's stylistic successor, both in morocco and russia.
Hering was obviously also binding in vellum by about 1800,
probably for Dulau (O.C.:
Tasso: *Aminta*, 1807: see Plate
X: "A" ticket).

HERING, *Charles, Jnr.*
Add.: 9 & 16 Newman St.
Refs.: ROB/DIR/22: 29: 32.
He is probably the C. Her(r)ing
referred to in SLB., pp. 108, 109
et seq. He may have died about
1837.

HERING, *E.*
Add.: 9 Newman St.
Refs.: ROB/DIR/20.

HERING, *Henry*
E.D.: 36.
Add.: 9 Newman St.
Refs.: PIG/DIR/36: 38: ROB/DIR/40.

HERING, *John*
(brother of C. Hering, Sr.)
(BS/HOWE/LBB. p. 46).
,, *James* (32).
Refs.: Timp/42. p. 835: COWIE/29
(no initial): PIG/DIR/32 (James):
38: ROB/DIR/20: 35 (James). (See
Plate XIII.)

HESSEY
(? see TAYLOR & HESSEY)
(BS.).
Add.: Fleet St.
Ref.: I have seen at Marks (late 1953) a green morocco bdg. (ca. 18/20) in the Lewis style with a cream ticket printed in black, where he only claims to be "bookseller", but he may have been connected with Taylor & Hessey.

HEWITT, *Thomas*
(BS. &).
Add.: Gt. Alie St., Goodman's Fields.
Refs.: PIG/DIR/23.

HICKLEY, *William*
Add.: 4 Upper James St., Golden Sq.
Refs.: PIG/DIR/40.

HICKSON, *Messrs.*
Add.: King St., Cheapside.
Refs.: SLB./p. 97.

HILL
E.D.: ? 94.
Refs.: Weber's *Fore-edge Paintings*, p. 81.

HILL, *Frederick*
Add.: 46 King St., Seven Dials.
Refs.: PIG/DIR/32.

HILL, *William R.*
(BS. &).
Add.: 3 Princes St., Drury Lane (29): 19 Princes St., Red Lion Sq. (32).
Refs.: COWIE/29: 31: 32: PIG/DIR/28: 32: 38: ROB/DIR/32: PO/DIR/40.

HINCKLEY, *James*
Add.: 86 Earl St. East, Lisson Grove.
Refs.: PIG/DIR/36.

HIND(E), *James*
(& ST. in 1832).
Add.: 18 Cannon St. (28): 15 St. Swithin's Lane (36).
Refs.: COWIE/29: PIG/DIR/28: 32: 36: 38: ROB/DIR/29: 32: 35: 40: PO/DIR/40.

HINE, *James*
Add.: 15 St. Swithin's Lane.
Refs.: COWIE/29: 31: 32.

HINTON, *Samuel/Elizabeth*
(BS/HOWE/LBB. p. 47).

HINTON, *Thomas*
Add.: 20 Charlotte St., Blackfriars.
Refs.: JOHN/17.

HIPKINS, *Joseph*
(& ST.).
Add.: 24 Cannon St., Ratcliff.
Refs.: PIG/DIR/24: ROB/DIR/20: 22:

PLATE XIX   LOVEJOY   (*10″ × 12″*)

PLATE XX   MEYER $(9\frac{1}{2}'' \times 12'')$

Apprenticed to Thomas Chipp, and then to William Cater. Admitted as F.S.C. on 3.3.18.

HITCH, *Samuel*
(BS/HOWE/LBB. p. 47).

HOBCRAFT, *John*
(BS/HOWE/LBB. p. 47).

HODGSON, *Robert*
Add.: 22 Cursitor St., Chancery Lane.
Refs.: PIG/DIR/24.

HODGSON, *T. F.*
(Vellum Binder, PR., ST.).
Add.: 4 Cateaton St., near Guildhall.
Refs.: PIG/DIR/24.

HODGSONS
Add.: Wimpole St.
Refs.: Munby Coll. Label "Bd. by H, Wimpole St.". Calf, ca. 1830.

HOFMAN, *Charles*
Add.: 23 Seacoal Lane, Snow Hill.
Refs.: PIG/DIR/32.

HOGG
Refs.: Gaisford Cat. April, 1890, Nos. 1564 & 1567 mention bindings by him, which may be within our period.

HOLDSWORTH, *James*
(BS/HOWE/LBB. p. 48).

HOLLAND, *George*
,, *Emma* (32).
,, *Priscilla & Joseph* (35).
,, *Joseph P.* (40).
Add.: 5 Bull & Mouth St., Aldersgate St.
Refs.: COWIE/29: 31: PIG/DIR/24: 28: 32: 36: 38: ROB/DIR/29: 32: 35: PO/DIR/40: COWIE/7.

HOLLAND, *William*
Add.: 18 Well St., Wellclose Sq.
Refs.: PIG/DIR/36.

HOLLINGS, *James*
(see Anyon & Hollings).
Add.: 17 Charles St., Covent Gdn. (31): 37 Tavistock St. (38).
Refs.: COWIE/31: 32: PIG/DIR/32: 36: 38: ROB/DIR/32: 35: 40: PO/DIR/40.

HOLLOWAY, *Samuel*
(BS/HOWE/LBB. p. 48).

HOLMES, *Thomas*
(BS/HOWE/LBB. p. 48).

HOOD, *James H.*
Add.: 25 Red Lion Sq., Holborn.
Refs.: PO/DIR/40: COWIE/7.

HOOD, *Richard*
  ,,   R. & H. (ca. 40).
(Vellum Binder).
Add.: 12 Nicholl's Sq., Aldersgate
  St. (22): 8 Bridgwater Sq. (24):
  56 Bartholomew Close: No. 12
  (32).
Refs.: COWIE/29: 31: PIG/DIR/24:
  28: 32: ROB/DIR/22: 32: 35: PO/
  DIR/40: COWIE/7.

HOOD, *William*
(BS/HOWE/LBB. p. 48).
Refs.: AND/90.

HOOD & McCULLOCK
  ,,   James H. (37).
Add.: 9 Clare St., Drury Lane (28):
  25 Red Lion Sq. (40).
Refs.: COWIE/31: 32: PIG/DIR/28:
  32: 38: ROB/DIR/32: 40.

HOOKHAM, *Thomas Jordan*
(etc., etc.).
(BS/HOWE/LBB. p. 48).
Add.: 100 New Bond St. (84).
Refs.: O.C.: Attwood's *Analyses*,
  1784, f.c.g. with ticket: elaborate
  label, taken from *Letters of Abelard
  & Heloise,* 1785, giving his activities in great detail.

HOPWOOD, *John/Sarah*
(BS/HOWE/LBB. p. 48).
Refs.: BRI/DIR/91.

HORNBY, *Robert*
(& BS.).
Add.: 63 Basinghall St.
Refs.: PIG/DIR/32: ROB/DIR/32: 35.

HOWE, *M.*
Add.: Howe's Bldgs., Globe Fields.
Refs.: PIG/DIR/32.

HOWE, *John*
(& ST. in 40).
Add.: 7 Upper Marylebone St.
Refs.: PIG/DIR/38: ROB/DIR/40: PO/
  DIR/40: COWIE/7.
In Sept. 1952 Marks had a
sumptuous, though dull, binding
with his label which must have
been made about May 1842. It
had silk endpapers.

HOWELL, *Henry*
Add.: Well Ct., Queen St.
Refs.: PIG/DIR/38.

HOWELL, *James*
(Vellum Binder in 40).
Add.: 9 Bread St. Hill (24): 3 Sugar-
  loaf Ct., Garlick Hill (32): 1
  West St., W. Smithfield (40).
Refs.: PIG/DIR/24: 32: PO/DIR/40:
  COWIE/7.

HOWGILL, *Matt.*
(BB.'s Toolmakers).
Add.: 15 St. Andrew's Hill,
  Doctors' Commons.
Refs.: COWIE/29: 31: PIG/DIR/28.

HOWSHALL, *Charles*
(& BS.).
Add.: 24 Blackman St., Borough.
Refs.: PIG/DIR/23 : 24.

HOXTON (*Male Refuge*)
E.D.: 15 ?
Refs.: ABB/CBS.

HUBNER, *John Christian*
Add.: 9 Fan St., Goswell Rd.
Refs.: PIG/DIR/32.

HUGHES, *George*
(& ST.).
Add.: 23 Compton St., Hunter St.
Refs.: PIG/DIR/36.

HUNT, *John*
(Vellum BB.).
Add.: 11 Swan St.
Refs.: HOLD/11.

HUNT, *Sarah*
(ST. in 40).
Add.: 178 High Holborn.
Refs.: PIG/DIR/36 : 38 : ROB/DIR/40 :
COWIE/7.

HUNT, *Thomas & Sons*
(Vellum Binders).
Add.: 34 St. Mary Axe.
Refs.: COWIE/29 : 31 : PIG/DIR/24 :
28 : 32 : ROB/DIR/22 : 32.

HUNTINGTON, *Ebenezer*
    ,,   *Sarah* (23).
(ST., BS. &).

Add.: High St., St. Giles: 25
Grafton St., East, Fitzroy Sq.
(23).
Refs.: HOLD/11 : PIG/DIR/23 : 28.

HURES
Refs.: Huth Sale No. 867.

HURREN, *J.*
Add.: 45 Curtain Rd., Shoreditch.
Refs.: COWIE/31 : 32 : ROB/DIR/32 :
35.

HURST, *J.*
    ,,   *Henry* (36).
Add.: 6 Staple Inn Bldgs.
Refs.: ROB/DIR/35 : PIG/DIR/36 : 38.

HUTCHINGS, *George*
(BS/HOWE/LBB. p. 49).
    ,,   *George Thomas* (36).
Add.: 1 Poplar Row, O.K.R. (ca.
40).
Refs.: COWIE/29 : 31 : PIG/DIR/36 :
COWIE/7.

HUTCHIN(G)S & BERNARD
Add.: 5 Ivy St., Newgate St.
Refs.: PIG/DIR/24.

HUTCHINS, *Edward*
(see previous entry).
Add.: 5 Ivy Lane.
Refs.: ROB/DIR/20 : 22.

HUTCHINSON, *Edwin John Robert*
(& ST., BS.).

Add.: 2 Clerkenwell Close: 5 Eldon Place, Islington (40).

Refs.: PIG/DIR/38: ROB/DIR/35: 40: Apprenticed to John Luke Catmur, made a F.S.C. on 3.4.27.

ILBERRY, *James*
(& BS.).
Add.: 1 Gt. Titchfield St.
Refs.: PIG/DIR/28: 38: ROB/DIR/40.

IMRAY, *James*
Add.: 25 Budge Row.
Refs.: ROB/DIR/35.

INDGE, *John/John*
(BS/HOWE/LBB. p. 50).

INGRAM, *Jos.* (? see PYMM)
Add.: 2 Tooks Ct., Chancery Lane.
Refs.: PIG/DIR/24.
O.C.: (? Rowlands, S.): 2 Chiswick Press reprints 1818/19: ½ m. g. in C. Smith style.

ISACKE, *William*
Add.: 211 Edgware Rd.: 1 Parker St., Westminster (38): 18 Sherborne Lane, City (ca. 40).
Refs.: ROB/DIR/20: PIG/DIR/38: COWIE/7: LAB/JONES/"Bound by").

JACKSON, *Charles Frederick*
Add.: 2 Spring Place, Portsmouth St.
Refs.: PIG/DIR/32.

JACKSON, *J.*
(Vellum Binder).
Add.: 15 St. Peter's Hill, Doctors Commons.
Refs.: ROB/DIR/40: PO/DIR/40: COWIE/7.

JACKSON, *John*
(ST. &).
Add.: 56 Greek St.
Refs.: PIG/DIR/32.

JACKSON, *John*
Add.: 42 Gt. Chart St., Hoxton.
Refs.: PIG/DIR/36: 38: ROB/DIR/40: COWIE/7: WSM/KC/NEW/54/p. 13.

JACKSON, *John/John*
JACKSON & SON (22).
(BS/HOWE/LBB. p. 50).
Add.: *24* Villiers St. (11).
Refs.: HOLD/11: COWIE/29: 31: ROB/DIR/20: 22: PIG/DIR/24 (& Son): 22 (J.J.): J.J. Junior was apprenticed to John Bird and admitted as a F.S.C. 4.3.1817.

JACKSON, *John & William*
(BS., BB. & ST. in 31).
Add.: 87 Strand.
Refs.: PIG/DIR/28: PO/DIR/31.

JACKSON, *Thomas*
(see BS/HOWE/LBB. p. 50 under *John* Jackson).
Add.: 5 Newcastle Ct., Temple Bar.

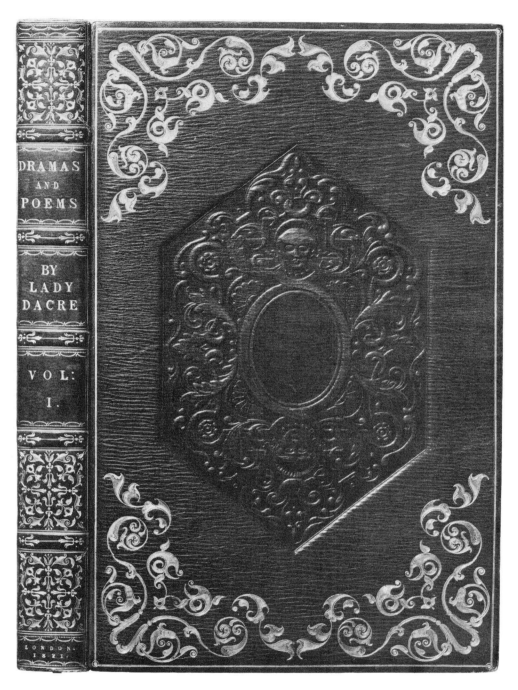

PLATE XXI   MURTON $(5\frac{1}{2}'' \times 8\frac{3}{4}'')$

PLATE XXII   SMITH, C.   (5″ × 8″)

JACKSON & WHITE
  ,,   *John* (38).
  Add.: 20 Queen St., Gt. Windmill St.
  Refs.: COWIE/29: 31: PIG/DIR/32: 36: 38: ROB/DIR/29: 32: 35: PO/DIR/40.

JACQUES, *B.*
  Add.: 30 Lower Sloane St., Chelsea.
  Refs.: COWIE/31: 32: ROB/DIR/32: 35.

JACQU(I)ERY, *John* (28)
  ,,   *Charlotte* (36).
  Add.: 20 Mansell St., Goodmans Fields (29): Chamber St., Goodmans Fields (36).
  Refs.: COWIE/29: 31: PIG/DIR/28 (John): 36 (C.): ROB/DIR/29.

JAMES
  Add.: St. George's Market.
  Refs.: COWIE/29: 31.

JAMES, *Edmund*
  Add.: 13 Market St., Boro Rd.
  Refs.: PIG/DIR/32.

JAMES, *Henry*
  (Vellum Binder & ST.).
  Add.: 24 Bow Lane, Cheapside.
  Refs.: COWIE/29: 31: PIG/DIR/28.

JAMES, *Henry*
  E.D.: ? 04.
  Refs.: JBO/AE.

JAMES, *Philip John*
  Add.: 6 Northumberland Place, Commerical Rd. East: Back Rd., Shadwell, & Limehouse Causeway (36): 10 Mount Terrace, Commercial Rd. E. (38).
  Refs.: PIG/DIR/36: 38: PO/DIR/40.

JEFFERIES, *Joseph*
  (BS/HOWE/LBB. p. 51).

JEFFREY, *John*
  Add.: 4 Greek St., Soho.
  Refs.: PIG/DIR/38.

JEFFREYS, *Edwards T.*
  Add.: 14 Sun St., Bishopsgate.
  Refs.: COWIE/29: 31: ROB/DIR/29.

JENKINS & CECIL
  Refs.: Huth Sale No. 920: BM. C. 56: crushed mor. gilt on Udall's *Floures*. Bdg. probably post 1840.

JENNINGS, *R.*
  (BS. &).
  Add.: 2 Poultry.
  Refs.: O.C.: Bacon's Essays. Sharpe 22. Olive m. g. in the C. Lewis/C. Smith tradition.

JENNINGS, *S.*
  Add.: 22 Warwick Lane, Newgate St.
  Refs.: ROB/DIR/22.

JESSUP, *Stephen*
(BS/HOWE/LBB. p. 51).

JEWELL, *Stephen*
(BS. &).
    Add.: 8 Hemmings Row, St. Martin's Lane.
    Refs.: ROB/DIR/29: 32: PIG/DIR/32.

JEWSON, *Isaiah*
(BS/HOWE/LBB. p. 51).

JOHN, *John*
    Add.: 3 Duke St., W. Smithfield.
    Refs.: PIG/DIR/32.

JOHN, *John*
    Add.: 34 Princes St., Soho.
    Refs.: PIG/DIR/32.

JOHNS, *Charles*
    ,,   *Gelly* (36).
    (Straw hat maker in 40).
    Add.: 56 Redcross St., Cripplegate.
    Refs.: COWIE/29: 31: PIG/DIR/28: 32: 36: 38: ROB/DIR/29: 32: 35: 40: PO/DIR/40.

JOHNSON
(BS/HOWE/LBB. p. 52).
    L.D.: May just spill over into the period.
    Refs.: See large number of his bindings mentioned in the 1886 Woodhall Library Sale: e.g. 7, 405, 413, 461, 478, 540, 553, 742, 1174, 1309, 1413, 1612, 1740, 1793, 1838, 1888, 1994, 2034, 2108, 2295, 2502, 2507, 2510, 2527, 2577. Of these, No. 1174 and No. 1828 (not described as bound by Johnson) have now been located in the Yale University Library (see Plate XIV). They are calf bindings, both similar, with plain sides and gilt-ornamented spines: in poor condition, but authenticated by Wodhull's autograph notes "bound by Johnson 1766". Bound extensively for Thomas Payne, e.g., 240 books in T.P.'s 1777 Cat. (BS/HOWE/LBB/ADD).

JOHNSON, *Charles*
    Add.: 15 Leicester St., Seven Dials (20): 27 Warwick St., Golden Sq. (29): 13 Leicester St. (31) & (40): 13 Beak St., Haymarket (35).
    Refs.: COWIE/29: 31: PIG/DIR/32: 36: 38: ROB/DIR/20: 29: 35: PO/DIR/40: COWIE/7.

JOHNSTON, *Richard*
    Add.: 6 Bateman's Row: Charles St., St. James' Sq. (29: no initial).
    Refs.: COWIE/29: 31: JOHN/17.

JONES, *Charles Samuel*
(Gilder & Marbler).
    Add.: 9 Maiden Lane, Covent Gdn.
    Refs.: PIG/DIR/36: PO/DIR/40.

JONES, *John*
(BS. &).
Add.: 56 Bartholomew Close.
Refs.: ROB/DIR/35.

JONES, *John*
(BS., ST. &).
Add.: 3 Duke St., W. Smithfield.
Refs.: PIG/DIR/28 : ROB/DIR/29.

JONES, *John*
Add.: 6 Cooper's Ct., Gt. Windmill
St.
Refs.: PIG/DIR/36 : ROB/DIR/35 : 40 :
PO/DIR/40.

JONES, *John*
(& ST.).
Add.: 34 Princes St., Soho.
Refs.: PO/DIR/40.

JONES, *Robert P.*
Add.: 3 Huish Ct., Water Lane,
Blackfriars.
Refs.: COWIE/29 : 31 : ROB/DIR/20 :
29 : PIG/DIR/32.
A "Robert Jones" was a F.S.C.
by 1813.

JONES, *Samuel*
Add.: 9 Kingsland Rd.
Refs.: PIG/DIR/38.

JONES, *Sophia*
Add.: 32 Angel St., St. Martin's-le-
Grand.
Refs.: PIG/DIR/28.

JONES, *William*
(BS. &).
Add.: 1 Earl St., Blackfriars.
Refs.: PIG/DIR/23.

JOSSE, *W. P.*
(Vellum Binder).
Add.: 10 Bond Ct., Walbrook.
Refs.: ROB/DIR/35.

JULLION, *Francis*
(BS/HOWE/LBB. p. 52).

JULPHS, *Thomas*
(BS. &).
Add.: 46 Penton St., Pentonville.
Refs.: PIG/DIR/23 : 28.

KAINES, *George/Mary*
(BS/HOWE/LBB. p. 53).
,,   *Mrs. M.* (& BS.) (30).
,,   *George Francis* (36).
Add.: 20 New Rd., St. George's E.
(28) (& 40) : 4 Lower Chapman
St., S.G.E. (36).
Refs.: HOLD/11 : PIG/DIR/23 : 24 :
(G) : 28 : 32 : 36 : ROB/DIR/40 :
PO/DIR/40.

KALTHOEBER, *Christian Samuel*
(BS/HOWE/LBB. p. 53).
Refs.: SLB./p. 93/4 mentions a
W. Kalthoeber, possibly a son of
the above. (See Plates XV and
XVI.)

KAPPELMANN
(BS/HOWE/LBB. p. 53).

KAY, *Charles & Co.*
  „   *& Grove* (40).
  Add.: 2 Leathersellers Bldgs.,
    London Wall.
  Refs.: COWIE/31: 32: PIG/DIR/32:
    38: ROB/DIR/32: 35: 40: PO/DIR/
    40.

KAY, *George*
  Add.: 2 Somerset St., Portman Sq.
  Refs.: PIG/DIR/32.

KEATS, *J.*
  (& ST.).
  Add.: 17 Paradise Row, Chelsea.
  Refs.: LAB/JONES.

KEKWITH, *Timothy*
(BS/HOWE/LBB. p. 53).

KELLEY, *James*
  Add.: 15 Castle Ct., Strand.
  Refs.: PIG/DIR/28.

KELLY, *George*
(BS/HOWE/LBB. p. 53).

KELLY, *John I.*
(BS/HOWE/LBB. p. 53).
  Refs.: BR/BM/IV/45, p. 10 appears to
    muddle up the two Johns.

KELLY, *John II*
(BS/HOWE/LBB. p. 54).

Add.: 7 Water St., Strand.
Refs.: HOLD/11.

KELLY, *John*
(see also Kelly & Goddard).
(Book and Music Binder).
E.D.: 30 (date of establishment on
  label).
Add.: 15 Gower Pl., Euston Sq.
Refs.: PIG/DIR/36: 38: ROB/DIR/35:
  40: PO/DIR/40: COWIE/7.
O.C.: Delavigne: *Fille du Cid*, 40
  (label): LAB/PEARSON.

KELLY, *William H.*
  (BS/HOWE/LBB. p. 54).
  (& ST. in 40).
  „   *& Sons* (? 25–35).
  Refs.: COWIE/29: 31: PIG/DIR/24:
    28: 32: 36: 38: ROB/DIR/20: 22:
    29: 32: 35: 40: PO/DIR/40:
    COWIE/7: LAB/KNA "K. & Sons"
    between 25–35.

KELLY & GODDARD
  Add.: 8 Cromer St., Brunswick Sq.
    15 Gower Pl., Euston Sq. (ca. 33).
  Refs.: COWIE/31: 32: ROB/DIR/32:
    WSM/HC/NEW/54 p. 15.

KELLY & SONS
(Makers of Kelliegram bindings).
  Refs.: BM. Card: BR/BM. March,
    1891, p. 10: Bookbinding Trade
    Journal II. p. 70.

KEMP, *Alfred*
(ST. in 40).
Add.: 7 Brydges St., Covent Gdn.
(32): 3 Orange Row, Kenning-
ton Rd. (38).
Refs.: PIG/DIR/32: 38: ROB/DIR/40.

KEMSHEAD, *Stephen*
(PR. &).
Add.: 5 Portsmouth Pl., Ken-
nington Lane & 30 Mansion
House St.
Refs.: PIG/DIR/28.

KEY, *James*
Add.: 2 Sermon Lane (29): 4 Ivy
Lane, Newgate St. (32): 9 War-
wick Sq. (36): 7 Oxford Arms
Passage, Warwick Lane (ca. 40).
Refs.: COWIE/29: 31: PIG/DIR/32:
36: 38: ROB/DIR/29: PO/DIR/40:
COWIE/7.

KILBY, *George Thomas*
Add.: 49 Tabernacle Walk.
Refs.: PIG/DIR/32.

KILE, *Frederick*
(BS/HOWE/LBB. p. 54).
(see Oxford binder of same name:
CR/BB. p. 102).
Refs.: SCH. S. de R. IV/22: HOLD/11.
O.C.: Tooke's *Diversions of
Purley*, 2 vol., 1798: f. russia
gilt. Ticket "Bd. by F.K., Gt.
Marylebone St.".

KILPACK, *Thomas*
(& BS. in 28).
Add.: 379 Strand (28): 24 South-
ampton St., Strand (29).
Refs.: COWIE/29: 31: PIG/DIR/28:
ROB/DIR/29.

KING, *P. S.*
E.D.: ? 10.
Add.: 2 Bridge St., Westminster.
Refs.: Ticket seen at Seligman's on
outline drawings album dated
1795 and with Lady Hamilton's
name on leather label on side.

KING, *Robert/J.*
(BS/HOWE/LBB. p. 54).
Refs.: HOLD/11.

KING, *Robert*
Add.: 18 Jewin St., Aldersgate St.
(28): 21 Redcross Sq., Cripplegate (32): 21 Redcross St.,
Cripplegate (40): 21 Jewin St.
(40).
Refs.: COWIE/29: 31: PIG/DIR/28:
32: 36: 38: ROB/DIR/29: 35: 40:
PO/DIR/40.

KINGWELL, *Richard*
(& Vellum Binder).
Add.: Green Arbour Sq., Old
Bailey.
Refs.: COWIE/29: 31: PIG/DIR/32.

KITCAT, *Abraham*
Add.: 22 Bartlett's Bldgs.
Refs.: PO/DIR/28.

KITCAT, *George/George*
      (BS/HOWE/LBB. p. 55).
  ,,   *George & James* (36).
Refs.: HOLD/11 : COWIE/29 : 31 : PIG/
  DIR/32 : 36 : 38 : ROB/DIR/20 : 29 :
  32 : 35 : 40 : PO/DIR/40 : COWIE/7.
See also *The House of Kitcat*, by
John Adam, 1948.

KNAPP, *George James*
  Add.: 10 Green St., Blackfriars Rd.
  Refs.: COWIE/29 : 31 : PIG/DIR/24 :
  28 : 32 : 36 : 38 : ROB/DIR/22 : 32 :
  35 : 40 : PO/DIR/40 : COWIE/7.
Apprenticed to Robert Jones and
then to John Parsons : admitted a
F.S.C. 6.6.20.

KNIBB, *Francis*
  Add.: 12 Newgate Market : 22
  Warwick Sq. (36) : 35 St. John's
  Sq. (42).
  Refs.: ROB/DIR/35 : 42 : PIG/DIR/36.

KNIGHT, *Henry H.*
  Add.: 11 Shoe Lane, Fleet St.
  Refs.: PO/DIR/40.

KNIGHT, *John*
      (BB.'s Toolmakers).
  ,,   *James* (40).
  Add.: 5 Parsonage Walk, Newing-
  ton : 39 Chandos St., Covent
  Gdn. (40).
  Refs.: COWIE/29 : 31 : PIG/DIR/36 :
  ROB/DIR/40 : PO/DIR/40.

KNIGHT, *J. Jnr.*
  (BB.'s Toolcutter).
  Add.: 63 Chandos St., Covent Gdn.
  Refs.: PIG/DIR/32 : 40 : LAB/PEARSON.

KNIGHT, *S.*
  Add.: 3 Fleet Lane, Farringdon St.
  Refs.: PO/DIR/40.

KNOCK, *John*
  ,,   *Mrs. Maria F.* (35).
  Add.: 8 Wells St., Cripplegate.
  Refs.: COWIE/31 : PIG/DIR/32 : 36 :
  38 : ROB/DIR/29 : 32 : 35 : 40 :
  PO/DIR/40.

KNOTT, *Thomas*
  (BS., BB. & ST.).
  Add.: 26 Warwick St., Golden Sq. :
  302 Regent St. (32).
  Refs.: HOLD/11 : PIG/DIR/32.

KRONHEIM
  (see Leeuw & Kronheim : also C.
  Ramsden : *French Bookbinders*, p.
  114).

LACEY, *John*
      (BS/HOWE/LBB. p. 56).
  ,,   *Mrs. Esther* (32).
  Add.: 25 Little Wild St., Lincolns
  Inn (20) : 25 Gt. Wild St. (38) :
  Little (40 ?).
  Refs.: COWIE/29 : 31 : PIG/DIR/24 :
  28 : 32 : 38 : ROB/DIR/20 : 22 : 32 :
  35 : 40 : PO/DIR/40 : COWIE/7.

LAIRD, *William*
　Add.: 2 Little Nelson Place, Old
　　Kent Rd.
　Refs.: PIG/DIR/38.

LAND, *William*
　(Pocketbook Maker in 1828).
　Add.: 2 Nelson Place, Old Kent
　　Rd.: 13 Kent Place, Old Kent Rd.
　　(32): 3 West St., Walworth Rd.
　　(ca. 40).
　Refs.: PIG/DIR/28: 32: 36: COWIE/7.

LANE, *John*
　(BS/HOWE/LBB. p. 56).
　Add.: 215 Upper Thames St.
　Refs.: PIG/DIR/28.

LANE, *M.*
　Add.: 7 Panyer Alley, Paternoster
　　Row.
　Refs.: ROB/DIR/32: 35.

LANGFORD, *William*
　(& ST.).
　Add.: 131 Aldersgate.
　Refs.: JOHN/17: Apprenticed to F.
　　Jullion and admitted as F.S.C. on
　　26.9.1817.

LANGLEY, *John*
　(BS/HOWE/LBB. p. 56).
　Add.: 4 Chapter House Ct., St.
　　Paul's.
　Refs.: HOLD/11: COWIE/29: 31: PIG/
　　DIR/24: 28: ROB/DIR/22: 29.

LANGSTON, *E.*
　Add.: 2 Paget Pl., Waterloo Rd.
　Refs.: COWIE/31: 32: ROB/DIR/32.

LARKIN, *Arthur*
　Add.: 59 Wood St., Cheapside.
　Refs.: PIG/DIR/32.

LARKIN, *Robert J.*
　Add.: 15 Primrose St., Bishopsgate.
　Refs.: ROB/DIR/40: PO/DIR/40.

LARKIN, *Robert William*
　(BS. in 40).
　Add.: 21 Norfolk St., Middlesex
　　Hospital: 40 Newman St., Ox-
　　ford St. (35).
　Refs.: COWIE/31: 32: PIG/DIR/32:
　　38: ROB/DIR/32: 35: 40: PO/DIR/
　　40: COWIE/7.

LARKIN, *William*
　　(BS/HOWE/LBB. p. 56).
　　(see CECIL).
　　,,　*Esther* (36).
　Add.: 2 Evangelist Ct., Ludgate Hill
　　(36).
　Refs.: HOLD/11: ROB/DIR/20: PIG/
　　DIR/28: 36.

LA ROCHE
　(BS/HOWE/LBB. p. 56).

LATHAM
　(Pressmaker).
　Add.: Old St.
　Refs.: COWIE/32

LATTY, *George*
  Add.: 24 Nassau Place, Commercial
  Rd.
  Refs.: PIG/DIR/28.

LAUFFERT, *C.*
  E.D.: 10 ?
  Refs.: *Bibliotheca Lusitana*, 1741–59.
  BM. G. 338/41. The first vol. is
  signed on spine "C. Lauffert, J."
  The style of the full russia binding is typical of the English
  binding of about 1810–15 and the
  "J" at the end would probably
  mean "Junior". There is another
  russia binding in the Christie
  Bequest at Manchester University signed "Lauffert, J" on spine,
  dating about 1825.

LAURIE, *Thomas/William*
  (BS/HOWE/LBB. p. 56/7).

LAW, *James*
  (& ST.).
  Add.: 12 Little Charlotte St.,
  Blackfriars.
  Refs.: ROB/DIR/35.

LAW, *Robert Phelps*
  (& ST.).
  Add.: 2 King St., Borough.
  Refs.: PIG/DIR/38 : ROB/DIR/40.

LAWFORD, *George*
  (BS/HOWE/LBB. p. 57).

Add.: 4 Saville Place, Old **Bond**
  St. (28 : BS.) : No. 6 (36 : BB.).
  Refs.: PIG/DIR/28 : 36.

LAXTON, *John*
  (Vellum Binder).
  Add.: 48 King St., Soho.
  Refs.: PO/DIR/40.

LEACH, *Thomas*
  Add.: 18 Vineyard Gdns., **Coppice**
  Row, Clerkenwell.
  Refs.: COWIE/31 : 32 : PIG/DIR/32 :
  ROB/DIR/32 : 35.

LEADER, *J.*
  (Toolcutter).
  Add.: 8 Little Knightrider St., **City.**
  Refs.: PIG/DIR/38 : ROB/DIR/40.

LEADLEY, *Miles*
  Add.: 27 Warwick Lane (38) : 10
  Oxford Arms Passage, **Warwick**
  Lane (40).
  Refs.: PIG/DIR/38 : PO/DIR/40.

LEAVER, *Francis*
  Add.: 16 Lower Knightrider **St.**
  (24) : No. 15 (28).
  Refs.: PIG/DIR/24 : 28.

LEE
  (BS/HOWE/LBB. p. 57).

LEE, *J.*
  „ *Susannah* (32).
  „ *James* (35).

PLATE XXIII   STAGGEMEIER & WELCHER $(9\frac{1}{2}'' \times 11\frac{1}{2}'')$

PLATE XXIV   STRONG, W. $(3\frac{3}{4}'' \times 5\frac{3}{4}'')$

Add.: 13 Ranelagh St., Pimlico
(24): 13 Lower R.S. (28).
Refs.: COWIE/29: 31: PIG/DIR/24:
28: 32: ROB/DIR/29: 32: 35.

LEE, *John*
Add.: 8 City Rd.
Refs.: PIG/DIR/32.

LEE, *Samuel*
(& ST.).
Add.: 71 Freeschool St., Horsley
Down.
Refs.: COWIE/29: 31: PIG/DIR/28:
32: 36: 38: ROB/DIR/29: 40.

LEE, *William*
Add.: 29 New North St., Red
Lion Sq.
Refs.: PIG/DIR/38: ROB/DIR/40. May
be the W. L. apprenticed to
William Axelby, and then to
Henry Lawrence and admitted a
F.S.C. on 6.4.1819.

LEECH, *John*
Add.: 21 Francis St., Tottenham
Ct. Rd.
Refs.: ROB/DIR/29.

LEIGH, *Samuel*
(BS/HOWE/LBB. pp. 57 & 67 under
Matthews, & SLB./p. 37).

LEIGHTON, *Archibald II*
(BS/HOWE/LBB. p. 57 & SLB./p. 113).
Add.: 55 Exmouth St., Spafields

(24): 11 Vineyard Gdns. (29):
3/4 Ashby Gdns., Northampton
Sq. (40).
Refs.: COWIE/29: 31: PIG/DIR/24:
28: 36: 38: ROB/DIR/29: 40: PO/
DIR/40.
BB. VOL. I, pp. 49 & 99.

LEIGHTON, *Euphemia & Sons*
    ,,   *& Eccles* (40).
Add.: 54/5 Exmouth St., Spafields.
Refs.: PIG/DIR/32: 36: 38: PO/DIR/
40.

LEIGHTON, *George*
(BS/HOWE/LBB. p. 57).
Add.: Vineyard Gdns., Clerkenwell.
Refs.: COWIE/29: 31: ROB/DIR/29:
32: 35: PIG/DIR/31 (Vellum Binder only).

LEIGHTON, *George & Son*
(BS/HOWE/LBB. p. 58).

LEIGHTON, *J.*
(& ST.).
Add.: 19 High St., Camden Town.
Refs.: PO/DIR/40.

LEIGHTON, *John*
            (BS/HOWE/LBB. p. 57).
    ,,   ,,   *& Sons* (32).
    ,,   *& Son* (40).
Refs.: COWIE/29: 31: PIG/DIR/24:
28: 32: 36: 38: ROB/DIR/29: 32:
35: 40: PO/DIR/40.

LEIGHTON, *John, Jr.*
(BS/HOWE/LBB. p. 58.).
Add.: 24 Norfolk St., Middlesex
Hospital.
Refs.: PIG/DIR/28.

LEIGHTON & BROWN
(BS/HOWE/LBB. p. 57 & SLB/p. 83).

LEIGHTON & SON
(BS/HOWE/LBB. p. 58).
Add.: 54 Exmouth St., Spafields
(29).
Refs.: ROB DIR/29 : 35 : COWIE/7.

LEISHMAN, *T.*
(BS/HOWE/LBB. p. 58).
Refs.: May have worked at 33 St.
James' St. ca. 1820 (BS/HOWE/LBB/
ADD), or even earlier, as I have a
Common Prayer of 1814 bd. by
him in black mor.
O.C.: Brown mor. gilt on
Clarke's *Tomb of Alexander*: 05,
carries the same major blind tool
and a similar gilt tool as previous
binding quoted (see Plate XVII).

LEMON, *J.*
(& ST.).
Add.: 5 Lowndes Pl., Holloway.

LETELLIER, *Charles*
Add.: 61 Chamber St.
Refs.: PIG/DIR/32.

LEEUW & KRONHEIM
(see Kronheim).
(BB.'s Toolmakers).
Add.: 90 Hatton Gdn.
Refs.: PO/DIR/40.

LEVER, *Charles*
Add.: 6 Cole Place, Gt. Dover St.,
Borough.
Refs.: PIG/DIR/32 : 36.

LEVI, *Humphrey*
Add.: South St. or Side, Finsbury
Market.
Refs.: COWIE/29 : 31 : ROB/DIR/29.

LEWER, *Henry*
Add.: 33 Lower Ransleigh St.,
Pimlico : No. 4 (40).
Refs.: COWIE/31 : 32 : PIG/DIR/32 :
38 : ROB/DIR/32 : 35 : 40 : PO/DIR/
40 : COWIE/7.

LEWIS, *Charles* (dec. 15.1.36)
(BS/HOWE/LBB. p. 58).
Add.: (? earliest) 4 Middle Scotland
Yard (see Ovid's *Epistles*. BM.
17157 : ticket only).
Refs.: COWIE/29 : PIG/DIR/28 : 32 :
36 : 38 : ROB/DIR/20 : 22 : 29 : 32 :
35 : 40 : PO/DIR/40 : COWIE/7 :
SLB. pp. 109 : 113 : Free of in-
dentures in 1807. Brassington :
History of Art of Bookbinding,
1894, says he had two brothers,
George and Frederick, who were
also bookbinders.

LEWIS, *John*
(BS/HOWE/LBB. p. 59). (The John
Lewis in the City is probably
different.)
Add.: Leicester St., Swallow St.
(20): 1 Buckingham Pl., Fitz-
roy Sq. (29).
Refs.: COWIE/29: 31: PIG/DIR/36:
38: ROB/DIR/20: 29: 32: 35: 40:
PO/DIR/40.

LEWIS, *John*
Add.: 39 Goodge St. (28): 43 Lime
St. (32): 36 Addle St., Wood St.
(40).
Refs.: PIG/DIR/32: 36:38: ROB/DIR/
40: PO/DIR/40.

LEWIS, *T.*
(ST. &).
Add.: 53 Minories.
Refs.: ROB/DIR/20.

LEWIS, *William*
(BS/HOWE/LBB. p. 59 & XXXV &
SLB. passim).

LEWIS & SPRIGG
(Successors of W. Lewis)
(& Leather Dealers).
(BS/HOWE/LBB. p. 59).
Add.: 30 Gt. Pulteney St.
Refs.: PO/DIR/17.

LIDDON, *James*
Add. 16 Cloisters, St. Bartholo-
mew's Hospital (17): 23 Banner
St., St. Luke's (20): 2 Knowles
Ct., Little Castle Lane (36).
Refs.: COWIE/29: 31: JOHN/17:
ROB/DIR/20: 22: 29: 32: 40: PIG/
DIR/24: 32: 36: PO/DIR/40:
COWIE/7.

LIDDON, *John*
(Vellum Binder).
Add.: 5 Bull & Mouth St. (20):
2 Lillypot Lane, Noble St. (29).
Refs.: COWIE/29: 31: ROB/DIR/20:
22: 29: 32: 40: PIG/DIR/24: 32:
36: PO/DIR/40.

LIGHTUP, *James*
(Vellum Binder).
„ *Richard & George* (40).
Add.: 141 Houndsditch (11): 4
Mitre St., Aldgate (29): 2
Houndsditch (40): 15 Minories
(ca. 40).
Refs.: HOLD/11: COWIE/29: 31: 32:
PIG/DIR/32: ROB/DIR/32: 35: PO/
DIR/40: COWIE/7.

LIMBIRD, *John*
Add.: 143 Strand.
Refs.: PIG/DIR/32.

LINDNER, *John*
(BS/HOWE/LBB. p. 60)
(see Fargher & Lindner).
(Also I. V.: James: & D.: quoted
in BS/HOWE/LBB. p. 60, the first
two as gold beaters.)
Refs.: HOLD/11: COWIE/29: 31.

LINDO
Add.: Charles St., Hoxton.
Refs.: COWIE/29 : 31.

LINDSAY, *Alexander*/ ? LINDSEY
(BS/HOWE/LBB. p. 60).

LIST, *Frederick Herbert*
(& ST.).
Add.: 17 Catherine St., Limehouse
Fields.
Refs.: PIG/DIR/36 : ROB/DIR/40.

LISTER, *George*
(BS/HOWE/LBB. p. 60).

LLOYD
(? see Lloyd & Wallis: & Lloyd,
Wallis & Lloyd).
E.D.: 21 (?)
Add.: 36 Chandos St., Strand.
Refs.: HOB/ABB/ Pl. 109, p. 154.

LLOYD, *Edmund*
(given as BS. & ST.).
Add.: 23 Harley St. (PO/DIR/17):
63 Gt. Marylebone St. (JOHN/17).
Refs.: PO/DIR/17 : JOHN/17.
O.C.: Southey: *Thalaba*, 14: 3rd
edition: 2 vol. Green st. gr.
morocco, signed on margin of
front E.P. of Vol. I: Ded. by
Lady Byron to Sarah (? Siddons)
dated 30.4.17.

LLOYD & WALLIS
Refs.: Huth Cat. No. 4726: HOE.
Cat. II. 1047 reports a calf binding
on a 1696 book.

LLOYD, WALLIS & LLOYD
Refs.: SCH/S. de R./IV: No. 515.

LOCK, *William*
(BS. & in 28).
Add.: 23 White Hart Pl., Ken-
nington Cross (28): 37 Union
Row, New Kent Rd. (35): 4
Borough Rd. (40).
Refs.: PIG/DIR/28 : 32 : 36 : 38 : ROB/
DIR/35 : 40 : PO/DIR/40 : COWIE/7.
O.C.: Fisher: *Syria*, etc.: 3 vol.
1836/9: ½ c.g. label "Bd. by/
W.L./4 B.R/near the Obelisk".

LOCKYER, *Samuel*
(Vellum Binder).
(BS/HOWE/LBB. p.60).

LOGAN, *Thomas*
(& ST. in 28).
Add.: 8 Harrow Rd. (28): 56
Hatton Gdn. (38).
Refs.: PIG/DIR/38 : ROB/DIR/40 : PO/
DIR/40.

LOME, *Alex.*
Add.: 15 Dean St., Tooley St.
Refs.: COWIE/31 : 32.

LORIMER, *Antony*
Add.: 18 Gloucester St., St. John

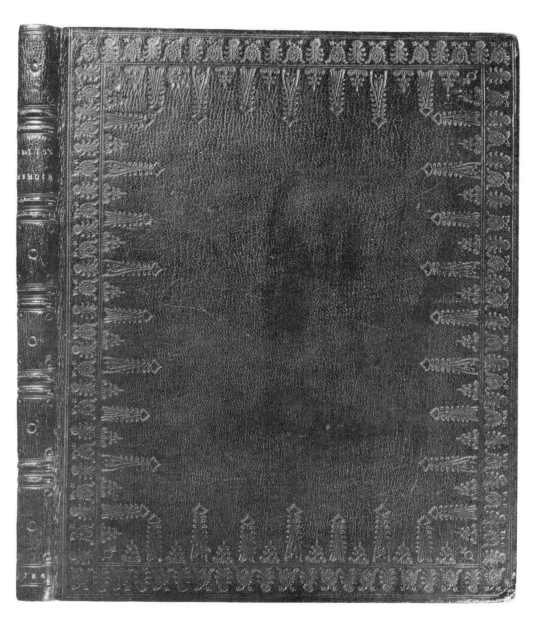

PLATE XXV   WALTHER $(9\frac{1}{2}'' \times 11\frac{3}{4}'')$

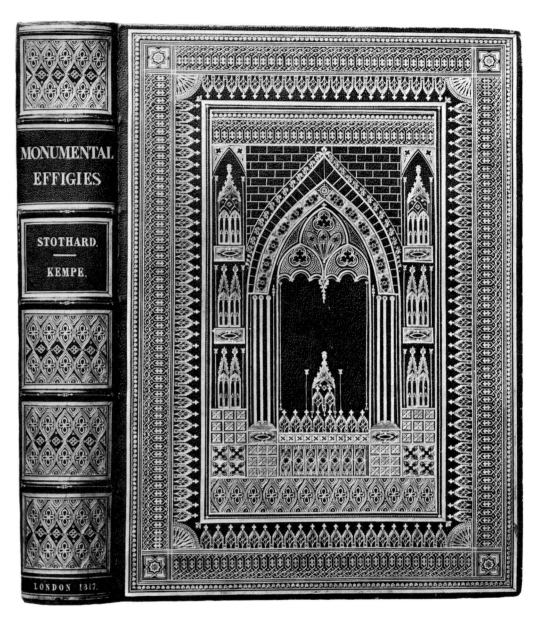

PLATE XXVI   WICKWAR   (*14″ × 19″*)

St. Rd.: 20 Bedford Sq. East
(ca. 40).
Refs.: ROB/DIR/35: COWIE/7.

LOVE, *Ambrose*
(& ST.).
Add.: 28 Charlotte St., White-
chapel.
Refs.: PIG/DIR/36.

LOVE, *William*
(& ST.).
Add.: 81 Bunhill Row.
Refs.: ROB/DIR/20: 22 (BS.).

LOVEDAY, *William*
Add.: 4 Princes St., Lincolns Inn.
Refs.: PIG/DIR/32.

LOVEJOY, *J.*
(BS/HOWE/LBB. p. 61 & SLB./
passim).
Refs.: HOLD/11 (Elizabeth) BS.
7 New Bridge St., Vauxhall and
William at the same address as
ST.
PIG/DIR/28 (see Plate XIX).

LOVEKIN, *Charles*
(BS/HOWE/LBB. p. 61).
Refs.: HOLD/11 (which gives him as
John): PIG/DIR/24: ROB/DIR/22:
ABB/CBS.

LOVETT, *A. Henry*
Add.: 35 Wardour St. (36): 19
Dean St. (40).

Refs.: PIG/DIR/36: ROB/DIR/40: PO/
DIR/40.

LOVETT, *John*
Add.: 134 Aldersgate St.
Refs.: PIG/DIR/24.

LOW, *John*
(BS/HOWE/LBB. p. 62).
Add.: 14 Little Queen St., Lincolns
Inn Fields (32): 1 Gray's Inn
Passage, Red Lion St. (ca. 40).
Refs.: O.C.: *Public Characters*, 2
vol. 1827. Ticket "J.L./BS./&
B./ 14 Little Queen St., Lincolns
Inn Fields" may(?) be by the
same, f.c.g. HOLD/11. See also
PIG/DIR/32: 38: ROB/DIR/40: both
at 14 Little Queen St.: COWIE/7.

LOW, *Peter*
(BS/HOWE/LBB. p. 62).
Add.: 7 Bull & Mouth St., Alders-
gate (24).
Refs.: COWIE/29: 31: JOHN/17:
ROB/DIR/32: PIG/DIR/24: 28.

LOW, *Richard*
(BS/HOWE/LBB. p. 62).
Refs.: HOLD/11.

LOW, *Sampson*
(BS. & library).
Add.: 42 Lamb's Conduit St.
Refs.: PIG/DIR/28.
O.C.: St. Pierre: *Paul & Virginia*,
1820, f.c.g. (ticket): Ticket in my

O.C. giving S. Low as BS. and BB.: taken from the 1830 Aldine Ed. of Burns' *Poems*, bd. in linen.

LOWE, *Alexander*
Add.: 15 Dean St., Tooley St.
Refs.: ROB/DIR/32.

LOWE, *R.*
(see Coxhead).
Add.: 8 Three Tun Passage, Newgate St.
Refs.: Ticket on Vol. II, 1815, of M. Park's *Travels*: Sotheby Sale 30.7.51/192: "R. Lowe, Binder, etc.".

LOWRIE, *Thomas*
Add.: 5 New Inn Passage.
Refs.: BRI/DIR/91: HOLD/11 (Lawrie).

LUCIN, *William*
(& ST.).
Add.: 15 George St., Mansion House.
Refs.: JOHN/17.

LUCKIN & *Son*
Add.: 21 Bartholomew Close.
Refs.: ROB/DIR/35.

LUGHTON & *Son*
Add.: 15 Cold Bath Sq.
Refs.: HOLD/11.

LYALL, *Charles*
Add.: 17 Marshall St., Golden Sq.
Refs.: PIG/DIR/32.

LYCETT, *Edward*
„   & ADLARD (21).
Add.: 27 Nelson St., City Rd. (17): 5 Windsor Terrace, City Rd. (26): 5 Wilmington Sq., Spafield (30): 15 Bartholomew Close (32).
Refs.: HOLD/17: 22/4: COWIE/29 (L only): 31: ROB/DIR/21 (L & A): 26/27: 29: 30: 32: 33: PIG/DIR/28: 32.
LAB/KNA. ca. 25: Roscoe: *Works*, 10 vol. 1806, f.m.g., ca. 16, with ticket at N.S. address seen at Josephs, April, 1952. E. L., Jnr., was admitted as a F.S.C. by redemption on 2.11.24.

LYS, *Michael*
E.D.: 28.
Add.: 4 Warwick Lane, Newgate St.
Refs.: PIG/DIR/28.

MACARTHUR
Add.: Bull Inn Ct., Strand.
Refs.: HOLD/11.

MACCOMBIE, *G. J.*
(BS. &).
Add.: 17 Barbican.
Refs.: ROB/DIR/40.

McCROMBIE, *George*
  Add.: 64 John St., Tottenham Ct.
  Rd.
  Refs.: PIG/DIR/38.

McCULLOCH, *Henry*
  Add.: 8 ?
  Refs.: JOHN/17.

McCULLOCH, *John*
  Add.: 33 St. John's Sq.: No. 30
  (38): 11 Temple St., Whitefriars
  (ca. 40).
  Refs.: PIG/DIR/36: 38: (No. 30):
  ROB/DIR/40: PO/DIR/40: COWIE/7:
  WSM/HC/NEW/54. p. 17.

McDANELL, *James*
  (BS. &).
  Add.: 1 Charterhouse St.
  Refs.: ROB/DIR/29.

MACDONALD, *John*
  Add.: 15 Villiers St., Strand: 18
  Sussex St., Tottenham Ct. Rd.
  (40).
  Refs.: COWIE/29: 31: ROB/DIR/29:
  32: PIG/DIR/32: PO/DIR/40.

MACE, *Benjamin*
  (BS/HOWE/LBB. p. 62).

MACFARLANE, *Andrew/John Young*
              (BS/HOWE/LBB. p.
              63).
  ,,   *& Son* (29).
  ,,   *& Sons* (35).

Add.: *10* Old Bailey (29).
Refs.: COWIE/29: 31: PIG/DIR/24:
  32: 36: 38: ROB/DIR/20: 22: 29
  (& Son): 32: 35 (& Sons) 40:
  PO/DIR/40: COWIE/7.
The first MacFarlane may have
been Andrew *George*. His son
Andrew, who had been appren-
ticed to him, became a F.S.C. on
2.5.1820.

MACFARLANE, *James*
  (BS/HOWE/LBB. p. 63).
  Add.: Shirelane (at some time, says
  Timperley).
  Refs.: TIMP/42, p. 942.

MACKAY, *Robert*
  Add.: Upper Rosoman St., Clerk-
  enwell.
  Refs.: PIG/DIR/28.

MACKAY, *Thomas & Son*
  Add.: 11 Kirby St., Hatton Gdn.
  Refs.: COWIE/29: 31: ROB/DIR/22:
  PIG/DIR/24.

MACKENZIE, *Hector*
  Add.: 40 Kenton St., Brunswick
  Sq.
  Refs.: ROB/DIR/40.

MACKENZIE, *John*
  (BS/HOWE/LBB. p. 63).
  Refs.: COWIE/29: 31: PIG/DIR/28:
  32: 38: ROB/DIR/20 (Crown St.):
  29: 32: 35: PO/DIR/40.

O.C.: Graffigny: *Lettres Péru-viennes*, 1747, mottled c. g.

MACKENZIE, *Joshua*
(& Ink Maker & ST.).
Add.: 7 Dean St., Fetter Lane.
Refs.: JOHN/17: ROB/DIR/20.

MACKENZIE, *J. & Son*
Refs.: SCH/S. de R./IV, 65.

MACKENZIE, *Joseph*
(BS/HOWE/LBB. p. 63).

MACKFARSON
(BS/HOWE/LBB. p. 63).

MACKIE, *F. Sr.*
Add.: 7 Seymour Place, Bryanston Sq.
Refs.: COWIE/31: 32: ROB/DIR/35.

MACKIE, *George/Robert*
(BS. & etc.).
(BS/HOWE/LBB. p. 64).
Add.: 30 Greek St., Soho.
Refs.: PIG/DIR/23: 24: 28: 32: 36:
ROB/DIR/20: 22: 29: 32: 35.

MACKIE, *J.*
(see BS/HOWE/LBB. p. 63, under Mackie, G/R.).

MACKINLAY, *John*
(BS/HOWE/LBB. p. 64 & SLB. passim).
Refs.: The copy of the First Folio

Shakespeare in the Soane Museum contains a long note by John Britton. After its purchase by James Boswell the younger in 1822 from the Kemble Sale, it was washed, inlaid and bound at a cost of 60 gs. by Mackinlay between 1822 and 1825, (when it was acquired by Soane). It is a magnificent performance in olive green mor., with some gilding, but mostly blindstamped (very finely). A notable feature is the architectural fan ornament in gilt in each of the four corners of the sides. Undoubtedly a F.S.C., since Charles Walther is recorded as his apprentice.

McMURRAY, *William*
Add.: 2 Lillypot Lane, Noble St. (32): 2 Oat Lane (38): 2 Lillypot Lane (40).
Refs.: PIG/DIR/32: 36: ROB/DIR/35: 40: PO/DIR/40: COWIE/7.

MACNAIR, *Alexander*
(BS/HOWE/LBB. p. 64).
Refs.: O.C.: *Itinerary of Archbishop Baldwin*, 2 vol. 06, f.m.g. label "Macnair/Bookbinder/8/Queen St./ Golden Sq./ Gentlemen's Libraries/Repaired." HOLD/11 gives his initial as "J". There is a particularly fine specimen in the Ehrman Collection.

MAC(C)OMIE, *Alexander*
 (They may be two binders. They are spelt with one or two "Cs").
 Add.: 7 Angel Ct., Gt. Windmill St. (29) & (36): 6 Percy St., Tottenham Ct. Rd. (28) & (32).
 Refs.: COWIE/29: 31: PIG/DIR/28: 32: 36: ROB/DIR/29: 32: 35: PO/DIR/40: COWIE/7.

MADDOX, *John Webb*
 (PR. in 40).
 Add.: 3 Dock Head, Bermondsey.
 Refs.: PIG/DIR/38: ROB/DIR/40.

MAGUIRE, *James*
 (BS/HOWE/LBB. p. 64).

MAINE, *James*
 Add.: 44 Stanhope St., Clare Mkt.
 Refs.: PIG/DIR/38.

MANDERSON, *William*
 Add.: 40 Gower Place, Euston Sq.
 Refs.: PIG/DIR/38.

MANN, *Robert Sandyman*
 (BS/HOWE/LBB. p. 64 mentions a Mann, without initials or address, under date of 1813).
 Add.: 4 Warwick Sq., Newgate St. (Robert & Samuel: 20): Robert S.: 5 Wardrobe Pl., Doctors Commons (22): Warwick Sq., Newgate St. (29): 9 Huish Ct., Water Lane, Blackfriars (32).
 Refs.: COWIE/29: 31: PIG/DIR/24: 28: 32: 36: ROB/DIR/20: 22: 29.

MANSELL, *Samuel*
 (& ST.).
 Add.: 59 Aldermanbury.
 Refs.: AND/90.

MARCHANT (? *William*)
 Add.: Gold Lion Ct., Aldersgate St.
 Refs.: COWIE/29: 31.
 A "William Marchant" was a F.S.C. by 1812.

MARCHANT, *Charles*
 (BS/HOWE/LBB. p. 64).
 (Vellum Binder in 1824).
 Refs.: HOLD/11: COWIE/29: 31: PIG/DIR/24: 28: 32: 38: ROB/DIR/20: 22 (E. St.): 29: 35: 40: PO/DIR/40: The signed binding, BM. 30. e. 8 is a handsome st. gr. mor. gt., with ships, etc. on spine, and, from the address on the label, almost contemporary with the book: Oddy's *European Commerce*, 05.

MARKWELL, *J. T.*
 Add.: 46 Gt. Titchfield St., Oxford St.
 Refs.: PO/DIR/40.

MAR(R)ABLE, *John*
 (BS. &).
 Add.: 14 Finsbury St. (32): 21 Castle St., Finsbury (35).
 Refs.: PIG/DIR/32: 36: 38: ROB/DIR/32: 35: 40.

MARROW, *Luke*
Add.: 5 Denmark Ct., Exeter St.,
Strand (28): 3 Cecil Ct. (36):
No. 8 (40).
Refs.: COWIE/29: 31: PIG/DIR/28:
32: 36: 38: ROB/DIR/29: 32: 35:
40: PO/DIR/40.

MARSH, *John*
(BS. in 40).
Add.: 5 Leigh St., Red Lion Sq.:
No. 3 (36).
Refs.: COWIE/31: 32: PIG/DIR/36:
ROB/DIR/32: 40.

MARSH, *Robert*
(BS/HOWE/LBB. p. 64).

MARSHALL, *Charles*
(BS. &).
Add.: 1 Clement's Inn.
Refs.: PIG/DIR/23.

MARSHALL, *George L.*
Add.: 5 Charles St., Middlesex
Hospital.
Refs.: COWIE/31: 32: PIG/DIR/32:
ROB/DIR/32.

MARSHALL, *Thomas*
Add.: 4 St. Andrew's Pl., Doctors
Commons.
Refs.: PIG/DIR/28.

MARSHALL, *William*
(BS/HOWE/LBB. p. 65).

MARTIN
Add.: Gough St., Gray's Inn Lane.
Refs.: COWIE/29: 31.

MARTIN
Add.: Westminster Rd.
Refs.: COWIE/29: 31.

MARTIN, *David*
Add.: 13 Fountain Ct., Strand.
Refs.: COWIE/31: 32: PIG/DIR/32:
36: 38: ROB/DIR/32: 35: 40: PO/
DIR/40.

MARTIN, *Henry/Thomas*
(BS/HOWE/LBB. p. 65).

MARTIN, *James (I & II)*
(BS/HOWE/LBB. p. 66).
Refs.: ROB/DIR/20: PIG/DIR/28 (at
Craven St.).

MARTIN, *James*
    „   *& Son* (? 32).
    „   *David Watson* (36).
Add.: 10 Fore St. (28): 16 Westmoreland Pl., City Rd. (29–
40): 84 St. John St. Rd. (D.W.
36).
Refs.: COWIE/29: 31: PIG/DIR/28:
32: 36: 38: ROB/DIR/29: 32: 35:
40: PO/DIR/40.

MARTIN, *James*
Add.: 1 Payne St., White Conduit
St.
Refs.: PIG/DIR/32: 36.

MARTIN, *Richard & Charles* (29).
   ,,   *Richard* (32).
  Add.: 7 Princes St., Barbican.
  Refs.: COWIE/31: 32: PIG/DIR/32:
    36: ROB/DIR/29: 32: 40: PO/DIR/
    40: COWIE/7.

MARTIN, *Robert*
(& BS.).
  Add.: 4 Church Lane, Marylebone.
  Refs.: PIG/DIR/32: ROB/DIR/32.

MARTIN, *Robert*
(BS/HOWE/LBB. p. 66).

MARTIN, *Samuel*
(BS/HOWE/LBB. p. 66).

MARTIN, *Thomas*
  Add.: 8 Cock St., St. Martin's-le-
    Grand: 14 Fetter Lane, Holborn
    (40).
  Refs.:   PIG/DIR/28:   PO/DIR/40:
    COWIE/7.

MARTIN & DENNY
  Add.: 14 Angel Ct., 335 Strand.
  Refs.: PIG/DIR/28.

MASON, *George*
(ST. &).
  Add.: 5 North Audley St.
  Refs.: PO/DIR/17.

MASON, *James*
(BS/HOWE/LBB. p. 66).

MASON, *William*
  Add.: 34 Homer St., Marylebone.
  Refs.: COWIE/31: 32: PIG/DIR/28:
    ROB/DIR/32.

MATON, *Charles*
  Add.: 8 Craven St., City Rd.
  Refs.: ROB/DIR/20.

MATTHEWS, *Geo. King*
  Add.: 22 Warwick Lane, Newgate
    St.
  Refs.: COWIE/29: 31: PIG/DIR/24:
    28: 32: 36: 38: ROB/DIR/29: 32:
    35: PO/DIR/40.

MATTHEWS, *James*
(BS/HOWE/LBB.   p.   67   &   SLB.
  passim).

MATTHEWS, *Thomas*
(Vellum Binder and Gilder).
  Add.: 17 Frith St., Soho.
  Refs.: COWIE/29: 31: ROB/DIR/20:
    22: PIG/DIR/24.

MAUGHAN, *Francis*
(BS/HOWE/LBB. p. 67).

MAYER, *George*
  Add.: Globe Terrace, Bethnal
    Green.
  Refs.: PIG/DIR/36.

MAYNARD, *Samuel*
  Add.: 91 Crown Ct., Fleet St.
  Refs.: PIG/DIR/32.

MEAD, *Nathaniel*
(Vellum Binder).
Add.: 93 High St., Whitechapel.
Refs.: COWIE/31 : 32 : ROB/DIR/32 :
35.

MEDES, *G. W.*
Add.: Church St., Camberwell.
Refs.: LAB/JONES ("Bound by").

MEIKLE, *W.*
Add.: 11 Regent St., Westminster.
Refs.: COWIE/29 : 31 : ROB/DIR/29.

MERTON
Add.: Broad St., Golden Sq.
Refs.: COWIE/29 : 31.

MERTON
Add.: Long Acre.
Refs.: COWIE/29 : 31.

MEYER, *Charles*
(BS/HOWE/LBB. p. 69).
(BS. &). (By app^t. to the Queen
& Princesses).
Add.: *2 Hemming's Row, St.
Martin's Lane (19).
Refs.: HOLD/11 : *SCH/S. de R./IV.
58. *Intellectual Sentiments*, 19,
cream m.g. shows that he was
still binding at his first address.
O.C.: Grammont: *Memoires*,
f.m.g. (n.d.) (see Plate XX).
There is a lovely specimen in the
Geo. III bequest at the BM. 83. k.
15, with blue mor. spine and

surround, blue silk sides, paper
appliqués and yellow silk
doublures.

MEYTON
(BS/HOWE/LBB. p. 69).

MILLAR, *J.*
(BS/HOWE/LBB. p. 69 & SLB. pp. 61
& 68).
Refs.: WSM/KC/NEW.

MILLER
Add.: 29 Maiden Lane, Covent
Gdn.
Refs.: PIG/DIR/24.

MILLER
Add.: 7 West St., Seven Dials.
Refs.: LAB/JONES : WSM/KC/NEW/A.
Ticket: "M/BB./No. 7 W.S.
S.D./Opposite the Chapel/Lib-
raries repaired/and beautified".

MILLER, *J.*
Add.: 6 Bridge Rd., Lambeth.
Refs.: LAB/JONES ("Bound and Sold
by / Miller / bookseller, etc. /
next Astley's Theatre / Lam-
beth").
O.C.: Marmontel: *Belisaire*.
London. 05. marbled calf. Label
"Bound & Sold/by J. Miller
/BS., ST./& Paper Hanger/6
Bridge Rd., Lambeth".

MILLER, J.
Add.: 16 St. Martin's Lane.
Refs.: AND/90.

MILLER, James
(Vellum Binder).
Add.: 52 Drury Lane.
Refs.: ROB/DIR/35.

MILLER, William (29)
,,   Peter (32).
Add.: 3 Little Windmill St. (29):
65 Poland St. (36): No. 1 (40).
Refs.: COWIE/29: 31: PIG/DIR/28:
32: 36: 38: ROB/DIR/29: 32: 35:
40: PO/DIR/40.

MILLS, John
Add.: 18 Lower Northampton St.,
Clerkenwell (28): 6 Allen St.,
Goswell Rd. (29).
Refs.: COWIE/29: 31: PIG/DIR/28:
36: ROB/DIR/29.

MILLS & Son
(ST., BS. &).
Add.: 368 Oxford St.
Refs.: HOLD/11.

MILTON, John
Add.: 13 Devonshire St. W.
Refs.: PIG/DIR/32.

MITCHELL (? William Otto)
Add.: 33 Old Bond St.
Refs.: LAB/JONES.
O.C.: Life of Ld. Hill, 45 f. green,

m. g. A William Otto M.,
apprenticed to G. T. Trickett,
was made a F.S.C. on 6.12.31.

MOFFAT & Son
(& Polyartists (sic) in 1840).
Add.: Gt. May's Bldgs.
Refs.: PIG/DIR/28: ROB/DIR/40: PO/
DIR/40.

MONTAGU, Richard
(BS/HOWE/LBB. p. 69 & p. XXXV).
Refs.: A number of bindings by him
are probably correctly attributed
in the Cat. of the Severne
(Wodhull) Cat., Jan. 11–21, 1886,
e.g., Nos 646, 851, 955, 1224,
2089, 2502. They are all in
russia or calf. See also Dibdin,
N.E. & S. Tour, p. 1052.

MOORE, R. P.
Add.: 23 Store St., Bedford Sq.
Refs.: Binding & label seen on book
at Josephs (March 51) dated 1798
but binding probably 20 years
later.
O.C.: Chapone: Improvement of
Mind, 22, f.c.g. (label torn).

MOORE, Samuel
,,   J. (32).
Add.: 33 Bull & Mouth St.,
Aldersgate St.
Refs.: COWIE/29: 31: ROB/DIR/29:
32 (J): PIG/DIR/32.

MOORE, *Thomas Richard*
(BS/HOWE/LBB. p. 69).

MOORE, *William*
Add.: 3 Denmark Ct., Strand.
Refs.: HOLD/11.

MORAN
(BS/HOWE/LBB. p. 69).

MOREHEN, *E. P.*
(& Gilder & Marbler, 40).
Add.: 18 New Union St., Little
Moorfields: 5 Bartholomew
Close (ca. 40).
Refs.: PIG/DIR/38: ROB/DIR/40: PO/
DIR/40: COWIE/7.

MORGAN, *Isaac*
(BS. &).
Add.: 18 Crown St., Moorfields.
Refs.: HOLD/11.

MORRIS, *Charles*
(Toolcutter).
Add.: 44 Kirby St., Hatton Gdn.
Refs.: PIG/DIR/36: 38: PO/DIR/40.

MORRIS, *Joseph & Co.*
  „   *King & Gooding* (ca. 40).
(Toolcutters).
Add.: 35 Ludgate St.
Refs.: PIG/DIR/38: PO/DIR/40:
COWIE/7. Arnett's *Bibliopegia*,
1835, states that by then the firm
had nearly 20,000 tools and
ornaments.

MORRISON, *James*
(Bookclasp Maker).
Add.: 44 Prince's St., Leicester Sq.
Refs.: ROB/DIR/20.

MOURQUE, *John*
(Vellum Binder).
Add.: 5 New Ct., London Wall.
Refs.: PIG/DIR/24.

MUDIE, *Thomas*
(Circ. Lib. &).
Add.: 39 Cheyne Walk, Chelsea.
Refs.: HOLD/11.

MULLINS
(Pressmaker).
Refs.: Ca. 1794: see LBB/HOWE,
p. 81.

MUNDAY, *Edward*
Add.: 4 Red Lion Ct., Fleet St.
Refs.: ROB/DIR/35.

MURRAY, *David*
Add.: 179 Sloane St.
Refs.: PIG/DIR/32.

MURRAY, *David/Maria*
(BS/HOWE/LBB. p. 70).

MURRAY, *James*
(& Solid Sketch-book Maker in 40).
Add.: 11 Gt. St. Andrew St.,
Seven Dials: No. 37 (40).
Refs.: PIG/DIR/36: ROB/DIR/35: 40:
PO/DIR/40.

MURRAY, *John J.*
(BS/HOWE/LBB. p. 70).
Refs.: HOLD/11.

MURRAY, *Matthew*
    ,,   *M. & Son* (29).
Add.: 22 Charles St., Hatton Gdn.
Refs.: COWIE/29:31: JOHN/17: ROB/
    DIR/29.

MURTON, *Charles*
(ST. & Printseller in 40).
Add.: 50 Long Acre (21): 9 Broad
    St., Golden Sq. (22): 6 Gt. New-
    port St., Long Acre (29): 12 St.
    Martin's Ct. (38).
Refs.: COWIE/29: PIG/DIR/32: 38:
    ROB/DIR/22: 29: 40.
O.C.: Lady Dacre's *Dramas*,
    1821, 2 vol. f.m.g. (see Plate
    XXI): *Nov. Test. Gr.*, 1632: f.c.g.
    stamped "Bound by C. Murton,
    50 Long Acre". A fine binder,
    specialising in blind stamping.

NAPPER, *John*
(BS/HOWE/LBB. p. 70).
Add. 4 Robin Hood Yard, Leather
    Lane (31): No. 5 (40): 13 Everett
    St., Brunswick Sq. (ca. 40).
Refs.: COWIE/31: 32: PIG/DIR/36:
    38: ROB/DIR/32: 35: 40: PO/DIR/
    40: COWIE/7.

NAYLOR, *Charles, Jr.*
Add.: 44 Stanhope St., Clare Mkt.
Refs.: PIG/DIR/32.

NEAL (NEALE), *Joseph*
(BS/HOWE/LBB. p. 70).
Refs.: HOLD/11.

NELSON, *David/J.*
(BS/HOWE/LBB. p. 70).
Refs.: HOLD/11 which gives initial
    as "J".

NELSTROP, *Richard*
(BS. in 32).
Add.: 9 or 17 Worship St., Fins-
    bury.
Refs.: COWIE/29: 31: PIG/DIR/28:
    32: ROB/DIR/29: 32.

NEVETT, *James William*
Add.: 82 Shoe Lane (35): 3 Holland
    St., Blackfriars (38): 1 Johnson's
    Ct., Fleet St. (ca. 40).
Refs.: PIG/DIR/38: ROB/DIR/35: 40:
    PO/DIR/40: COWIE/7.

NEVETT (or NEVITT), *Joseph*
(BS/HOWE/LBB. p. 70).
    ,,   *Charles & Joseph* (36).
Refs.: COWIE/29: 31: PIG/DIR/24:
    28: 36: ROB/DIR/22: 29.

NEWBERRY, *Charles*
(Vellum Binder & Gilder).
Add.: 12 Crosskeys Sq., Little
    Britain: 74 Basinghall St. (35).
Refs.: COWIE/31: 32: PIG/DIR/32:
    ROB/DIR/32: 35: PO/DIR/40.

NEWBERY & CARNON
   Refs.: See Munby Coll. & Sadleir:
   Evolution of Publishers' Binding
   styles, p. 10.

NEWSON, *George*
   Add.: 65 Newman St., Oxford St.
   & Caroline St., Bedford Sq.
   Refs.: COWIE/29: 31: PIG/DIR/32:
   36: 38: ROB/DIR/29: 32: 35: 40:
   PO/DIR/40.

NICHOLS, *William*
   Add.: 10 Ireland Row, Mile End
   Rd.
   Refs.: PIG/DIR/36.

NICKOLDS, *John*
   (BB.'s Toolcutter & graining plates).
   Add.: 15 Buckingham Pl., Fitzroy
   Sq.
   Refs.: PIG/DIR/32.

NIGHTINGALE, *Henry*
   (& ST.).
   Add.: Windsor Terrace, near Eaton
   St., Pimlico.
   Refs.: PIG/DIR/28.

NIMMO, *John*
   (& Medical & General BS. & ST.).
   Add.: 10 Gt. Maze Pond, Bow.
   Refs.: PIG/DIR/28.

NIMMO, *Richard*
   (SLB. p. 22).
   Add.: 5 Hart St., Covent Gdn.
   Refs.: PIG/DIR/38.

NIMMO, *Walter (or Watkins)*
   (SLB. passim).
   Add.: Blackfriars.

NIMMO, *Walter, Jr.*
   (SLB. p. 22.   ? never a master).

NOON, *William*
   (BS/HOWE/LBB. p. 71 & SLB.
   passim).

NOONE, *G. E.*
   Add.: 7 Rathbone Place.
   Refs.: COWIE/29: 31: ROB/DIR/29.

NORMAN, *G.*
   E.D.: 40 ?
   Add.: 6 Kirby St., Hatton Gdn.
   Refs.: Signature seen at Marks in
   1948: COWIE/7: See E.C. Lowe
   Cat. 153/No. 381.

NORMAN, *George*
   Add.: 5 Prujean Sq., Old Bailey
   (32): 1 Warwick Sq. (38).
   Refs.: PIG/DIR/32: 38: ROB/DIR/40:
   PO/DIR/40.

NUNN, *James*
   (BS/HOWE/LBB. p. 72).
   Refs.: PIG/DIR/28 gives him as book-
   seller only at old address in Gt.
   Queen St.

NURSEY, *George*
   Add.: 8 Adelaide St., Strand.
   Refs.: PIG/DIR/36.

NUTT, *William*
Add.: 12 Craven Bldgs., Drury Lane.
Refs.: PIG/DIR/38: ROB/DIR/40: PO/DIR/40: COWIE/7: Huth Cat. Nos. 4281: 8035.

OLD, *John*
(BS/HOWE/LBB. p. 72).
Refs.: HOLD/11: ROB/DIR/20: 22: PIG/DIR/24: 28.

OLIVER, *James*
(BS/HOWE/LBB. p. 72).
Refs.: HOLD/11.

OLLEY, *John*
(Vellum Binder: 40).
Add.: 14 Nicholls Sq., Aldersgate St.: 109 Upper Thames St. (40): 38 Gracechurch St. (ca. 40).
Refs.: ROB/DIR/35: PO/DIR/40: COWIE/7.

OMASH, *Richard*
Add.: 12 London Rd.
Refs.: PIG/DIR/28.

ORGER & MERYON
(BS. &).
E.D.: ? 34.
Add.: 174 Fenchurch St.
Refs.: O.C.: Rogers' *Poems*, 34, maroon chag. g. Though bearing a ticket on which they describe themselves as "BS. & BB.", I suspect this is a publisher's binding.

ORTON, *John*
Add.: 2 Little St. Mary Axe.
Refs.: PIG/DIR/38: ROB/DIR/40: PO/DIR/40: COWIE/7.

OTTRIDGE
(BS/HOWE/LBB. p. 73).
Add.: Gt. Warner St. (11).
Refs.: HOLD/11.

OXLADE, *John*
Add.: 31 Water Lane, Fleet St.
Refs.: COWIE/29: 31: ROB/DIR/29.

OXLADE, *William*
(BS/HOWE/LBB. p. 73).

PAAS
Refs.: Sotheby's Cat. 11.10.54, No. 23, Frank Bauer, gardener at Kew Gardens (1798) mentions having paid £1 1s. 0d. to Paas for binding Thomson's *Dictionary*.

PAAS (or PASS) (*John*) & Co.
(BB.'s Toolmakers).
Add.: 26 High Holborn: No. 44 (32).
Refs.: COWIE/29: 31: PIG/DIR/28: (as John Pass & Co., engravers and copper-plate printers at No. 26 High Holborn): 32: ROB/DIR/29.

PALMER, *Thomas*
Add.: 31 Earl St., E. Lisson Grove: 13 Princess St., L.G. (ca. 40).

Refs.: PIG/DIR/36: ROB/DIR/35: COWIE/7. A "Thomas Palmer" was apprenticed to John Arnott, and admitted a F.S.C. on 8.1.1825.

PALMER, *Thomas William*
(BS/HOWE/LBB. p. 73).

PALMER & GLAISHER (28)
,, *Thomas Dove* (31).
Add.: 11 Little Titchfield St., Portland Pl. (28): 6 Gt. Chesterfield St., Marylebone (36).
Refs.: COWIE/31: 32: PIG/DIR/28: 32: 36: 38: ROB/DIR/32: 35: 40: PO/DIR/40: COWIE/7.

PALWORTH & *Sons*
Add.: 14 Queen's Row, Pimlico.
Refs.: COWIE/29: 31: ROB/DIR/29.

PARK(E), *Gaden, Gaven, John or George*
(BS/HOWE/LBB. p. 73).
Add.: 7 Titchfield St., Soho.
Refs.: HOLD/11: COWIE/29: 31: PIG/DIR/24: 28: 32: 36: ROB/DIR/20: 22: 29: 32: 35.

PARKER, *James Mitchell*
Add.: 183 High St., Borough.
Refs.: PIG/DIR/36.

PARKINS, *John*
(& ST.).
Add.: 4 & 5 Little Tufton St.,

Westminster (29): 2 Church St. (35).
Refs.: COWIE/29: 31: PIG/DIR/32: 36: 38: ROB/DIR/29: 32: 35: 40.

PARSON & *Son*
(BS. &).
Add.: 166 Fleet St.
Refs.: PO/DIR/17: In my O.C. is a calf gilt binding, on John Owen: *Fashionable World Displayed*: 4th edition, 1803, with label "Parson/binder" but no address.

PARSONS, *John*
(BS/HOWE/LBB. p. 74).

PASSMORE, *William*
(BS. & 35).
Add.: 26 Hanover St., Walworth Rd. (31): 17 Manor Pl., Walworth Rd. (36).
Refs.: COWIE/31: 32: PIG/DIR/32: 36: 38: ROB/DIR/32: 35: COWIE/7.

PATTIE, *James*
(BS. & publisher in 1840).
Add.: 4 Brydges St., Strand.
Refs.: PIG/DIR/38: ROB/DIR/40.

PAWLEY, *Richard*
Add.: 4 Union St. (or Ct.), Holborn Hill: 4 Upper Union Ct., High Holborn (32).
Refs.: COWIE/29: 31: PIG/DIR/32: 36: 38: ROB/DIR/29: 32: 35.

PAYNE, *John T.*
Add.: 31 Tabernacle Walk, Finsbury.
Refs.: COWIE/31: 32: PIG/DIR/36: 38: ROB/DIR/32: 35: 40: PO/DIR/40: COWIE/7.

PAYNE, *Roger*
(BS/HOWE/LBB. p. 74).
Refs.: Howe's suggestion that Payne may have been employed by McKinlay towards the end of his life is confirmed by Item 163 in the Wheeler Sale Cat. of 1932. The binding is tree-calf on E. Gibbon's *Misc. Works*, 2 vol., 1796, and although Payne died in 1797, the vols. contain an account for the binding in the name of Payne & McKinlay, dated 1805, which would tend to show that McKinlay attached value to his short association with Payne. Signed examples of his work are in the Ld. Rothschild and Storer (Eton College) Collections. He also bound a great deal for Wodhull. (See 1886 Cat. passim).

PAYNE, *Thomas*
(BS/HOWE/LBB. p. 74).
Refs.: BM. C 69 e. 6.

PAYNE, *William*
(BS/HOWE/LBB. p. 74).
Refs.: HOLD/11.

PAYNE & MACKINLAY
(see Payne, R.).
Refs.: Wheeler Cat. 163, which says that the bill of these binders is contained in the first volume. HOLD/11 mentions P. & M. as BS. at 86/87 Strand. The existence of Payne, the binder, and Payne, the bookseller, presents great possibilities of confusion.

PEACOCK
(BS/HOWE/LBB. p. 75).
Refs.: SLB. p. 62. Seems to have been a master as early as 1794.

PEACOCK & MANSFIELD
(? see Peacock).
Refs.: O.C.: *Common Prayer.* Murray 45. Elab. inlaid vellum binding, silk end-papers, stamped signature on recto of end fly-leaf. (Now in BM. Aug. 54).

PEARCE, *Edward*
(Book, etc. Gilder).
Add.: 6 Castle Ct., Strand.
Refs.: PIG/DIR/28.

PEARCE, *James William*
(BS. &).
Add.: 204 Piccadilly.
Refs.: PIG/DIR/23.

PEARSON, *Thomas Squire*
(BS/HOWE/LBB. p. 75).

PEARSON & WEEDON
Add.: 24 Thomas St., Hackney Rd.
Refs.: PIG/DIR/28.

PECK, *Thomas*
(BS/HOWE/LBB. p. 75).

PECK, *Thomas*
Add.: 16 Cowper St., City Rd.
(32): 8 Warwick Sq., City (ca.
40).
Refs.: PIG/DIR/36: 38: ROB/DIR/35:
PO/DIR/40: COWIE/7: BR/BM/IV/29.
p. 13.

PEERS, *David Frinder*
Add.: 6 Warwick Sq., Newgate St.
Refs.: COWIE/29: 31: ROB/DIR/20:
22.

PEERS, *David Trinder*
(BS/HOWE/LBB. p. 75).

PENNY, *Henry*
(Vellum Binder).
Add.: 10 Old Bailey.
Refs.: PIG/DIR/32: COWIE/7.

PENNY, *James*
(see William P. BS/HOWE/LBB. p.
75).
Add.: 1 St. Andrew's Hill.
Refs.: ROB/DIR/29: 32: PIG/DIR/32
(No. 39).

PENNY, *William* (see WAKELIN)
(BS/HOWE/LBB. p. 75).
Refs.: COWIE/29: 31.

PENSTONE, *John*
Add.: 22 Sidmouth St., Gray's Inn
Rd.
Refs.: ROB/DIR/29.

PERKS, *William*
(ST. &).
Add.: 21 St. Martin's Lane.
Refs.: HOLD/11.

PERRY, *Thomas*
(BS/HOWE/LBB. p. 76).

PESMAN, *Isaac*
(PR. in 28).
Add.: 63 Cromer St.
Refs.: COWIE/29: 31: PIG/DIR/28:
ROB/DIR/29.

PHARAOH's, *J. B., Library*
Refs.: LAB/JONES ("Bound by").

PHELPS, *Joseph*
(BS/HOWE/LBB. p. 76).

PHELPS & SIMPSON
,,   *G. R.* (24).
,,   *George Henry* (24).
(Vellum Binder).
Add.: 27 Martin's Lane, Cannon
St.
Refs.: COWIE/29: 31: JOHN/17:
PIG/DIR/24: 28: 32: ROB/DIR/20:
22: 32: 35: COWIE/7: PO/DIR/40.

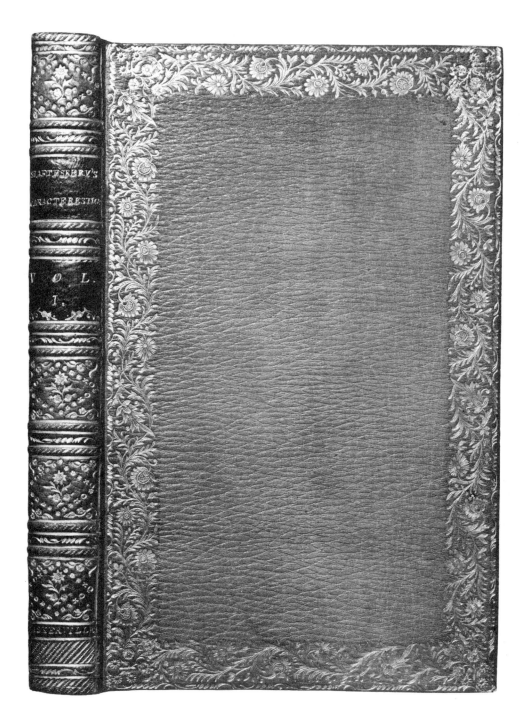

PLATE XXVII   WIER $(6'' \times 9\frac{3}{4}'')$

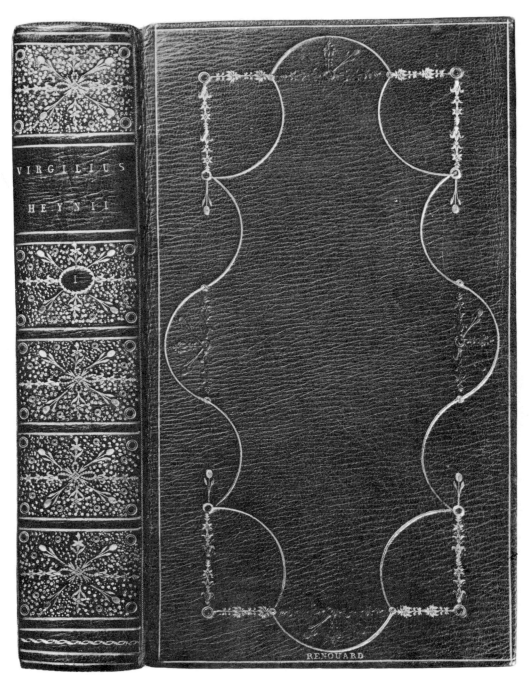

PLATE XXVIII ANON (5" × 9")

PHILANTHROPIC
          MANUFACTORY
E.D.: 08 ?
Add.: St. George's Fields.
Refs.: O.C.: Nield's *Account of Debtors,* 1808, cont. tree calf: Ticket "Bd. at the/P.M./S.G.F.".

PHILLIMORE, *Richard*
(BS/HOWE/LBB. p. 76).

PHILLIMORE, *Richard*
Add.: New Cross.
Refs.: HOLD/11: PIG/DIR/32 (? two different binders).

PHILLIPS, *Thomas*
Add.: Britannia St., City Rd. (? 31): 12 Plumber St., City Rd. (ca. 35).
Refs.: COWIE/31: 32: PIG/DIR/32: 38: ROB/DIR/32: 40: COWIE/7: BM. 1052. 1. 15: AE/COLL/LAB (ca. 35): WSM/KS/NEW/A (ticket).

PHILLIPS, *Benjamin/William*
(BS/HOWE/LBB. p. 76).
Refs.: HOLD/11.

PICKERING, *George*
Add.: 12 Blenheim St., Oxford St.
Refs.: ROB/DIR/35.

PICKWORTH, *John*
Add.: 43 Kirby St., Hatton Gdn.
Refs.: COWIE/29: 31: PIG/DIR/28: 32: 36: ROB/DIR/29: 32: 35.

PIKE, *William* (11)
          (Bookclasp Makers).
  „   *William & Son* (29).
  „   *John & William* (36).
Add.: 28 Hosier Lane, W. Smithfield (11): 8 Oxford Arms Passage, Warwick Lane (23).
Refs.: HOLD/11: COWIE/29: 31: PIG/DIR/23: 28: 36: 38: ROB/DIR/29: 40: PO/DIR/40: COWIE/7.

PILGRIM, *Philip*
(BS/HOWE/LBB. p. 76).

PINKNEY, *Albert*
Add.: 20 Old Walnut Tree Walk.
Refs.: PIG/DIR/32.

PINKNEY, *Herbert*
          (BS/HOWE/LBB. p. 76).
  „   *John* (35).
Refs.: COWIE/29: 31: PIG/DIR/28: ROB/DIR/29: 32: 35.

PIPPING, *William/Benjamin*
(BS/HOWE/LBB. p. 76).
Refs.: COWIE/29: 31: ROB/DIR/20: 22: PIG/DIR/28.

PLANT, *Charles*
Add.: 8 Cumming St., Pentonville.
Refs.: PIG/DIR/36.

PLAYER, *George*
Add.: 1 Harvey's Bldgs., Strand.
Refs.: PIG/DIR/36.

PLAYER, *Henry*
(BB.'s Toolmaker).
Add.: 8 Hemming's Row.
Refs.: ROB/DIR/20.

PLAYER, *Nicholas*
(BS/HOWE/LBB. p. 104).
(Edgegilder).
Add.: 5 Hudson's Ct., Strand (29).
Refs.: COWIE/29: 31: PIG/DIR/28:
SLB./p. 97.

POLLEY, *John*
(Vellum Binder).
Add.: 11 Church St., Strand.
Refs.: PIG/DIR/24.

POLWARTH, *John/John II*
(BS/HOWE/LBB. pp. 77
& XXXIV & VI).
,,   *John & Robert.*
(ST.).
Refs.: HOLD/11: PIG/DIR/32.

POLWARTH & SONS (20)
(& ST.).
,,   *Robert* (36).
,,   *H.* (40).
Add.: 14 Queen's Row, Pimlico:
No. 8 (38).
Refs.: ROB/DIR/20: 22: PIG/DIR/36:
38: ROB/DIR/40: COWIE/7.

PONDER & PALMER
(Vellum Binders).
Add.: 30 Marsham St.
Refs.: HOLD/11.

POOLE, *John*
(BS/HOWE/LBB. p. 77).

POOLE, *Joseph*
Refs.: Described himself as a BB. of
4 Aldersgate Bldgs., when registering on 22.2.29 a son, George
Henry, born to his wife Phoebe
on 26.4.28 (Harl. Soc. Vol. 44,
St. Pancras, Soper Lane).

POOLE, *Nathaniel*
(Bookclasp Maker).
Add.: Oxford Arms Passage, War-
wick Lane.
Refs.: HOLD/11.

POOLER, *Richard*
(ST. &).
Add.: 6 Gt. Tower St.
Refs.: PIG/DIR/28: PO/DIR/31.

POORATT, or PORRETT, *John
Coulson*
(BS/HOWE/LBB. p. 77).
Refs.: COWIE/29: 31: PIG/DIR/28:
ROB/DIR/29.

POPE, *George E.*
,,   ,,   *Henry* (40).
Add.: 18 Warwick Sq.
Refs.: PIG/DIR/38: PO/DIR/40.

POPE, *James*
Add.: 12 Church St., Hackney.
Refs.: COWIE/31 : 32 : PIG/DIR/32 :
ROB/DIR/32 : 35 : PO/DIR/40.

PORTER, *Thomas*
Add.: 9 Clarence Gdns., Regent's
Park.
Refs.: PIG/DIR/36.

POTTER, *J.*
,,   *& Son* (32).
,,   *Charles* (40).
        (& BS. & ST.).
Add.: 16 Warwick Pl., Kingsland.
Refs.: COWIE/31 : PIG/DIR/38 : ROB/
DIR/32 : (& Son) : 35 : PO/DIR/40 :
COWIE/7.

POTTER, *T. J.*
Add.: 68 Tabernacle Walk.
Refs.: COWIE/31 : 32 : COWIE/7.

POUNCEBY, *James*
(also spelt Pownceley & Pownaby).
(BS/HOWE/LBB. p. 77).
    (It is difficult to trace the relation-
ship, if any, between the various
binders of closely similar name).
Add.: 2 Red Lion St., Spitalfields
(24) : 2 New Union St., Moorfields (35) : 8 Pool Terrace, Bath
St., City Rd. (36) : 62 Curtain
Rd. (38).
Refs.: COWIE/29 : 31 : 32 : PIG/DIR/
24 : 36 : 38 : ROB/DIR/20 : 22 : 35.

POUNCEY & *Sons*
Add.: 65 Long Acre.
Refs.: PIG/DIR/32.

POWNCEBY, *John*
Add.: 4 Radnor St., St. Luke's.
Refs.: PIG/DIR/28.

POWNCEBY, *John William*
Add.: 14 Maiden Lane, Wood St.
(28) : 36 Union St., Little Moor-
fields (31).
Refs.: COWIE/31 : PIG/DIR/28 : 32 :
ROB/DIR/32.

POWTER, *William*
(BS/HOWE/LBB. p. 77).

POYNTON
(BS., ST. &).
Add.: 2 Knightsbridge (ca. 25) :
10 Water St., Blackfriars (35).
Refs.: P/Label : ROB/DIR/35.

PRATT, *Joseph*
Add.: 49 York St., Westminster.
Refs.: PIG/DIR/36.

PRATT, *William Pitt*
(& BS.).
Add.: 20 Russell Ct., Drury Lane
(23) : 9 Clarence Gdns., Regent's
Park (36) : 30 Carey St., Lincolns
Inn (38).
Refs.: COWIE/29 : 31 : PIG/DIR/23 :
24 : 28 : 32 : 36 : 38 : ROB/DIR/29 :
32 : 35.

PRESTON, *Ralph*
(Gilder & Marbler, & dealer in
BB.'s tools).
Add.: 28 Maiden Lane, Covent
Gdn.
Refs.: COWIE/29: 31: PIG/DIR/28:
32: 36: 38: ROB/DIR/40: PO/DIR/
31: 40: COWIE/7.

PRICE, *James*
Add.: 25 Ivy Lane, Newgate St.
Refs.: PO/DIR/40.

PRICE, *John*
Add.: 7 Craven's Bldgs., Drury
Lane (32): 5 Took's Ct., Chancery
Lane (40).
Refs.: COWIE/32: PIG/DIR/36: 38:
ROB/DIR/32: 35: 40: PO/DIR/40.

PRICE, *William*
(BS/HOWE/LBB. p. 78).

PRICE, *William*
Add.: 11 Berwick St., Soho.
Refs.: PIG/DIR/28.

PRINCE, *Benjamin*
(BS/HOWE/LBB. p. 78).
Refs.: HOLD/11: COWIE/29: 31:
ROB/DIR/20: 22: PIG/DIR/24: 28.

PRINCE, *J.*
(? see Price, John).
Add.: 7 Craven Bldgs., Drury Lane.
Refs.: COWIE/31.

PROCTOR, *John*
Add.: 54 Bartholomew Close.
Refs.: PIG/DIR/24.

PROCTOR, *Joseph*
E.D.: 10 ?
Refs.: Gum. Cat. XII/344.

PROCTOR, *Joshua or John*
Add.: 11 Westmoreland Bldgs.
Refs.: COWIE/29: 31: JOHN/17
(John): ROB/DIR/20.

PROUDFOOT, *J. Thomas* (17)
(BS/HOWE/LBB. p.
78).
(& BS. 29).
,,   *& Son* (36)
,,   *Thomas* (40).
Add.: 89 Wardour St. (20): 63
Mortimer St., Cavendish Sq.
(38): 73 George St., Euston Sq.
(ca. 40).
Refs.: HOLD/11 (J.): COWIE/29: 31:
PIG/DIR/23: 24: 28: 36: 38: ROB/
DIR/20: 22: 29: 32: 35: 38: PO/
DIR/40: COWIE/7. Calf binding
on 1st. ed. Stendhal's *Rouge et
Noir*, 1831 (Grolier 49/51. p. 965).

PUBLIC, *Elizabeth Lovejoy*
(see Lovejoy).
E.D.: 12 ?
Add.: 7 New Bridge St., Vauxhall.
Refs.: HOB/ABB: p. 146.

PLATE XXIX   ANON $(9'' \times 11\frac{1}{4}'')$

PLATE XXX   ANON   (*6″ × 9″*)

PUGH, *Joseph J.*
  Add.: Wharf Rd., City Rd. (29).
  14 Northampton Pl., New
  North Rd. (38): 14 King St.
  Terrace, New North Rd. (40).
  Refs.: COWIE/29: 31: PIG/DIR/38:
  ROB/DIR/29: 40: PO/DIR/40.

PURDY, *Edward*
  Add.: Dean St., Fetter Lane: 22
  Took's Ct., Cursitor St., Chan-
  cery Lane (28).
  Refs.: COWIE/29: 31: PIG/DIR/28:
  32: ROB/DIR/20: 22: 29: 32: 35:
  LAB/JONES.
  O.C.: Moore, T.: *Lalla Rookh*,
  17 f. blue c.g.

PYMM & INGRAM
  ''   *George* (24).
  Add.: 5 Buckingham St., Strand:
  33 Villiers St., Strand (28):
  Upper Crown St., Westminster
  (40): 32 Villiers St. (ca. 40).
  Refs.: COWIE/29: 31: PIG/DIR/24:
  28: 32: 36: ROB/DIR/22: 29: 32:
  35: PO/DIR/40: COWIE/7 (two
  Pymms mentioned without initials at last two addresses given
  above): SLB. p. 92.

QUELCH, *Henry*
  (BS., BB., etc.).
  Add.: 24 East St., Walworth.
  Refs.: PIG/DIR/28.

QUINN, *James*
  (BS/HOWE/LBB. p. 78).

RACKHAM
  E.D.: 12 (?)
  Refs.: Sotheby Sale, 12.6.50/No.
  127, f.m.g. silk endpapers.

RAE (RAY), *Robert/Stuart*
  (BS/HOWE/LBB. p. 79).
  Refs.: HOLD/11: COWIE/29: 31:
  PIG/DIR/24: 28: 32: 36: 38: ROB/
  DIR/20: 22: 32: 35: 40: 41: 42:
  43: PO/DIR/40: COWIE/7.

RAE, *W.*
  Add.: 3 Crown Ct., Pall Mall.
  Refs.: PIG/DIR/28.

RAINES, *Thomas*
  Add.: 39 Hart St., Bloomsbury
  (35): 11 Pickett St., Strand (40):
  24 Gt. Ormond St. (ca. 40).
  Refs.: PIG/DIR/36: 38: ROB/DIR/35:
  40: PO/DIR/40: COWIE/7.

RAINSFORD, *Octavius*
  Add.: 5 Barclay St., Somers Town.
  Refs.: PO/DIR/40: ROB/DIR/41.

RANKIN
  (Edgegilder).
  (BS/HOWE/LBB. p. 104).

RAPER, *Thomas*
  (BS/HOWE/LBB. p. 79).

RAVEN
  Add.: 29 Greenhill's Rents: ? Bars.
  Ref.: COWIE/31: rubbed ticket seen

on elaborate mor. binding about 1820/5 at W.T. Spencer (July, 1954).

RAVENSCROFT, *John/Hannah* (28) (BS/HOWE/LBB. p. 79).
Refs.: HOLD/11 : Hannah appears at the same address in PIG/DIR/28.

RAVENSCROFT, *Temple/W.* (BS/HOWE/LBB. p. 79).

RAY, *Stuart* (see RAE).

RAYSON, *William*
Add.: 28 Leadenhall St. (28) : 4 Brown's Bldgs., St. Mary Axe (31).
Refs.: COWIE/29 : 31 : 32 : PIG/DIR/ 28 : ROB/DIR/29 : 32.

READ, *Samuel*
(Vellum Binder in 35).
Add.: 22 Gt. Bell Alley : 95 London Wall (35).
Refs.: PIG/DIR/32 : ROB/DIR/35.

REDFORD & ROBINS
Add.: 96 London Rd.
Refs.: PIG/DIR/32.

REDWELL, *Mary*
Add.: 6 Sherrard St., Golden Sq.
Refs.: PIG/DIR/38.

REED, *S.*
(ST. &).
Add.: 444 Strand.
Refs.: HOLD/11.

REEPE, *Raham* (BS/HOWE/LBB. p. 80).

REESE, *Thomas*
Add.: Vauxhall Place.
Refs.: HOLD/11.

REEVE, *Joseph Boulton*
Add.: 11 Water Lane, Fleet St.
Refs.: PIG/DIR/36.

RELTON, *Henry Edward*
(BB.'s Toolmaker : BB. & Engraver in 32).
Add.: No. 24 (17) : 44 Kirby St., Hatton Gdn.
Refs.: JOHN/17 : COWIE/29 : 31 : PIG/DIR/28 : 32.

REMNANT, *Frederick*
Add.: 92 Bartholomew Close.
Refs.: 29 : 31 : 32 : PIG/DIR/28 : 32 : ROB/DIR/29 : 32.

REMNANT, *Frederick*
    b. 1780 : d. 30.5.1853.
    (BS/HOWE/LBB. p. 80).
    „   & *Edmonds* (31) q.v.
Add.: 9 Lovell's Ct., Paternoster Row (24).
Refs.: COWIE/29 : 31 : PIG/DIR/24 : ROB/DIR/29 : 35.

REMNANT, *Thomas*
(BS/HOWE/LBB. p. 80).

REMNANT & EDMONDS
 (BS/HOWE/LBB. pp. 80/1
 ,, & *Co.* (40).
E.D.: 31.
Add.: 9 Lovell Ct., Paternoster
Row.
Refs.: COWIE/31: PIG/DIR/32: 36:
38: ROB/DIR/32: 40: PO/DIR/40:
COWIE/7: Arnett's *Bibliopegia*,
1835, p. 126, says that they
introduced in 1829 the so-called
arabesque binding by whole
plates which was later used widely
for albums, etc.

RENNIE
(BS/HOWE/LBB. p. 81).

RESTELL, *William*
(& BS. in 28).
Add.: 25 Bear Lane, Church St.,
Blackfriars Rd. (28): 23 or 33
Charlotte St., Blackfriars Rd.
(29).
Refs.: COWIE/29: 31: PIG/DIR/28:
36: 38: ROB/DIR/29: 40: 41: 42.
LAB/JONES "Bound by". I have a
label reading "WR/BB./No. 23/
C.S./B.R." removed from a tree
calf bdg. on Burney's *Hist. of
Music*, 1782, which the donor
assures me is contemporary. If so,
there may have been a W.R.,

Senior, and his son may have
moved to Charlotte St. on his
death.

REYNOLDS, *John*
Add.: 38 Robert St., Bedford
Row.
Refs.: PIG/DIR/36.

REYNOLDS, *T.*
Add.: 157 Oxford St. (30): No.
137 (? 96).
Refs.: AE/f./LAB: Munby Coll.:
Label: "Bd. by T.R., 137 O.S."

REYNOLDS, *William*
(& BS. 40).
Add.: 11 Church Row, Aldgate:
No. 7 (40): 6 Elder St., Finsbury
(ca. 40).
Refs.: PIG/DIR/38: PO/DIR/40:
COWIE/7.

RHODES, *Thomas*
(BS/HOWE/LBB. p. 81).

RICE, *Edward*
(BS/HOWE/LBB. p. 81).

RICH, *Cornelius*
(BS/HOWE/LBB. p. 81).
Add.: 7 Christopher Ct., St.
Martin's-le-Grand (40): 21 Old
Fish St., Doctors Commons (ca.
40).

Refs.: COWIE/29: 31: (vellum binders): PIG/DIR/28: PO/DIR/40: COWIE/7.

RICHARDS, *Alexander*
(BS/HOWE/LBB. p. 81).

RICHARDS, *Henry*
(& BS.).
Add.: 29 Gt. Castle St., Cavendish Sq. (17): 14 Gt. Portland St. (20).
Refs.: JOHN/17: ROB/DIR/20: 22 (ST.).
O.C.: Duras: Eureka. 24: $\frac{1}{2}$ c.g.

RICHARDS, *William*
Add.: 5 Oat Lane, Noble St. (36): 21 Old Change (38).
Refs.: PIG/DIR/36: 38: ROB/DIR/40: 41: 42: PO/DIR/40: COWIE/7.

RICHARDSON
(BS/HOWE/LBB. p. 81).

RICHARDSON, *Bezelia*
(BS/HOWE/LBB. p. 81).

RICHARDSON, *Edmund, Richard & James*
,,   *Edmund & James* (35).
,,   *J. & E.* (40).
Add.: 14 St. Swithin's Lane, City.
Refs.: PIG/DIR/36: 38: ROB/DIR/35: 41: 32: PO/DIR/40: COWIE/7.

RICHARDSON, *Robert*
Add.: 3 Britannia St., Gray's Inn Rd. (28): Birchin Lane & Cornhill (31).
Refs.: COWIE/31: 32: PIG/DIR/28: 32: 36: ROB/DIR/32: 35.

RICHMOND, *J.*
Add.: 123 Jermyn St., St. James'.
Refs.: HOLD/05.

RIEBAU, *George*
(BS/HOWE/LBB. p. 82).
(BS., BB. & ST. in 1828).
Refs.: COWIE/29: 31: ROB/DIR/20: 22: PIG/DIR/28.

RIGBY, *Robert*
(BS. & ST. 40).
Add.: 31 Hatfield St., Blackfriars (28): 41 George St., Gt. Surrey St. (35).
Refs.: COWIE/29: 31: PIG/DIR/28: 32: 36: 38: ROB/DIR/29: 35: 40: 41: 42: PO/DIR/40.

RILEY, *Charles*
(BS/HOWE/LBB. p. 82 & XXXVI).
Refs.: SCH/S. de R/IV. 27: Sotheby 22.5.50, No. 86: HOLD/11: mentions a Charles Rieley (*sic*) at 15 St. John's Sq.

RILEY, *Charles*
(& Bookedge Marbler).
Add.: 13 Addle Hill, Doctors

Commons (28): 2 St. Andrew's Hill, City (29).
Refs.: COWIE/29: 31: PIG/DIR/28: 32: 36: 38: ROB/DIR/29: 32: 35: 40: 41: 42: PO/DIR/40.

RILEY, *Geo.*
Add.: 48½ Paternoster Row.
Refs.: PO/DIR/40.

RILEY, *Horatio*
(Gilder and Marbler in 38).
Add.: 29 Greenhill's Rents, Smithfield Bars.
Refs.: PIG/DIR/36: 38: ROB/DIR/35: 40: PO/DIR/40.

RILEY, *Thomas*
Add.: 3 Cross St., Hampton St., Walworth.
Refs.: PIG/DIR/28.

RING, *Robert*
Add.: 21 Jewin St.
Refs.: PIG/DIR/36.

RIPPEN, *Jane*
Add.: 21 Theobalds Rd.
Refs.: JOHN/17.

RITCHIE, *Benjamin*
Add.: 2 New Ct., London Wall.
Refs.: PIG/DIR/32.

RIVIERE, *Robert*
d. 1882.
(also of Bath, see CR./BB./p. 140).

Refs.: COWIE/7: AE/f.: BB. VOL. I, p. 150: BR/BM/IV/44/p. 5, which says that after ill-success in Bath in 1829 he started on his own in Great Queen St. and moved in 1840 to Piccadilly.

ROBERTS, *David*
(BS/HOWE/LBB. p. 82).
Add.: 19 Bartholomew Close (20): 22 Castle St., Falcon Sq. (28).
Refs.: ROB/DIR/20: 22: PIG/DIR/24: 28.

ROBERTS, *David*
„ *& Fisher* (35).
Add.: 11 Redcross Sq., Cripplegate.
Refs.: COWIE/29: 31: ROB/DIR/29: 35.

ROBERTS, *Robert*
(BS/HOWE/LBB. p. 82 & XXXVI).

ROBERTS, *Sarah*
Add.: 11 Redcross Sq. and 22 Castle St., Falcon Sq.
Refs.: PIG/DIR/32: 36 (C. St. only): 38: ROB/DIR/35: 40: PO/DIR/40.

ROBERTS & FISHER
(see ROBERTS, *Sarah*).
Add.: 11 Redcross Sq. (36): 22 Little Bartholomew Close (40).
Refs.: PIG/DIR/36: 38: ROB/DIR/40: 41: 42: PO/DIR/40.

ROBERTSON, *Alexander*
    Add.: 29 Hyde St., Bloomsbury.
    Refs.: PIG/DIR/36 : 38 : ROB/DIR/35.

ROBERTSON, *Peter* (11)
    ,,   *Charles* (20).
    ,,   *& Son* (24) & (38).
    Add.: 18 Rolls Bldgs., Fetter Lane.
    Refs.: HOLD/11 : COWIE/29 : 31 : PIG/
    DIR/24 : 28 : 36 : 38 : ROB/DIR/20 :
    22 : 29 : 32 : 35 : 40 : PO/DIR/40 :
    COWIE/7.

ROBERTSON, *Hugh*
    (BS. &).
    Add.: 1 Cross Ct., Drury Lane.
    Refs.: PIG/DIR/28.

ROBINS, *Joseph & Sons*
    Add.: 57 Tooley St.
    Refs.: PIG/DIR/32.

ROBINSON, *Henry*
    Add.: 10 Mt. Pleasant (32): 2
    Plumbers Ct., High Holborn (35).
    Refs.: PIG/DIR/32 : 38 : ROB/DIR/35 :
    40.

ROBINSON, *Maria or Mary*
    Add.: 21 Old Change.
    Refs.: COWIE/29 : 31 : PIG/DIR/28 :
    32 : 36 : ROB/DIR/22 : 29 : 32 : 35.

ROCHE, *Mary*
    Add.: 21 Bridgwater Sq.
    Refs.: PIG/DIR/38.

RODEN
    E.D.: ca. 20.
    Add.: 18 Bedford St.
    Refs.: AE/COLL/LAB.

RODGER (or ROGERS, *Thomas*
    (& ST.).
    Add.: 53 Rathbone Place.
    Refs.: PIG/DIR/32 : ROB/DIR/32.

RODWELL, *James*
          (BS/HOWE/LBB. p. 83).
    ,,   *Maria* (36).
    ,,   *James* (? *II*) (40).
    Add.: As in Howe, but he seems to
    have also been a bookseller at 46
    New Bond St., first in his own
    name as "Successor to Mr.
    Faulder"★ and later as "Rodwell
    & Martin" (see ticket under
    Dawson & Lewis on Milton: 16).
    Refs.: HOLD/11 : COWIE/28 : 32 :
    AE/COLL/LAB.
    O.C.: Lambert's *Hist. of London*,
    4 vol. 06: f.c.g.: Heyne's *Ver-*
    gilius, 09: (both with Warwick
    Sq. label): Voltaire: *Henriade*,
    1790, f.m.g. (bookseller's ticket
    as above★): handsome dark blue
    mor. gilt BM. G. 10, noted as
    bound in 1808: small rectangular
    label "Bd. by/I.R.". PIG/LON/
    DIR/28 gives Rodwell & Martin
    as book and printsellers at 46 New
    Bond St. and 40 Argyle St., and
    also J. Rodwell as bookbinder at
    6 Sherrard St., Golden Sq.

ROB/DIR/29: 32: 35: 40: PIG/DIR/
32: 36 (Maria): PO/DIR/40.

RODWELL, *R.*
(? BS. only).
Add.: 436 Oxford St.
Refs.: PO/DIR/17.

ROE, *Charles*
Add.: 16 Cornwall Rd., Lambeth.
Refs.: ROB/DIR/29.

ROGERS, *John*
Add.: 2 Duke St., Westminster.
Refs.: COWIE/29: 31: ROB/DIR/20
(W): 22 (J).

ROOKE
Add.: Weymouth St., New Kent
Rd.
Refs.: COWIE/29: 31.

ROSE & *Son*
(BS/HOWE/LBB. p. XXXVI).
Add.: Catherine St., Strand.
Refs.: COWIE/29: 31.

ROW, *Walter*
(? BS. only).
Add.: 28 Gt. Marlborough St.
Refs.: PIG/DIR/28: PO/DIR/31.

ROWBOTHAM, *J.*
(& Indiarubber Binder).
Add.: 70 Castle St. East, Oxford St.
(41): 19 Newman St. (?).
Refs.: PO/DIR/40: COWIE/7: LAB/
JONES.

ROWE, *Lewis*
Add.: 31 Hatton Wall.
Refs.: HOLD/11.

ROWE & WELLER
Add.: Fleet St.
Refs.: Noted as dating about
1814–30.

ROWLEY, *George*
    „   E. (36).
    „   J. & G. (40).
Add.: 2 Wardrobe Terrace, Doctors Commons: 5 Porter St.
Refs.: COWIE/29: 31: PIG/DIR/28:
32: 36: 38: ROB/DIR/29: 35: 40:
PO/DIR/40. SLB. p. 44: Jaffray
says that he was one of Lovejoy's
workmen and took over his
masonic tools.

ROWLEY, *J. G.*
Add.: 8 Oxford Arms Passage,
Warwick Lane.
Refs.: ROB/DIR/35.

ROYLE, *John*
    „   J. H.
        (& ST. in 1832: & BS. in
        40).
Add.: 212 Tottenham Ct. Rd. (32):
10 Judd St., New Rd. (36).
Refs.: PIG/DIR/32: 36: 38: ROB/DIR/
40: PO/DIR/40.

RUMFITT, *John*
Add.: 33 Castle St., Leicester Sq.
Refs.: PIG/DIR/38: COWIE/7.

RUNTING, *William*
  Add.: 22 Took's Ct., Cursitor St., Chancery Lane (35): No. 6 and 14 Castle St., Holborn (38): latter address only (40): 7 East Harding St., Shoe Lane (40).
  Refs.: PIG/DIR/36: 38: ROB/DIR/35: 40: PO/DIR/40.

RUSSELL, *Alexander*
            (BS/HOWE/LBB. p. 83).
  „   *Susan* (32).
  „   *& Spencer* (35).
  Add.: 14 Bridgwater Sq., Barbican.
  Refs.: COWIE/29: 31: PIG/DIR/24: 28: 32: 36: 38: ROB/DIR/20: 22: 29: 32: 35.

RUSSELL, *Geo.*
  Add.: 5 Porter St., Soho: 3 Newman St. (32).
  Refs.: COWIE/29: 31: PIG/DIR/24: 28: 32: ROB/DIR/20: 22.

RUSSELL, *Richard*
  (& ST.).
  Add.: March St., Walthamstow.
  Refs.: HOLD/11.

RUTTER, *Josiah*
  (BS/HOWE/LBB. p. 83).

SALLIS, *William*
  Add.: 5 Cross Key Ct., Little Britain.
  Refs.: PIG/DIR/32.

SAMS
  (BS. &).
  Add.: 62 Pall Mall (? 15): 1 St. James' St. (18).
  Refs.: Sotheby Cat. 24.7.51/76: Ticket in ROB/DIR/20 at Bishopsgate Institute: "S/BS. & B./ 1 St. J. St./opposite the Palace".
  O.C.: Paley's *Nat. Theology*, 15.
  f.c.g. (ticket).

SANDERS, *Charles*
  Add.: 28 Fleet Lane, Old Bailey.

SANDERS, *Joseph*
  Add.: 3 Little Shire Lane, Temple Bar.
  Refs.: PIG/DIR/28: 36.

SANFORD, *William*
  (Gilder & Marbler).
  Add.: 40 Maiden Lane.
  Refs.: PO/DIR/40.

SANTRY, *Cornelius Michael*
  Add.: 245 High St., Borough.
  Refs.: COWIE/29: 31: PIG/DIR/28: 32: 36: 38: ROB/DIR/29: 32: 35: 40: PO/DIR/40.

SAUNDERS, *Robert*
  Add.: 20 Albion Bldgs., Aldersgate St.
  Refs.: COWIE/29: 31: ROB/DIR/29: 32.

SAUZE
  Add.: 8 Little Carter Lane.
  Refs.: COWIE/29: 31: ROB/DIR/29.

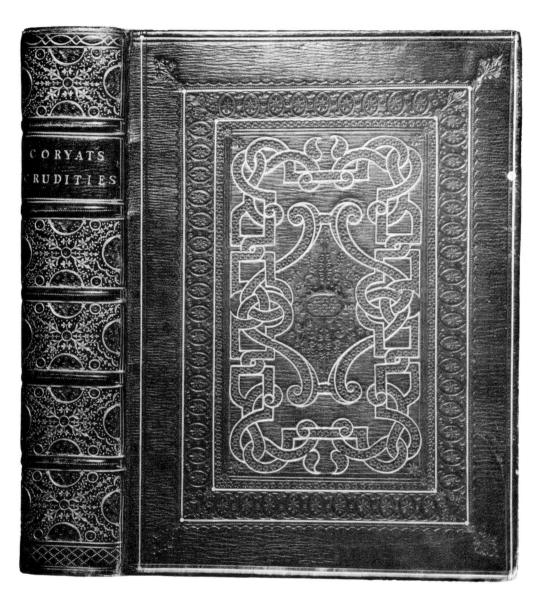

PLATE XXXI   ANON $(6\frac{3}{4}'' \times 9'')$

PLATE XXXII   ANON $(9\frac{1}{2}'' \times 11\frac{1}{2}'')$

SAUZE, *James*
(Vellum Binder).
Add.: 12 Little Knightrider St. (32):
29 New Union St. (40).
Refs.: PIG/DIR/32: PO/DIR/40.

SAW, *William*
Add.: 6 Russell Ct., Drury Lane:
36 Vere St., Clare Mkt. (40)
(May not be the same binder).
Refs.: ROB/DIR/35: 40: 41: 42
(R.C.): PIG/DIR/36: 38: PO/DIR/
40: COWIE/7.

SCHMIDT, *Gotte*
(Godfrey in 1838: Gottfried in 40).
Add.: 41 Belton St., Long Acre:
38 Long Acre (40).
Refs.: PIG/DIR/36: ROB/DIR/40: PO/
DIR/40.

SCHWEDER
Add.: ?
Refs.: The only known example of
his work (Lot 122 in Sotheby
Sale of 20.12.54) is in red silk and
contained in calf slip case signed
on spine: "Schweder, Binder,
1787".

SCOTT, *R.*
(BB.'s Toolmakers: Engraver of
brass ornaments to H.M. Library).
(BS/HOWE/LBB. p. 104 under
Brooke).
Add.: Corner of Newcastle St.,
Strand (29): 302 Strand (17).
Refs.: COWIE/29: 31: PO/DIR/27.

SCOTT, *William*
Add.: Old Change.
Refs.: PIG/DIR/32.

SCRIPPS, *James*
Add.: 5 South Molton St., Bond St.
Refs.: COWIE/29: 31: PIG/DIR/28:
32: 36: 38: ROB/DIR/29: 32: 35:
40: PO/DIR/40.

SEARE, *Samuel & Co.*
(Toolcutters & Engravers).
Add.: 44 High Holborn.
Refs.: PIG/DIR/36: PO/DIR/40.

SEARLE, *John/Mary Ann*
(BS/HOWE/LBB. p. 83 &
XXXVI).
(BS. 32).
,,   *William* (29) (see separate
entry).
,,   *Mary Ann* (28: also re-
appears in ROB/DIR/35).
Add.: 76 & 77 (Lower) Grosvenor
St.
Refs.: HOLD/11: PO/DIR/17: COWIE/
29: 31: PIG/DIR/24: 32: 36: LAB/
JONES.
O.C.: Ticket "Bound by J.S.:
76 Lower G.S." taken from a
1803 work, whose mottled calf
binding appeared to be con-
temporary. There was a John
Searle, ST. & BB. at 24 Brewer
St., Golden Sq., in 1790 (see
AND/90).

SEARLE, *William*
(BS/HOWE/LBB. p. 84).
(From the address he may be connected with previous entry).
Add.: 76 & 77 Lower Grosvenor St. (20): 19 Frith St. (38).
Refs.: ROB/DIR/20: 29: 35: 40: PIG/DIR/32: 36: 38: PO/DIR/40.

SEARLE, *William*
(BS/HOWE/LBB. p. XXXIV & 84).

SECAR (or SEEAR), *John*
Add.: 34 Shoreditch: 3 West Harding St. (32).
Refs.: COWIE/31: 32: ROB/DIR/20: 32: 35: PIG/DIR/32: 36: PO/DIR/40: Possibly a F.S.C. by 1813.

SEDDON, *James*
Add.: 23 Banner St., St. Luke's.
Refs.: PIG/DIR/28.

SELL, *T.*
(ST. &).
Add.: 73 St. Martin's Lane.
Ref.: PO/DIR/31.

SELLES
Add.: Little Britain.
Refs.: COWIE/29: 31.

SERGEANT, *Mr. & Mrs.*
    „   *John* (28).
Add.: 3 Albion Bldgs., Bartholomew Close (28): 11 Staining Lane (32).

Refs.: TIMP/42, p. 947: PIG/DIR/28: 32: 36: 38: ROB/DIR/40: PO/DIR/40: COWIE/7.

SHAKELTON, *Thomas*
Add.: 9 Baldwyn's St., City Rd.
Refs.: ROB/DIR/20.

SHARP, *Robert/John Thomas*
(BS/HOWE/LBB. p. 84).
Add.: 41 St. Andrew's Hill.
Refs.: HOLD/11.

SHARP, *Thomas*
(may be the same as John Thomas Sharp q.v.).
Add.: 3 Creed Lane.
Refs.: BRI/DIR/91.

SHARP & LAWSON
(BS/HOWE/LBB. p. 84 & SLB. p. 74).

SHAW, *Charles*
(Vellum Binder).
Add.: 29 Newcastle St., Strand.
Refs.: ROB/DIR/32: 35.

SHAW, *Charles Alfred*
    „   *Charles Alex. H.* (40).
Add.: 13 Serles Pl., Lincolns Inn Fields.
Refs.: COWIE/31: 32: ROB/DIR/32: 40: PO/DIR/40: COWIE/7.

SHAW, *E.*
    „   *Stephen* (32).
Add.: 22 Old Boswell Ct., Carey St.

Refs.: COWIE/31 : 32 : PIG/DIR/32 :
36 : ROB/DIR/32 (E) : 40 : PO/DIR/
40 : COWIE/7.

SHAW, *Joseph or John*
Add.: 2 Tennis Ct., Shoemakers
Row (32) : 8 Little New St.,
Shoe Lane (36).
Refs.: PIG/DIR/32 : 36 : ROB/DIR/35 :
PO/DIR/40.

SHAW, *Solomon*
Add.: 22 Old Boswell Ct., Carey
St.: 22 John St., Old Kent Rd.
(36).
Refs.: ROB/DIR/35 : PIG/DIR/36.

SHAW, *Thomas*
Add.: 6 Oxendon St., Haymarket.
Refs.: HOLD/11.

SHAW, *William*
Add.: 22 Old Boswell St., Lincolns
Inn Fields.
Refs.: ROB/DIR/35.

SHEPHERD, *John*
Add.: 26 Mitre St., New Cut.
Refs.: COWIE/29 : 31 : ROB/DIR/29.

SHEPHERD, *R. A.*
(BS. & 32).
Add.: 11 Charles St., Middlesex
Hospital : 16 Newman St. (35).
Refs.: COWIE/29 : 31 : ROB/DIR/29 :
32 : 35.

SHERRAT(T), *John*
Add.: 19 Hatfield St., Blackfriars.
Refs.: COWIE/29 : 31 : PIG/DIR/28.

SHERWOOD, *John*
,,   *John Woodhouse* (32).
,,   *John William* (36).
Add.: John St., Wilmington Sq.
(29) : 19 Albion Pl., Clerken-
well (32) : Boddy's Bridge,
Blackfriars Rd. (36).
Refs.: COWIE/29 : 31 : PIG/DIR/32 :
36 : ROB/DIR/29.

SHOVE, *J.*
(BS/HOWE/LBB. p. 85).

SIFTON
(BS/HOWE/LBB. p. 85).

SILVESTER, *William*
Add.: 112 Fleet St.
Refs.: PIG/DIR/38.

SIMMONDS, *George*
(BS/HOWE/LBB. p. 85).
Refs.: HOLD/11 (& PR.).

SIMMONS
(BS/HOWE/LBB. p. 85).

SIMMONS, *G.*
(BS. & ST.).
E.D.: 20 (?)
Add.: 63 Edgware Rd.
Refs.: P/Label : "Bound by".

129

SIMMONS, *J. W.*
Add.: Botolph Lane, Lower Thames St.
Refs.: COWIE/29: 31: ROB/DIR/22.

SIMMONS, *John*
(Vellum Binder & patent account book maker).
Add.: 18 London Wall.
Refs.: PIG/DIR/24.

SIMMONS, *P.*
(Vellum Binder).
Add.: 34 St. Mary Axe.
Refs.: ROB/DIR/35.

SIMMON(D)S, *Thomas*
Add.: 6 King St., Cloth Fair (32): 19 East Passage, Cloth St. (36): 19 Middle St., Cloth Fair (38).
Refs.: COWIE/29: 32: PIG/DIR/32: 36: 38: ROB/DIR/32: 35: PO/DIR/40: COWIE/7.

SIMMONS, *W.*
(BS/HOWE/LBB. p. 85).

SIMPSON, *George*
,,   & *Renshaw* (? after period).
Add.: 8 Stationers Ct., Ludgate St.: 25 Bread St. Hill (29): 21 Hampstead Rd.: & as before (36): H. Rd. only (38): B. St. Hill (40).
Refs.: COWIE/29: 31: PIG/DIR/28: 32: 36: 38: ROB/DIR/29: 32: 35: 40: PO/DIR/40: COWIE/7.

SIMPSON, *Thomas*
Add.: 16 Rolls' Bldgs., Fetter Lane.
Refs.: BRI/DIR/91.

SIMPSON & BURRUP/SIMPSON, *William*
(BS/HOWE/LBB. p. 86).

SIOR, *William*
(BS. &).
Add.: 12 South St., New Rd., St. Pancras.
Refs.: PIG/DIR/23: 24: ROB/DIR/29.

SIRETT, *Thomas*
Add.: 18 Dartmouth St., Westminster.
Refs.: PIG/DIR/36.

SLATER, *George*
Add.: 10 Cecil St., St. Martin's Lane.
Refs.: PIG/DIR/28.

SMITH, *Belinda*
(Vellum Binder).
Add.: 26 Little Trinity Lane, Queenhithe.
Refs.: COWIE/29: 31: PIG/DIR/24.

SMITH, *Alfred B.*
Add.: 54 St. John St. Rd.: 15 St. John's Lane (ca. 40).
Refs.: PIG/DIR/36: PO/DIR/40: COWIE/7.

SMITH, C.
  (? see Smith, Samuel Charles).
  Add.: 19 Oxendon St., Haymarket.
  Refs.: O.C.: Fenelon: *Télémaque*,
    1799, 2 vol.: f.c.g.: bound at
    least 10 years later: ticket "Bd.
    by/CS./OS/H": (see Plate XXII).

SMITH, *Charles*
  Add.: 12 Cecil St., Strand.
  Refs.: COWIE/29: 31: PIG/DIR/28:
    32: 36: ROB/DIR/29: 32: 35: 40.

SMITH, *Charles*
  Add.: 13 Church St., Soho (17):
    13 Litchfield St., Soho (20).
  Refs.: JOHN/17: ROB/DIR/20.

SMITH, *Daniel*
  Add.: 49 Brook St., West Sq.
  Refs.: PIG/DIR/36.

SMITH, *Daniel O.*
  Add.: 6/7 Church St., Blackfriars.
  Refs.: PIG/DIR/36: ROB/DIR/40.

SMITH, *Edward*
  (BS/HOWE/LBB. p. 86).
  Refs.: HOLD/11.

SMITH, *George*
  Add.: 18 Denmark St., St. Giles'.
  Refs.: COWIE/29: 31: PIG/DIR/28:
    ROB/DIR/29: 32.

SMITH, *George*
  Add.: 60 Kingsland Rd.
  Refs.: COWIE/29: 31: PIG/DIR/28:
    ROB/DIR/29: 32: 35.

SMITH, *George*
  Add.: 1 Bull's Head Ct., Newgate
    St.
  Refs.: COWIE/31: 32: PIG/DIR/32:
    ROB/DIR/32: 35.

SMITH, *George*
  Add.: 24 Duke St., Smithfield.
  Refs.: PIG/DIR/36: ROB/DIR/40: PO
    DIR/40: COWIE/7.

SMITH, *J.*
  „   *Joseph James* (28).
  Add.: 26 Little Wild St., Lincolns
    Inn Fields: No. 36 (38).
  Refs.: COWIE/31: 32: PIG/DIR/28:
    36: 38: ROB/DIR/35.

SMITH, *James*
  Add.: 7 Pennington Pl., Lambeth.
  Refs.: COWIE/29: 31: PIG/DIR/28:
    32: ROB/DIR/29: 32: 35.

SMITH, *James*
  Add.: 119 Fleet St.: No. 118 &
    7 Hercules Bldgs., Lambeth (40).
  Refs.: PIG/DIR/36: 38: ROB/DIR/35:
    40: PO/DIR/40.

SMITH, *John*
  (ST. & Vellum Binder).
  Add.: 40 Oxford St.: No. 49 (20).
  Refs.: PO/DIR/17: ROB/DIR/20.

SMITH, *John*
   (& Vellum Binder).
   Add.: 49 Long Acre: Gloucester
   Row, Walworth (22): ? No. 52
   (ca. 40).
   Refs.: COWIE/29: 31: 32: PIG/DIR/
   32: 38: ROB/DIR/22: 32: 35:
   COWIE/7.
   O.C.: *Army List*, f.m.g. label
   "Bd. by/S/49 L A".

SMITH, *John (or J. H.)*
   Add.: 3 or 16 Denmark Ct., Exeter
   St., St. Giles': 3 Exeter St.,
   Strand (36).
   Refs.: COWIE/29: 31: PIG/DIR/28:
   32: 36: 38: ROB/DIR/29: 32: 40:
   PO/DIR/40.

SMITH, *Joseph*
   „   *Jane* (35).
   Add.: 12 or 11 Lovell's Ct.,
   Paternoster Row.
   Refs.: COWIE/31: 32: ROB/DIR/32:
   35.
   O.C.: Stamp on S.P.C.K. publi-
   cation reading "J. Smith, Binder,
   May, 1830". May be this, or the
   Little Wild St. J. Smith. Binding
   similar to the J. Bird III bindings
   for S.P.C.K. with blind stamp
   obviously provided by them in
   each case.

SMITH, *Joseph*
   (Book Edgegilder).
   Add.: 5 Duke St., W. Smithfield.
   Refs.: PIG/DIR/28: ROB/DIR/29.

SMITH, *Joseph*
   „   *John* (32).
   „   *& Son(s)* (35).
   Add.: 14½ Albion Bldgs., Bartholo-
   mew Close.
   Refs.: COWIE/29: 31: JOHN/17
   (John): PIG/DIR/28: 36: 38: ROB/
   DIR/20: 29: 32: 35: PO/DIR/40.
   Munby Coll. Label ca. 1840 "and
   Son".

SMITH, *Joseph James*
   Add.: 26 Little Wild St., Lincolns
   Inn Fields: 3 Gate St., Lincolns
   Inn Fields: 5 Ivy Lane (40).
   Refs.: PIG/DIR/32: ROB/DIR/32: PO/
   DIR/40: BB/BM/V/50/p .5.

SMITH, *N.*
   Add.: 15 Church St., Soho.
   Refs.: ROB/DIR/20: PIG/DIR/24.

SMITH, *R.*
   Add.: 55 Baldwyn St., City Rd.
   Refs.: COWIE/31: 32: PIG/DIR/32:
   ROB/DIR/32.

SMITH, *Robert*
   Add.: 4 John St., Holland St.
   Refs.: ROB/DIR/35.

SMITH, *Robert*
   Add.: 80 Chancery Lane.
   Refs.: PIG/DIR/36: 38: ROB/DIR/35:
   40: PO/DIR/40.

SMITH, *Samuel Charles*
(? see Smith, C.).
(BS/HOWE/LBB. p. 87).
(He seems to have usually styled himself "C. Smith" q.v.).
Refs.: COWIE/29: 31.
SCH/S. de R/IV. 63/64. (The first of these has its sides stamped as O.C. Murton Binding and its spine as O.C. below.)
O.C.: Thurston's *Designs for Shakespeare* 12/15 f.m.g. Ticket "Bd. by/CS/13 Church St., Soho".

SMITH, *Thomas*
(Vellum Binder).
Add.: 26 Little Trinity Lane, Queenhithe.
Refs.: JOHN/17: ROB/DIR/20: 22.

SMITH, *William*
Add.: Upper North Pl., Gray's Inn Rd. (31): 5 Butcher Hall Lane (28).
Refs.: COWIE/31: 32: PIG/DIR/28: ROB/DIR/32.

SMITH, *William*
(& ST. in 36).
Add.: 2 Ivy Lane, Newgate St. (20): 81 Crown Ct., Blackfriars (38): 81 Dorset St., Salisbury Sq. (40): ? 5 Ivy Lane (ca. 40).
Refs.: COWIE/29: PIG/DIR/24: 28: 32: 36: 38: ROB/DIR/20: 22: 29: 32: 35: 40: PO/DIR/40: COWIE/7: LAB/KNA.

SMITH, *William*
Add.: 12 Greville St., Hatton Gdn.
Refs.: ROB/DIR/29: 32.

SMITH, *William*
Add.: 16 Albion Bldgs., Aldersgate.
Refs.: ROB/DIR/20.

SMITH, *William*
Add.: 52 Paternoster Row.
Refs.: PIG/DIR/32.

SMITH & JACKSON
(Vellum Binders).
Add.: 11 Little Carter St. (28): 15 Peter's Hill, Doctors Commons (31).
Refs.: COWIE/31: 32: PIG DIR/28: 32: ROB DIR/32: 35.

SMITH & *Son*
Refs.: O.C.: *Claims of Established Church*, 30. Basil, signed "S. & S., Binder, Oct. 1832". Typical S.P.C.K. binding. May well be the successor of J. Smith who was binding for the S.P.C.K. two years earlier.

SMYTH
Add.: Greville St., Hatton Gdn.
Refs.: COWIE/29: 31.

SNELGROVE, *John Simones*
(Vellum Binder).
Add.: New Sq., Minories (28): 23 Camomile St. (40).
Refs.: PIG/DIR/28: PO/DIR/40.

SOM(M)ERS, *Henry*
(BS/HOWE/LBB. p. 87).

SOMMERS, *James*
  Add.: 16 Dove's Ct., Swithin's
    Lane.
  Refs.: BRI/DIR/V/98.

SOPER, *John*
  Add.: 6 Greville St., Hatton Gdn.
  Refs.: ROB/DIR/35.

SOPER, *John*
  Add.: 6 Greville St., Hatton Gdn.
  Refs.: PIG/DIR/36.

SORRELL, *J.*
(BS/HOWE/LBB. p. 87).

SOUL, *Eli*
  Add.: 26 Tabernacle Walk, Fins-
    bury: No. 36 (38): No. 28 (ca.
    40): 24½ Wilson St., Finsbury
    (28).
  Refs.: PIG/DIR/28: 36: 38: ROB/DIR/
    35: 40: PO/DIR/40: COWIE/7.

SOUTER, *Isaac.*
  Add.: 4 Mitre Ct., London House
    Yd.: 11 Bell's Bldgs., Salisbury
    Sq. (ca. 40).
  Refs.: PIG/DIR/36: COWIE/7.

SOUTHAMS, *John*
  Add.: 16 Gloucester St., Queen's
    Sq.:
  Refs.: PIG/DIR/38.

SOUTHWORTH, *John*
(BS/HOWE/LBB. p. 87).

SPENCER, *Robert*
(& BS.).
  Add.: 15 Bridgwater Sq. (31):
    314 High Holborn (38): 14
    Bridgwater Sq. (40).
  Refs.: COWIE/31: 32: PIG/DIR/38:
    ROB/DIR/32: 40: COWIE/7: PO/
    DIR/40: P/Label.

SPILLING, *Thomas*
(Newsvendor in 1828).
  Add.: 52 St. John St. Rd.
  Refs.: PIG/DIR/28: 32: 36.

SPRATT, *John*
(ST. in 40).
  Add.: 38 Henry St., Hampstead &
    137 Tottenham Ct. Rd. (36):
    Latter address only in 40.
  Refs.: PIG/DIR/36: ROB/DIR/40.

SPURGIN, *George*
  Add.: 29 Lombard St.
  Refs.: PIG/DIR/28.

STACE, *Austin*
  Add.: 19 Mortimer St.
  Refs.: COWIE/29: PIG/DIR/28: 32:
    ROB/DIR/29.

STAGG, *Richard*
  Add.: 6 Seymour Ct., Covent Gdn.
    (28): 20 Gt. Newport St., Long
    Acre (31): 27 Devonshire St.,
    Queen's Sq. (ca. 40).

PLATE XXXIII   ANON $(4\frac{1}{4}'' \times 7\frac{1}{4}'')$

PLATE XXXIV   ANON $(5'' \times 8\frac{1}{4}'')$

Refs.: COWIE/31: 32: PIG/DIR/28:
32: 36: 38: ROB/DIR/32: 35: PO/
DIR/40: COWIE/7.

STAGGEMEIER, *L.*
STAGGEMEIER & WELCHER
WELCHER, *Samuel*
(BS/HOWE/LBB. p. 80).
Refs.: HOLD/11: WH/CAT. 165/6
(the first of these two bindings is
the only example known to me of
a binding with L. Staggemeier's
ticket in his own name only).
SCH/S. de R/IV/21: HOB/ABB. p. 144
(see Plate XXIII).

STAMPER, *H.*
(? out of period).
E.D.:   L.D.: ? 57.★
Add.: 17 Frith St., Soho.
Refs.: Huth Sale: Nos. 1410, 3300:
Sotheby Cat. 27.11.50, No. 180
appears to show that he was
binding as late as 1857.★

STANFIELD, *W.*
(ST. &).
E.D.: 98 (?)
Add.: 4 Duke's Ct., St. Martin's
Lane.
Refs.: Binding seen at Foyle's on
Langthorne's *Plutarch*. Marbled
sides & black straps on spine.

STAPELL, *Richard*
Add.: 46 George St., Bagnigge
Wells Rd.
Refs.: PIG/DIR/36.

STAPELLS, *Charles*
Add.: Wandsworth Rd.

STAPLES, *Richard*
Add.: 1 Charterhouse Ct.
Refs.: PIG/DIR/32.

STAPLES, *Thomas*
(BB.'s Toolmaker).
Add.: 30 Castle St., Holborn.
Refs.: PO/DIR/40.

STARLING
(BB.'s Toolmaker).
Add.: Norfolk St., Islington.
Refs.: COWIE/29.

STEARNE, *John*
(BS/HOWE/LBB. p. 88).

STEEL
(BS/HOWE/LBB. p. 89).

STEPHENSON, *James William*
Add.: 12 Charterhouse St.
Refs.: PIG/DIR/32.

STEPHENSON, *William*
        (BS. etc. in 1840).
    „   *James William* (28).
Add.: 36 Horseferry Rd. (? 12):
12 Parliament St. (25).
Refs.: PIG/DIR/28: 36: ROB/DIR/40:
PO/DIR/31 (J.W.). B.M.C. 17738.
Shabby $\frac{1}{2}$ calf on Gleig's *Subaltern*,
1825. Ticket "S/BB./& BS./12
P.S.". Thornton, R. J.: *Temple*

of Flora, 12. blue mor. gt. silk endpapers (Ticket): in Sotheby Sale 14.12.50, No. 343.

STEWART, *Henry*
   Add.: 9 High St., Marylebone.
   Refs.: COWIE/29: 31: PIG/DIR/28: ROB/DIR/29.

STEWART, *John*
   (BS/HOWE/LBB. p. 89).

STRAHAN, *Daniel Henry*
   Add.: Lower Crown St., Westminster (28): 11 Harrison St., Gray's Inn Rd. (29): 5 Tyler's Ct., Golden Sq. (36).
   Refs.: COWIE/29: 31: PIG/DIR/28: 32: 36: 38: ROB/DIR/29: 32: PO/DIR/40.

STRAHAN, *James*
   Add.: 4 Upper Union Ct., High Holborn.
   Refs.: PIG/DIR/36.

STRAKER, *Edward/Elizabeth*
   (BS/HOWE/LBB. p. 90).
   Add.: 3 Staining Lane Wood St. (28).
   Refs.: ROB/DIR/20: 22 (Eliz.): PIG/DIR/24: 28: An Ezra Straker, Jr., apprenticed to James Adlard, was made a F.S.C. on 6.12.25.

STRAKER & Co. (29)
   ,,   *William Robert*
   Add.: 35 Monkwell St., Cripplegate.
   Refs.: COWIE/29: 31: PIG/DIR/32: 36: 38: ROB/DIR/29 (& Co.): 32 (no "& Co."): 35 (& Co.): PO/DIR/40: COWIE/7.

STREET, *W.*
   (Vellum Binder).
   Add.: Bird-in-Hand Ct., Cheapside.
   Refs.: PO/DIR/40.

STRETCH, *Edward*
   (Vellum Binder in 40).
   Add.: 16 Upper Charlton St. (36): 73 St. Martin's Lane (40).
   Refs.: PIG/DIR/36: ROB/DIR/40: PO/DIR/40.

STRONG, *W.*
   Refs.: O.C.: *Rev. T. Wilson*, 1838. f.m.g. copy of 17th cent. binding (see Plate XXIV).

STROUD
   (BS., BB. & ST. in 28).
   Add.: 4 Warwick Row, Blackfriars.
   Refs.: COWIE/29: 31: PIG/DIR/28.

STRUTT, *Joseph*
   (also called Senior).
   Add.: 20 Little Queen St., Lincolns Inn (24): 25 Hyde St., Blooms-

bury (28): 1 Streatham St.,
Bloomsbury (36).
Refs.: PIG/DIR/24: 28: 32: 36: 38:
ROB/DIR/40: PO/DIR/40.

STRUTT, *Joshua* (or STURT)
(also called Joseph, Jr.).
Add.: 49 Gloucester St., Queen Sq.
(24) & (36) ditto: Red Lion Sq.
(29).
Refs.: COWIE/29: 31: PIG/DIR/24:
28: 32: 36: ROB/DIR/29: 32: 35.

STRUTT, *William*
Add.: 18 Charlotte St., Fitzroy Sq.
Refs.: ROB/DIR/40.

STUART, *C/J.*
„   *Joseph* (17).
(BS/HOWE/LBB. p. 90).
Refs.: HOLD/11 "To Lords' Journal
office" (*sic*): JOHN/17.

SULLIVAN, *Christopher*
„   *Charles*
(but not described as a
BB.).
Add.: 22 Charles St., Hatton Gdn.
Refs.: PIG/DIR/38: ROB/DIR/40: PO/
DIR/40.

SUMPTER, *William*
Add.: 174 High St., Poplar (28):
No. 97 (32): No. 87 (36).
Refs.: PIG/DIR/28: 32: 36: ROB/DIR/
35.

SUTHERLAND, *K.*
(BS., ST. &).
Add.: 136 Aldersgate St.
Refs.: HOLD/11.

SUTTABY, *Edward*
Add.: Hatfield St., Blackfriars (11):
10 Warwick St., Holborn (28).
Refs.: HOLD/11: PIG/DIR/28.
A George Edward S., apprenticed
to William S., was made a F.S.C.
on 7.12.30.

SUTTABY, *William*
(BS/HOWE/LBB. p. 91).

SWALE & *Co.*
Add.: 21 Gt. Russell St.
Refs.: ROB/DIR/29.

SYKES, *John*
(BS. &).
Add.: 15 Gt. Russell St.
Refs.: PIG/DIR/28.

SYMMONS, *Edward*
(called himself a ST. in 1828).
Add.: 57 Theobalds Rd.
Refs.: COWIE/29: 31: PIG/DIR/28:
ROB/DIR/29.

SYRETT, *Edward*
Add.: 65 Tabernacle Walk, Fins-
bury.
Refs.: PIG/DIR/28: ROB/DIR/29.

SYRETT, *George*
(BS/HOWE/LBB. p. 91).
Add.: 46 Banner St., St. Luke's.
Refs.: PIG/DIR/24 : 28.

SYRETT, *Wm.*
(BS/HOWE/LBB. p. 91).
Refs.: COWIE/29 : PIG/DIR/24.

TALBOT, *James B.*
Add.: 33 Bedford St., Commercial
Rd.
Refs.: PIG/DIR/32.

TALLENT, *Charles*
Add.: 5 Vine Pl., Old St. Rd.
Refs.: PIG/DIR/32.

TAPPY, *Michael/S.*
(BS/HOWE/LBB. p. 91/2).

TARNER, *Thomas & George*
  ,,   ,, (38).
        (ST. in 40).
Add.: 40 High St., Marylebone
(28) : 75 New Bond St. (36).
Refs.: PIG/DIR/28 : 36 : 38 : ROB/DIR/
40.
The Bond St. premises were in
1828 occupied by William Tarner
as a perfumer, while at the same
time Thomas was established as
ST., BS. and BB. at 40 High St.,
Marylebone.

TAYLOR
(Edgegilder).
Add.: Wardour St., Soho.
Refs.: COWIE/29 : 31.

TAYLOR
(BS/HOWE/LBB. p. 92).

TAYLOR, *Edward*
Add.: 5 Berwick St., Oxford St.
Refs.: ROB/DIR/35 : PIG/DIR/36.

TAYLOR, *George*
(Edgegilder).
(BS/HOWE/LBB. p. 104).
Refs.: PIG/DIR/23.

TAYLOR, *John*
(BS/HOWE/LBB. p. 92).
Add.: 141 High Holborn (36) (may
be a different person).
Refs.: PIG/DIR/36.

TAYLOR, *Richard*
Add.: 6 Vauxhall Bridge Rd.
Refs.: PIG/DIR/36 : 38 : ROB/DIR/35 :
40 : PO/DIR/40.

TAYLOR, *Richard T.*
(Vellum Binder).
Add.: 17 Devonshire St., Queen
Sq.
Refs.: COWIE/31 : 32 : PIG/DIR/24 :
28 : ROB/DIR/32 : 35.

TAYLOR, *Thomas*
  Add.: 63 Edgware St., St. Marylebone.
  Refs.: Label seen on 3 vol. Snarleyvow 37.

TAYLOR, *Wm./Sarah*
  (BS/HOWE/LBB. p. 92).
  Add.: 8 Holder St., Soho (32).
  Refs.: PIG/DIR/24 : 28 : 32.

TAYLOR & HESSEY
  (BS. & : see also Hessey).
  Add.: 98 Fleet St. (11).
  Refs.: HOLD/11 : This firm signed their bindings in various ways. (a) "T & H/BS, London" on the more obvious trade bindings, e.g., green mor. bdg. in O.C. on Mme. de Stael : *De la Litterature*, 2 vol. Colborn, 12 : (b) in gilt on outer edges of the two covers : (c) "Bd. by T. & H." on inside of edge of top cover on Vol. I and on inside of edge of lower cover on Vol. II of O.C. : W. Cowper's *Poems*, 2 vol. 10 : bound in cream morocco, with elaborate blind stamping : (d) "Bound by T. & H." on outer edge of upper cover : Mrs. Tighe's *Psyche*, etc., 3rd Ed., 11. Bd. in dark blue st. gr. mor. SCH/s. de R/IV. 45.
  There seems little doubt that T. & H. executed both trade and bespoke bindings.

TAYLOR & WATSON
  E.D. 10 (?)
  Add.: Upper Gower St.
  Refs.: Cohen (Marks) reports ticket on a set of *British Classics* sold at Sotheby's about 16.4.51. The address does not correspond to any of the *TAYLORS* or *WATSONS* in BS/HOWE/LBB.

TEPPER
  Add.: 46 Southampton Bldgs.
  Refs.: COWIE/7 : Weber's *Fore-edge Paintings*, p. 83.

TERRITT, *John*
  (In 1828 he gives himself only as a BS.).
  Add.: 62 Judd St., Brunswick Sq.
  Refs.: COWIE/29 : 31 : PIG/DIR/28.

TESSEYMAN, *Charles*
  (Print and Bookseller in 40).
  Add.: 43 Gt. Wild St. (36) : 5 Broad Ct., Bow St. (38).
  Refs.: PIG/DIR/36 : 38 : ROB/DIR/40 : PO/DIR/40 : COWIE/7.

THALL, *James Edwin*
  (Edgegilder).
  Add.: 15½ Peerless Row, City Rd.
  Refs.: PIG/DIR/38.

THOMAS & *Co.* (20)
  „   (29).
  Add.: Baldwyns Ct., Cloak Lane.
  Refs.: ROB/DIR/20 : COWIE/29 : 31.

THOMAS
(BS/HOWE/LBB. p. 92).

THOMPSON, *Charles*
(BS/HOWE/LBB. p. 92).
Refs.: PIG/DIR/24 : 28 : 32 : ROB/DIR/
29.

THOMPSON, *James*
(ST. &).
Add.: 14 Smithfield Bars.
Refs.: AND/90.

THOMPSON, *John*
Add.: 1 Cross St., Clerkenwell.
Refs.: COWIE/29 : 31 : PIG/DIR/24.

THOMPSON, *Jonathan*
(& ST. in 36).
Add.: 75 Aldersgate St. (24) : 114
Cheapside (32) : No. 124 & High
St., Stoke Newington (36).
Refs.: PIG/DIR/24 : 32 : 36.

THOMPSON, *John*
Add.: 6 West Harding St., Fetter
Lane.
Refs.: ROB/DIR/35.

THOMPSON, *Thomas*
Add.: Broad-wall, Blackfriars.
Refs.: HOLD/11.

THOMPSON, *Thomas*
Add.: Broad-wall, Blackfriars.
Refs.: HOLD/11.

THOMSON
(BS/HOWE/LBB. p. 93).

THOMSON, *John*
(BS. &).
Add.: 42 Upper Berkeley St.
Refs.: PIG/DIR/28.

THOMSON, *John*
(BS/HOWE/LBB. p. 93).

THORN, *Reuben T. or B.*
Add.: 59 Basinghall St. : Nos. 45 &
59 (ca. 40).
Refs.: ROB/DIR/35 : PIG/DIR/36 : 38 :
PO/DIR/40 : COWIE/7.

THORNE, *Reuben*
Add.: 59 Basinghall St.
Refs.: PIG/DIR/36 : 38.

THORNE, *Samuel*
(BS/HOWE/LBB. p. 93).
Refs.: AND/90 describes him as a
Vellum Binder).

THORPE, *John*
(Vellum Binder).
Add.: 2 Plough Yd., Seething Lane.
Refs.: COWIE/31 : 32 : PIG/DIR/28 :
32 : ROB/DIR/32 : 35.

THORP(E), *W. or W.T.*
(BS. &).
Add.: 10 University St., Tottenham
Ct. Rd.
Refs.: PIG/DIR/32 : ROB/DIR/32 : 35.

TIBBS, *Nathaniel*
(BS/HOWE/LBB. p. 93).

TICKETT (? same as TRICKETT)
Add.: John St., Westminster.
Refs.: COWIE/29: 31.

TIFFIN, *Thomas/Ann*
(BS/HOWE/LBB. p. 93).
Refs.: HOLD/11 still records Thomas
Tiffin at 134 Salisbury Sq.

TIFFIN, *Wilford/William*
(BS/HOWE/LBB. p. 93).

TILLEY
(BB.'s Toolmaker).
Add.: Marchmont Place, Little
Coram St.
Refs.: COWIE/29: 31.

TIMBURY
(BS/HOWE/LBB. p. 105).
(Toolcutters and Engravers).
Refs.: See HOWE for the various
changes of style in the firm.
Additional refs. are: Charles T.,
5 Cursitor St.: in 1840 the firm is
at Racquet Ct., and Frederick, as
engraver at the old address.
HOLD/11 (T. & Sons, 104 F.L.):
PO/DIR/17/40: ROB/DIR/40: COWIE/
29 mentions two Timburys at
Cursitor St. and Fetter Lane.

TOBY, *W.*
(BS. & 35).
Add.: 18 King's Rd. (20): 18
Asylum Terrace, King's Rd.,
Chelsea: Beaufort Terrace, King's
Rd. (35).
Refs.: COWIE/29: 31: ROB/DIR/20:
22: 32: 35.

TOMKINS
Add.: Serles Place, Lincolns Inn.
Refs.: COWIE/29: 31.

TOMLINSON, *Charles*
(see MACKINLAY, *John*).
Refs.: SLB./passim.

TOOVEY, *James*
Refs.: O.C.: Homer, Pickering ed.
f.m.g. 31: Huth Sale 176 et
passim: W. Lilly's *Hist. Baldwyn*
22 (Beauchamp Bookshop Cat.
1949).

TRAIG (TRAGE), *Charles*
(BS/HOWE/LBB. p. 94).
Refs.: COWIE/29: 31: ROB/DIR/20.

TRANAH, *John*
(& ST. in 36).
Add.: 13 Addle St., Aldermanbury:
No. 16 (32): 1 Crown Ct.,
Aldersgate St. (38).
Refs.: COWIE/31: 32: PIG/DIR/36:
38: ROB/DIR/32: 35: PO/DIR/40:
Apprenticed to W. E. Barry and
admitted a F.S.C. on 1.9.1818.

TREBLE, *J.*
Refs.: Weber's *Fore-edge Paintings*,
p. 81.

TRENDER, *John James*
Add.: 23 Wells St., Cripplegate.
Refs.: PO/DIR/40: COWIE/7.

TRENTER, *William*
Add.: 21 Pavement, Finsbury.
Refs.: PIG/DIR/32.

TREVETT, *Robert*
Add.: Finsbury Pl.
Refs.: PIG/DIR/28.

TRICKETT, *J/George/George
Theophilus*
(see also TICKETT).
(BS/HOWE/LBB. p. 94).
Add.: 7 John St., Westminster (20):
24 Gt. Smith St., Westminster.
Refs.: HOLD/11: PIG/DIR/23: 24:
36: 38: ROB/DIR/20: 32: 35(G):
40: PO/DIR/40 (George).
G.T.T. was apprenticed to An-
drew MacFarlane and admitted a
F.S.C. on 4.3.1823.

TUCK, *Henry*
„   „   *& Co.*
(Son of John Tuck, BS/HOWE/LBB.
p. 94).
Add.: Little St. Thomas Apostle.
Refs.: COWIE/29: 31: PIG/DIR/28:
which gives them as ST. &

Account Book Makers: ROB/DIR/
29.
Henry Tuck was apprenticed to
Joseph Bruce and admitted a
F.S.C. on 3.12.1823.

TUCK, *John*
(BS/HOWE/LBB. pp. 94/5).

TUCKER, *Jos.*
„   *J. & J.* (40).
Add.: 7 & 8 Little Warner St.,
Clerkenwell.
Refs.: COWIE/29: 31: PIG/DIR/24:
32: ROB/DIR/20: 22: 32: 35:
PO/DIR/40: COWIE/7.

TUCKETT, *J.* (?)
„   *Charles* (two).
„   *John.*
Add.: 47 Museum St. (28): 20
Little Russell St. (35 & possibly
29): 66 Great Russell St. (54).
Refs.: COWIE/29: 31: ROB/DIR/29:
32: 35: 40: PIG/DIR/32: 36: 38:
PO/DIR/38: COWIE/7: Esdaile in
AE/BML/p. 337 mentions two
Charles as British Museum
Binders, one 1825/65, and the
other 1865/75. Davenport's list
at the BM. calls the elder Tuckett
"J". He may be the father of the
elder Charles. John may have
taken over the Great Russell
Street business shortly after the
younger Charles was appointed

PLATE XXXV   ANON $(5\frac{3}{4}'' \times 8\frac{1}{2}'')$

PLATE XXXVI   ANON   (4″ × 6½″)

binder to the BM. One or both of the Charles sign on occasion as "Binder to the Queen".

TYLER, *Thomas*
(BS. &).
Add.: 24 Grafton St., Tottenham Ct. Rd.
Refs.: PIG/DIR/23.

UPFOLD, *William*
(Gilder & Marbler in 40).
Add.: 36 Union St., Little Moorfields: also 36 New Union St., Spitalfields: 43 Buttesland St., Hoxton (ca. 40).
Refs.: PIG/DIR/38: ROB/DIR/40: PO/DIR/40: COWIE/7.

UPTON, *James*
Add.: 1 Upper North Pl., Gray's Inn Rd.
Refs.: PIG/DIR/32: ROB/DIR/35.

UPTON & BEET
Add.: 46 New Bond St.
Refs.: I have one label "Sold by" and one "Bound by", and another with just the name and address on a very nice gr. mor. gilt binding, possibly "bd. by" U. & B., ca. 1800, on: *Lettere Amorose,* etc.

VAUGHAN, *R.*
Refs.: Huth Sale No. 2457.

VENNER, *Stephen*
(BS/HOWE/LBB. p. 95).

VERNON, *George*
Add.: 11 John St., Blackfriars Rd.
Refs.: PIG/DIR/36.

VICK, *Joseph*
Add.: 7 Nassau St., Soho.
Refs.: PIG/DIR/28.

VINCENT, *William*
Add.: 46 Hoxton Old Town.
Refs.: PIG/DIR/32.

VIRTUE, *James*
Add.: 7 Newcastle St., Farringdon Rd.
Refs.: PIG/DIR/36: 38.

WACEY, *George*
Add.: 22 Charles St., Hatton Gdn.
Refs.: COWIE/31: 32: PIG/DIR/32: ROB/DIR/32.

WADDINGTON, *Mary*
Add.: 26 Addle Hill (32): 6 Wardrobe Terrace: St. Andrew's Hill (36).
Refs.: PIG/DIR/32: 36: ROB/DIR/35.

WAKELING, *William/Elizabeth*
       ,,   *& PENNY.*
(BS/HOWE/LBB. p. 96).
(see PENNY).
Refs.: HOLD/11: PIG/DIR/24 (W. & P.): 28 (W.P.): ROB/DIR/22 (W.P.).

WAKELING, *Samuel*
(BS/HOWE/LBB. p. 96).

WALKER
  Add.: 10 Bagnio Ct., Newgate St.:
  10 Bath St. (32).
  Refs.: COWIE/29: 31: ROB/DIR/29:
  32: PIG/DIR/32.

WALKER & HOOD
  (Vellum Binder).
  Add.: 8 Water Lane, Fleet St.
  Refs.: AND/90.

WALKER, *Edward*
  Add.: 5 Silver St., Wood St.
  Refs.: PIG/DIR/28.

WALKER, *Henry*
  Add.: 7 Castle Ct., Strand (20):
  12 Lovell's Ct., Paternoster Row
  (22).
  Refs.: ROB/DIR/20: 22: PIG/DIR/24.

WALKER, *William*
  (BS/HOWE/LBB. p. 96).

WALKER, *William*
  (BS. & in 40).
  Add.: 27 Goswell Rd. (? which
  W.W.) (29): 7 Star Ct., Fen-
  church St.: 84 Aldersgate St. (32).
  Refs.: PIG/DIR/32: 38: ROB/DIR/29:
  32: 40.

WALLER, or WALTER, *William*
  (BS. &).
  Add.: Leigh St., Red Lion Sq. (23)

(Waller): 9 Russell Ct., Drury
  Lane (32).
  Refs.: PIG/DIR/23: 28: 32: ROB/DIR/
  32 (Walter).

WALLIS, *Elizabeth*
  Add.: 65 Union St., Hoxton New
  Town (28): 51 Moneyers St.,
  City Rd. (36).
  Refs.: PIG/DIR/28: 32: 36.

WALLIS, *John*
  Add.: 78 Shoreditch.
  Refs.: PIG/DIR/24.

WALTER, *William*
  Add.: 18 City Terrace, City Rd.
  Refs.: COWIE/29: 31: ROB/DIR/22:
  PIG/DIR/24: 28.

WALTERS
  Add.: 14 Duke Ct., Drury Lane.
  Refs.: COWIE/29: 31: ROB/DIR/20.

WALTHER, *Henry/Charles Davis*
  (or *David*).
  (Probably H.W. died before 1824).
  (BS/HOWE/LBB. p. 97).
  Add.: No. 11 (40).
  Refs.: COWIE/29: 31: 32: PIG/DIR/
  28: 32: ROB/DIR/20: 32: 35 (at
  20 C. St.): PO/DIR/40.
  O.C.: Nonni. *Dionisiaca.* 1569.
  f.m.g. SCH/S. de R/VI/18/20: C. F.
  Bishop, Sale, 216: T. Langley:
  Hundred of Desborough, 1797: L.
  P., citron mor. g. for Sir R. Colt

144

Hoare of Stourhead: Ellis (George): *Memoir . . . Black Sea & Caspian* (1807), blue mor. gilt, blind stamped on sides with steeples. (See Plate XXV). Usual printed label "Bd. by/ H.W." This is a key binding as it links up with a large number of bindings in the Storer Bequest at Eton College, which are unsigned but carry the distinctive steeple tools (3 varieties) very often in gilt. H.M. Nixon: *Twelve Books in fine bindings in the Library of J. W. Hely-Hutchinson*: Roxburghe Club: 1953. This "repetition" binding is signed and dated *1791* on the doublure joint.

Charles W. was apprenticed to John Mackinlay and then to Michael Stainton. Admitted as a F.S.C. on 3.8.1817.

WARD, *Charles*
  Add.: 66 Wells St.
  Refs.: PIG/DIR/32.

WARD, *Charles Edward*
  (Vellum Binder 35).
  Add.: 10 Three Kings Ct., Lombard St.
  Refs.: PIG/DIR/32: ROB/DIR/35.

WARD, *George W.*
  (Bookclasp Makers).
  Add.: 22 Red Cross Sq., Clerkenwell.
  Refs.: COWIE/29: 31: PIG/DIR/28.

WARD, *George*
  Add.: 23 Cock Lane, W. Smithfield.
  Refs.: ROB/DIR/22: PIG/DIR/24.

WARD, *George William*
  (Bookclasp Maker).
  Add.: 9 Wells St., Cripplegate.
  Refs.: PIG/DIR/36: 38: ROB/DIR/29: 32: 35: 40: PO/DIR/40.

WARD, *Stephen*
  (BS/HOWE/LBB. p. 98).
  Add.: 94 Dean St., Soho (20): 66 Wells St., Oxford St. (35): No. 15 (38): No. 31 (40): Haye's Ct., Soho (& printseller) (?)
  Refs.: COWIE/29: 31: PIG/DIR/24: 28: 38: ROB/DIR/20: 22: 35: PO/DIR/40.

WARD, *William*
  Add.: 23 Bartholomew Close.
  Refs.: COWIE/29: 31: PIG/DIR/24: 28: ROB/DIR/29.

WARNER
  (BS/HOWE/LBB. p. 98).
    ,,   *Stephen* (36).
  Add.: 6 Shepherdess Walk (36).
  Refs.: PIG/DIR/36.

WARREN
  E.D.: 18 (?)
  Add.: Old Bond St.
  Refs.: O.C.: Virgil: *Opera*: Rodwell & Martin, 1818.

WARREN, *Henry George*
  Add.: 9 Titchborne St., Quadrant.
  Refs.: PIG/DIR/36.

WARWICK, *Charles Antony*
  (BS/HOWE/LBB. p. 98).
  „   *Christopher* (20 or 22?).
  „   *William* (38).
  „   *Charles* (40).
  Add.: 4 Middle New St., Shoe Lane
  (20): 9 Rolls Bldgs. (no initial:
  ca. 40).
  Refs.: COWIE/29: 31: PIG/DIR/24:
  28: 32: 36: 38: ROB/DIR/20: 22:
  40: PO/DIR/40: COWIE/7. C.A.W.
  was admitted as a F.S.C. on
  6.10.1824.

WARWICK, *Francis*
  (BS/HOWE/LBB. p. 98).

WARWICK, *J.*
  (Vellum Binder).
  Add.: 2 Silver St., Wood St.
  Refs.: HOLD/11.

WATKINS
  E.D.: ? 30.
  Add.: 8 Paradise Row, Gravel Lane,
  Southwark.
  Refs.: LAB/KNA. ca. 30: COWIE/7.

WATKINS, *L. M.*
  „   *Thomas* (29).
  (Binder to B. & F. Bible
  Soc., 1832).
  „   *Mrs. Louisa* (40).

Add.: 47 St. John's Sq.
  Refs.: COWIE/29: PIG/DIR/36: 38:
  ROB/DIR/29: 32: 35: 40: PO/DIR/
  40: LAB/JONES: LAB/KNA: BM.
  1106. b. 7.

WATSON, *D.*
  (BS/HOWE/LBB. p. 98).

WATSON, *James*
  Add.: 12 or 13 Charles St., Covent
  Gdn. (28): 43 Maiden Lane,
  Southampton St. (36): 53 Long
  Acre (38).
  Refs.: COWIE/29: 31: PIG/DIR/28:
  32: 36: 38: ROB/DIR/29: 32: 35:
  PO/DIR/40.

WATSON, *John*
  Add.: 68 Princes St., Leicester Sq.
  Refs.: ROB/DIR/35.

WATSON, *John*
  Add.: 10 Pemberton Row, Gough
  Sq.
  Refs.: COWIE/29: 31: PIG/DIR/28:
  32: ROB/DIR/29: 32: 35.

WATSON, *John*
  Add.: 16 Dean St., Fetter Lane.
  Refs.: PIG/DIR/36: 38: ROB/DIR/35:
  40: PO/DIR/40.

WATSON, *John*
  Add.: 6 Bateman's Bldgs., Soho Sq.
  Refs.: PIG/DIR/36.

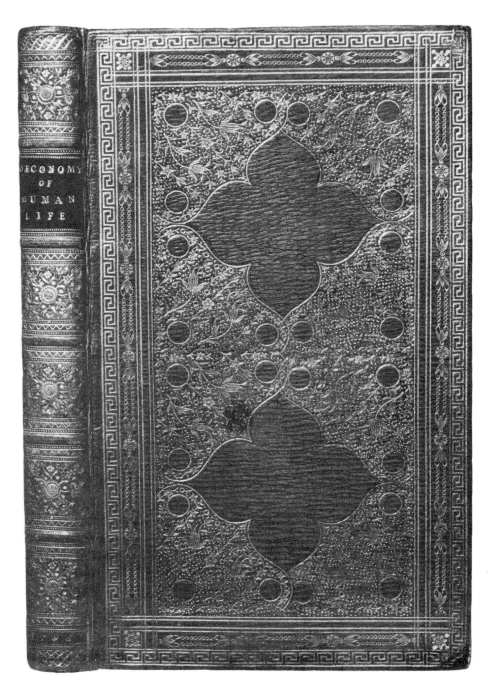

PLATE XXXVII   ANON $(4\frac{1}{2}'' \times 7\frac{1}{2}'')$

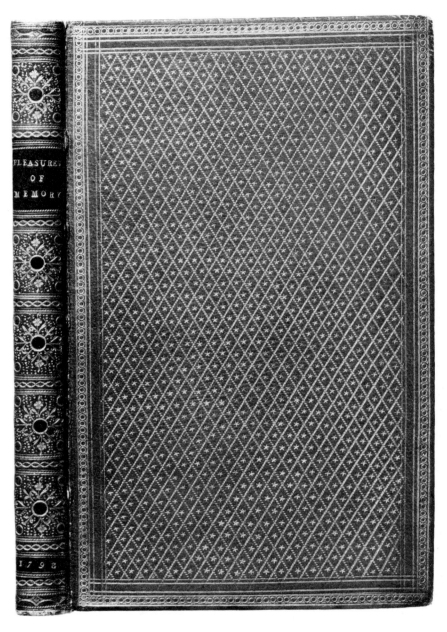

PLATE XXXVIII   ANON $(4'' \times 6\frac{1}{4}'')$

WATSON, *John*
,,   *Kechnie* (38).
Add.: 50 Cirencester Pl.
Refs.: PIG/DIR/36: 38: ROB/DIR/40:
PO/DIR/40.

WATTS, *Henry*
Add.: 25 Broad St., Golden Sq.
Refs.: PIG/DIR/38.

WEBSTER, *John*
(ST. &).
Add.: 421 Oxford St.
Refs.: HOLD/11.

WEEMYS & *Co.*
(see CLARKE & WEEMYS &
WEMYSS, *W.*).
Add.: Long Lane, Aldersgate St.
Refs.: P./Labels: COWIE/7.

WEIGHTMAN, *Andrew*
(BS/HOWE/LBB. p. 98).

WEIR *Family*
(see WIER).

WEIR, *David Hope*
(BS/HOWE/LBB. p. 99).
Refs.: May be the same as the
Richard Weir in Belfast 1820–24.
(See CR/BB. p. 249.)

WELCH
(BS/HOWE/LBB. p. 99).

WELCHER, *Samuel*
(BS/HOWE/LBB. p. 99).
Add.: 12 Villiers St., Strand.

Refs.: SCH/S. de R./IV/44.
The Soane copy of Chaucer's
Works, 1602, is in a splendid red
mor. binding by Welcher with
his ticket. With the exception
of the title the whole ornamentation is in very minute blind
stamping. An unusual feature is
that the boards are over ½″ thick,
with 2″ squares in the corners and
the rest of the edges bevelled off.

WELSH, *Jos.*
E.D.: ? 17.
Add.: 10 Queen St., Golden Sq.
Refs.: ROB/DIR/20: 22: PIG/DIR/24.
Ticket seen at Marks on *Young's
Night Thoughts* (1817) "Bound by
I. Welsh, 10 Queen St., Golden
Sq. Gents' Libraries cleaned and
repaired."

WEMYSS, *William*
(see WEEMYS & Co.).
(BS. &).
Add.: 15 Little Warner St., Cold
Bath Sq.).
Refs.: PIG/DIR/28.

WENN, *T.*
(Vellum Binder).
Add.: 6 Earl St., Finsbury.
Refs.: COWIE/31: 32.

WEST, *Benjamin*
Add.: 2 St. James Walk, Clerken-
well: St. James Bldgs. (37): St.
James West, Clerkenwell (? 39).

Refs.: PIG/DIR/32: ROB/DIR/37: PO/DIR/40: COWIE/7.
O.C.: Pope's *Poetical Works*, 39, f.m.g.: stamped address: Abbott's *Young Christian*, n.d. (ded. 58): SLB./p. 110.

WEST, *John*
Add.: 37 Anwell St., Spitalfields: 37 Anwell St., Claremont Sq. (36).
Refs.: COWIE/29: 31: ROB/DIR/29: 32: 35: PIG/DIR/36.

WESTLEY
Add.: John St., Smithfield.
Refs.: COWIE/29: 31.

WESTLEY, *Francis/Josiah*
(ST. &). (see also Westley, Son & Jarvis).
(BS/HOWE/LBB. pp. 99/100).
Add.: 15 Charles Sq., Hoxton & 11 Friar's St. (11).
Refs.: HOLD/11: COWIE/29: 31: PO/DIR/17: PIG/DIR/28: 32: 36: ROB/DIR/22: 32: 35: Labels are common. Two of F. Westley in O.C.

WESTLEY, *George*
(BS/HOWE/LBB. p. 100).
Refs.: COWIE/29: 31: JOHN/17: ROB/DIR/20: PIG/DIR/28.

WESTLEY, *Henry*
(BS/HOWE/LBB. p. 100).

WESTLEY, *Son &* JARVIS
(? successors to Westley, Francis/Josiah q.v.).
Add.: Friar St., Blackfriars (40).
Refs.: COWIE/7 (& Co.): Publisher's Binding on Jennings' *Album* (Marks 29.9.50): SLB./p. 110.

WESTLEY, *William (Russell)*?
Add.: 4 Ivy Lane, Newgate (32): 8 Warwick Sq., Newgate Mkt. (35): No. 1 (40).
Refs.: PIG/DIR/32: 36: 38: ROB/DIR/35: 40: PO/DIR/40: COWIE/7.
Apprenticed to George W., he was made a F.S.C. on 3.3.29.

WESTLEYS & CLARK
Refs.: Huth Sale No. 3382.

WHALLEY, *John*
Add.: 12 West St., Seven Dials.
Refs.: PIG/DIR/28.

WHARTON, *J.*
(& BS.).
Add.: 20 Charlotte Row, Walworth Rd.
Refs.: ROB/DIR/32: 35.

WHITE, *J.*
Add.: 24 Piccadilly (20): 24 Pall Mall (40).
Refs.: Huth Sale: No. 1579: Drawhandle imit. of Mearne, seen at Marks, 3.4.48: Sexton Cat. 43, No. 464 (ca. 37).

WHITE, *Thomas*
    „   „   D. (38).
    Add.: 93 Newman St., Oxford St.:
    25 Hart St., Bloomsbury (38).
    Refs.: ROB/DIR/35: PIG/DIR/36: 38.

WHITE, *W.*
    Add.: 89 Piccadilly.
    Refs.: PO/DIR/40.

WHITE, *William*
    Add.: 31 Frederick St., Hampstead
    Rd.
    Refs.: PIG/DIR/28.

WHITE, *William*
    (Engraver, PR. & BB.).
    Add.: 50 Queen St., Gt. Charlotte
    St., Blackfriars Rd.
    Refs.: PIG/DIR/28.

WHITEHEAD, *Thomas*
    (BS/HOWE/LBB. p. 101).
    Refs.: COWIE/29: 31: ROB/DIR/22:
    PIG/DIR/24.

WHITELAW, *George*
    Add.: 11 or 15 Nassau St., Middle-
    sex Hospital.
    Refs.: COWIE/31: 32: PIG/DIR/32:
    36: 38: ROB/DIR/32: 35: 40: PO/
    DIR/40.

WHITE, *Charles*
    (BS. &).
    Add.: 72 Myddleton St., Spafields
    (35): 3 Bouverie St., Fleet St.
    (38).

Refs.: PIG/DIR/36: 38: ROB/DIR/35:
40: PO/DIR/40.

WHITFIELD, *John*
    Add.: 12 Bartholomew Close.
    Refs.: PIG/DIR/36.

WHIT(T)AKER, *John*
           (BS/HOWE/LBB. p.
           100).
    „   *Elizabeth* (32).
    Add.: 11 Queen St. or Little Smith
    St., Westminster.
    Refs.: HOLD/11: PIG/DIR/28 (&
    printer in gold): 32 (E): ROB/DIR/
    32: HOB/ABB. p. 148: OLD/SH.
    p. 163: TIMP/42. p. 844. A bind-
    ing similar to that at Longlect,
    is in the Rylands (Spencer)
    Library.

WHITAKER, *Leonard*
    (BS/HOWE/LBB. p. 100).

WHITEHEAD, *Thomas*
    (BS/HOWE/LBB. p. 101).

WHITING, *Thomas*
    Add.: 8 Warwick Sq., Newgate St.:
    7 Oxford Arms Passage (ca. 40).
    Refs.: PO/DIR/40: COWIE/7.

WICKWAR & *Son* (29)
           d. Sept. 1854 (of
           cholera).
    „   *J.* (32).
           (BS. &).
    „   *J. & Co.* (40).

Add.: 3 Marylebone Lane, Oxford St.: 6 Poland St. (32).

Refs.: COWIE/29: PIG/DIR/36: ROB/DIR/29: 32: 35: 40: PO/DIR/40.

O.C.: Stothard's *Monumental Effigies*, 1817/32: f.m.g. Gothic spines, sides and insides (see Plate XXVI). Vellum end-papers. Signed on reverse of vellum guard. (Now in BM., Aug. 54.)

WIER, *Maria*
(BS/HOWE/LBB. p. 98).

Refs.: She was a skilful ruler and restorer, and also bound in the plainer Payne-Wier style, largely for M. Wodhull, many of whose bindings are attributed to her in the Severne-Wodhull Sale Cat.

WIER (WEIR), *Richard or Davy*
(BS/HOWE/LBB. p. 98/9).

Refs.: See Article by the author in the *Book Collector*, Dec. 1953. His bindings are now easily recognisable (see Plate XXVII). Since my article Mr. H. W. Davies has shown me a binding from the McCarthy Library which from its sides is un-doubtedly by Wier, but has the title on the spine lettered in upright capitals, dog-tooth inside edges and other distinctly French features. It was probably done soon after Wier's arrival at Toulouse. Another binding on Jebb: *Vita Mariae Reg.* 1725 in the Rylands Library also shows how Wier built up his own style from the French.

WILKINSON, *Rowland*
Add.: 6 Ivy Lane, Newgate St.
Refs.: COWIE/31: 32: ROB/DIR/32.

WILKINSON, *R. H.*
Add.: 1 Prujean Sq., Old Bailey.
Refs.: COWIE/29: 31: ROB/DIR/22: PIG/DIR/24.

WILLEY, *W.*
(& BS., ST.).
Add.: near Crescent, Clapham Common.
Refs.: PO/DIR/40.

WILLIAMS, *C.*
Add.: 11 or 19 Albion Bldgs., Aldersgate St.
Refs.: COWIE/29: 31: ROB/DIR/29.

WILLIAMS, *J.*
Add.: Duchy St., Strand.
Refs.: ROB/DIR/20.

WILLIAMS, *James*
Add.: 7 Bull & Mouth St., St. Martin's-le-Grand.

Refs.: COWIE/31: 32: PIG/DIR/32: 36: 38: ROB/DIR/29: 32: 35: 40: PO/DIR/40.

WILLIAMS, *John*
Add.: 1 High St., Kensington.
Refs.: COWIE/31: 32: PIG/DIR/32: ROB/DIR/32: 35.

WILLIAMS, *Thomas*
Add.: 20 White St., Little Moorfields.
Refs.: ROB/DIR/20: 22: PIG/DIR/24: 28.

WILLIAMS & DYKE (32)
  „   *William* (38).
Add.: Duchy Pl., Strand.
Refs.: PIG/DIR/32: 38: ROB/DIR/35: 40: PO/DIR/40 (W. & D.): COWIE/7.

WILLIS
(BS. &).
Add.: 5 Cloisters, Bartholomew Hospital.
Refs.: HOLD/11.

WILLIS, *Stephen*
Add.: 36 Kenton St., Brunswick Sq.
Refs.: PIG/DIR/38: ROB/DIR/40.

WILMORE, *John*
(& periodicals).
Add.: 7 Francis St., Lambeth.
Refs.: PIG/DIR/32.

WILSON, *Edward*
Add.: 6 Gt. Distaff Lane.
Refs.: PIG/DIR/36.

WILSON, *J.*
Add.: 2 Martlett Ct., Covent Gdn.
Refs.: COWIE/31: 32: ROB/DIR/32: 35.

WILSON, *John*
        (BS/HOWE/LBB. p. 102).
  „   *W. & H.* (ca. 40).
Add.: 19 Blackmore St. (11): 88 Royal Exchange (?): 19 Foley Pl. (? 24).
Refs.: HOLD/11: COWIE/29: 31: PIG/DIR/24: 28: 32: 36: 38: ROB/DIR/22: 29: 32: 35: 40: COWIE/7 (W. & H.): OLD/SH161/2.
O.C.: Weber's *Marie Antoinette*, 05/12: f.m.g.: Tickets on 2 first vols.: none on Vol. 3, and different binding.

WILSON, *Joseph*
Add.: 22 & 33 Ray St., Clerkenwell Green.
Refs.: PIG/DIR/32: 36: 38: ROB/DIR/35: 40: COWIE/7.

WILSON, *William*
Add.: 15 Crown Ct., Covent Gdn.
Refs.: PIG/DIR/28.

WILTON, *William*
(BB.'s Toolcutter).
Add.: 1 Sarah Pl., Clerkenwell.
Refs.: PIG/DIR/32.

WILTON, *William*
Add.: 2 New Turnstile, Holborn
(32): 6 Cursitor St., Chancery
Lane (40).
Refs.: PIG/DIR/32: PO/DIR/40.

WINCKWORTH, *James*
Add.: 12 Albemarle St., Clerken-
well.
Refs.: PIG/DIR/32.

WINGFIELD, *Thomas*
(BS/HOWE/LBB. p. 102).

WINGRAVE, *John*
(BS/HOWE/LBB. p. 102).

WINGROVE, *David*
(& ST.).
Add.: 44 Commercial Rd.
Refs.: PIG/DIR/36: 38: ROB/DIR/40:
PO/DIR/40: COWIE/7.

WINN, *Thomas*
(Vellum Binder).
Add.: 6 Earl St., Finsbury & 27
Camomile St.: 10 Sun St.,
Bishopsgate (ca. 40).
Refs.: PIG/DIR/32: ROB/DIR/32:
COWIE/7.

WISE, *A. K.*
„ *A. Robert*
(Gilder & Marbler) (40).
Add.: 21 Albion Bldgs., Bartholo-
mew Close: 18 Bartholomew
Close (40).
Refs.: ROB/DIR/35: PO/DIR/40.

WISE, *John Lewis*
(BS/HOWE/LBB. p. 102).
Refs.: HOLD/11.

WOHLMAN, G.
(BS./HOWE/LBB. p. 102).

WOLTER, *Thomas* (32)
„ *William* (36).
Add.: 12 Duke Ct., Drury Lane
(32): 52 Drury Lane (36).
Refs.: PIG/DIR/36: ROB/DIR/32: 35:
PO/DIR/40: COWIE/7.

WOLTERS
(BS/HOWE/LBB. p. 102).
Refs.: See Coxhead, J.

WOLTERS & BRAND
(BS/HOWE/LBB. p. 102).

WOOD, *William*
(BS/HOWE/LBB. p. 102).

WOODBURN, *H.*
(BS/HOWE/LBB. p. 103).
Add.: 112 St. Martin's Lane.
Refs.: BM. G. 3508. Nice $\frac{1}{2}$
russia bdg. on Miller's *Doncaster*:
ca. 05. Label (8 point star)
"Bd. by/H.W/112 S.M.L."

WOODEN, *James*
Add.: 14 Colman St. Bldgs.
Refs.: PIG/DIR/24: 28.

WOODEN, *William*
    Add.: 8 Queen's Pl., Lincolns Inn
    Fields.
    Refs.: PIG/DIR/28.

WOODFALL, *Fred*
    Add.: 26 York St., Westminster.
    Refs.: COWIE/29: 31: ROB/DIR/22:
    PIG/DIR/24.

WOODGATE, *George*
        „   „   *Roan* (32).
    Add.: 56 Bunhill Row (20): 21
    James St., Old St. (28): 40
    Cowper St., Finsbury (32): 60
    Tabernacle Walk, Finsbury (36):
    35 Noble St., City (38).
    Refs.: COWIE/29: 31: ROB/DIR/20:
    PIG/DIR/28: 32: 36: 38. Possibly
    an earlier G.R.W. was appren-
    ticed to Francis Allchin and
    admitted as a F.S.C. on 3.9.1817.
    George W., apprenticed to John
    Samuel Close, was made a F.S.C.
    on 6.2.27.

WOODGATE, *Thomas*
    (BS. in 1840).
    Add.: 60 Tabernacle Walk, Fins-
    bury.
    Refs.: PIG/DIR/38: ROB/DIR/40.

WOODMAN, *William/James*
    (BS/HOWE/LBB. p. 103).

WOODS, *E. J.*
    Add.: 8 Upper Rosoman St.,
    Clerkenwell.
    Refs.: PIG/DIR/28.

WOODS, *Robert*
    (ST. in 40).
    Add.: 22 Whitecross St., Cripple-
    gate.
    Refs.: PIG/DIR/36: ROB/DIR/40.

WOOLMER, *Edward Robert*
    Add.: 1 Robert St., Waterloo Rd.
    Refs.: ROB/DIR/35: PIG/DIR/36.

WOOLNOUGH, *Charles*
    Add.: 18 Hill St., Finsbury (22):
    6 Bateman Row, Shoreditch
    (? 28).
    Refs.: COWIE/29: 31: PIG/DIR/24:
    28: 36: ROB/DIR/22: 29: 32: 35:
    40: PO/DIR/40: COWIE/7.

WOOLNOUGH, *Stephen*
    Add.: 7 Upper James St., Golden
    Sq. (20): 51 Marshall St., Golden
    Sq. (35).
    Refs.: COWIE/29: 31: PIG/DIR/24:
    28: 32: 36: 38: ROB/DIR/22: 29:
    32: 35: 40: PO/DIR/40: COWIE/7.

WORSFOLD, *Hanna*
    Add.: 23 East Pl., Lambeth.
    Refs.: PIG/DIR/32.

WORTHINGTON, *James*
   Add.: 3 High St., Kensington:
   3 Mayfield Pl. (ca. 40).
   Refs.: ROB/DIR/35: PO/DIR/40:
   COWIE/7.

WOTTER, *Thomas*
   Add.: 12 Duke St., Drury Lane.
   Refs.: COWIE/31: 32.

WRIGHT, *C.*
   Add.: Charlotte Terrace.
   Refs.: COWIE/29: 31: Huth Cat.
   No. 4223.

WRIGHT, *John*
   Add.: 21 Noel St., Wardour St.:
   Nos. 14 & 15 (ca. 40).
   Refs.: PIG/DIR/36: 38: ROB/DIR/35:
   40: PO/DIR/40: COWIE/7.
   O.C.: Hofland: *Angler's Manual*,
   39, f.m.g., Gosden tools. He was
   a binder of the highest order but
   in the main falls outside our
   period.

WRIGHT, *John*
   Add.: 106 Crawford St.
   Refs.: PIG/DIR/38.

WRIGHT, *Joseph*
   (BS. &).
   Add.: 8 Little Woodstock St.,
   Marylebone.
   Refs.: PIG/DIR/32: 36: 38: ROB/DIR/
   35: Apprenticed to John Old, he
   was made a F.S.C. on 7.8.27.

WRIGHT, *Peter*
   (& BS. 32).
   (BS/HOWE/LBB. p. 103).
   Add.: 7 High St., Bloomsbury.
   Refs.: ROB/DIR/32: 35.

WRIGHT, *William*
   Add.: 5 Northampton Bldgs.,
   Clerkenwell (35): 3 King St.,
   Holborn (40).
   Refs.: PIG/DIR/36: ROB/DIR/35: 40.

WYAN, *Edward*
   (Vellum Binder).
   Add.: 26 Little Trinity Lane.
   Refs.: HOLD/11.

WYLDE, *Wm.*
   Add.: 33 Duke St., W. Smithfield.
   Refs.: PIG/DIR/24.

WYLY, *Christopher or/and Charles*
   (BS/HOWE/LBB. p. 103).
   Add.: 36 Warwick Lane (11).
   Refs.: HOLD/11 (Charles): ROB/DIR/
   20: 22: PIG/DIR/24: 28: The JOHN/
   17 Ref. is to *Charles.*

WYLY, *Robert*
   (BS/HOWE/LBB. p. 103).
   Refs.: HOLD/11.

WYNN, *E.*
   (Vellum Binder).
   Add.: 26 Little Trinity Lane,
   Queenhithe.
   Refs.: PO/DIR/17.

PLATE XXXIX   ANON $(4\frac{3}{4}'' \times 7\frac{1}{2}'')$

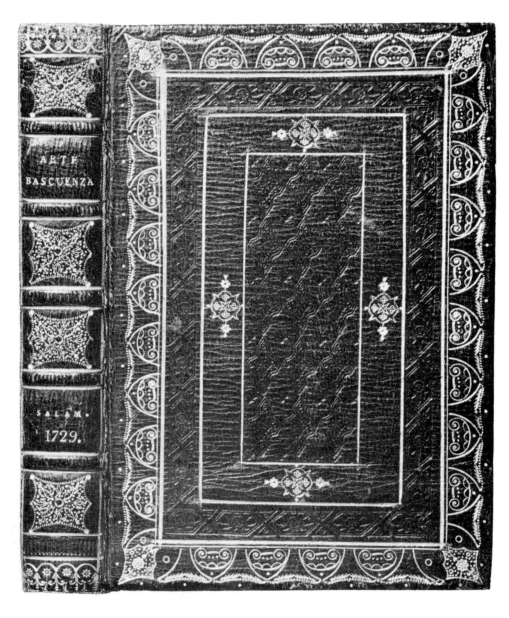

PLATE XL   ANON $(4\tfrac{1}{4}'' \times 6'')$

YARINGTON, *Henry*
 (BS. &).
 Add.: 54 Broad St., Golden Sq.
 Refs.: PIG/DIR/29.

YEO, *Margery*
 Add.: St. Martin's Lane.
 Refs.: HOB/ABB. App. XI, p. 194.

YOUNG
 Add.: Hatfield St., Blackfriars.
 Refs.: COWIE/29: 31.

YOUNG, *James*
 Add.: 23 Cleveland St., Fitzroy Sq.
 Refs.: COWIE/29: 31: ROB/DIR/22:
  PIG/DIR/24.

YOUNG, *William*
 (Vellum Binder).
 Add.: 5 Vine St., Minories (28):
  29 New Sq., Minories (31).
 Refs.: COWIE/31: 32: PIG/DIR/28:
  32: ROB/DIR/32: 35: PO/DIR/40.

ZAEHNSDORF
 Add.: 90 Drury Lane.
 Refs.: COWIE/7 (see article in DICT.
  NAT. BIOG.): BR/BM/IV/37 p. 8
  gives his first individual working
  date as 1842.

ZANDER, *Augustus*
 Add.: 4 Ann St., Spafields.
 Refs.: PIG/DIR/32.

NOTES